who knew?

CUSTOMERS' CHOICE!

Your Favorite Time- and Money-Saving Tips Ever

who knew?

CUSTOMERS' CHOICE!

Your Favorite Time- and Money-Saving Tips Ever

BRUCE LUBIN & JEANNE BOSSOLINA-LUBIN

CASTLE POINT PUBLISHING

Cover and interior design by Lynne Yeamans
Layout and design by Susan Livingston

Castle Point Publishing
58 Ninth Street
Hoboken, NJ 07030
www.castlepointpub.com

ISBN: 978-0-9850374-2-0

Printed and bound in the United States of America

2 4 6 8 10 9 7 5 3 1

Please visit us online at www.WhoKnewTips.com

Contents

Dedication and Introduction

First, a big THANK YOU to our readers, friends, and fans! This book wouldn't be possible without you.

Since we wrote down our first household tip almost twenty years ago (store your eggs upside down!), we've been searching near and far for more tips to share with you. Sometimes, they seem to find us—like friends matter-of-factly saying, "Well *of course* I always use baby wipes instead of replacements for my wet mop!" Other times, you'll find us hounding the short-order cook at the local diner for all his pancake secrets. And lately, we've been getting some great tips on Facebook and through our website, WhoKnewTips.com! (A recent favorite: Smear car wax on your headlights and breaklights at the beginning of winter to keep away snow and grime!)

Since HSN has introduced us to so many of you, we wanted to make a book for you—our HSN customers! We've compiled your best-loved, most-requested tips, as well as some of our own favorites that will save you time and money. We've also added more than 1,000 brand-new tips that we've gotten from readers, learned from the pros, or accidentally discovered during our day-to-day lives of raising three boys who have never learned to take their shoes off before coming into the house.

We hope the tips inside help make frugal fun, and that you'll enjoy the hints and tricks from other members of the Who Knew? family! Don't forget to let us know your favorites that have been passed down from family and friends. Join the Who Knew? community online at WhoKnewTips.com (or find us at Facebook.com/WhoKnewTips or Twitter.com/WhoKnewTips). And of course, if you have a question about anything you find inside one of our books, let us know! We're here to help.

Thriftily Yours,
Jeanne and Bruce

PART 1

WHO KNEW?
HOW-TO

We're all for reducing household mayhem! So here's everything you need to know to easily solve the everyday problems that annoy you. Did you know that you can make dried-out masking tape usable again by microwaving it? Or that you can use a hair dryer to keep the coals on your grill going? If you've ever wanted to make your house smell wonderful without spending a cent, keep your cookies chewy for weeks, or quickly get pet hair off the couch, you'll love this section. We'll also tell you our readers' tips on how to unkink earbud headphones (page 12), get screws into stripped holes (page 65), unstick photos (page 81), get those last crumbs out of the bottom of your purse (page 139), and much more! Get ready to tackle daily to-dos more easily than ever before!

CHAPTER 1

EVERYDAY PROBLEMS SOLVED!

Fix Stuck Plugs

If an electric plug on an appliance fits too snugly and
is difficult to pull out, rub its prongs with a soft lead
pencil, and it will move in and out more easily.

Cell Phone Saver

Here's a trick that could save you hundreds: If your cell
phone gets wet, first take the battery out and dry it
with a paper towel. Then bury the phone and the battery in a bowl of uncooked rice for 24 hours. The rice
will draw the rest of the water out of the phone, and
hopefully it will be back in business again.

Bring Your Phone Back to Life

Left your cell phone in your hot car, and now it won't
work? Just turn on the car's air conditioner, and direct
it at the phone. When you get home, continue cooling
the phone until it is no longer hot to the touch, and
then put it in an airtight bag and stow it in the fridge
(not freezer) for 5 minutes. Your phone should work
fine again now!

Pump Up the Volume

Have trouble hearing music through your mobile device's speakers? Just place it in a bowl (preferably an aluminum or stainless steel one). The sides of the bowl will amplify the sound.

Reader's Tip

If you have teenagers who always seem to have headphones on, they'll love this trick. If your headphone cords are hopelessly kinked and tangled, wrap them gently around the outside of a coffee mug several times, then tape them so they're held close to the sides. Next, fill the mug with boiling water and let sit. By the time the water has cooled, the warmth will have unkinked the cords.   —MAGGIE FELD, WYOMING, MI

Old Cassette Cases Are Good for Something!

Looking for a container to store iPod earbud headphones where they won't get tangled? Coil the cord and then place it inside an old cassette case. Your headphones will be safe, and your friends can admire the *Flashdance* soundtrack decoration on the outside. So retro!

Make-Up On-the-Go

If your eyeliner or lip pencils are too long for your make-up case, break them in half to form two smaller pencils and sharpen them both. You'll not only save space, but you'll have a backup if one pencil goes missing. Don't have a make-up case? Use a repurposed mint tin!

Checkbook Covers Turned Organizers

When you receive new checks in the mail, don't throw away the plastic cover that often comes with them. Instead, use it as an organizational tool to store receipts, itineraries, or other papers that find their way into your purse or wallet.

What to Do with Wet Umbrellas

Need a cover to store your wet umbrella while you're on the go? Look no further than the end of your driveway. The plastic bags newspapers come in are waterproof and the perfect size.

Easy Fix for Some Broken Umbrellas

Before you throw away an umbrella, see if you can fix it by sewing the fabric back onto the metal arm—easily accomplished with a simple sewing kit!

Reader's Tip

If you discover a couple of photos stuck together, don't lose hope! They can be unstuck. Warm them with a hairdryer set on low and very slowly pull apart. Allow to cool, then press them under some heavy books to keep them flat.

—DAYANA DOMINGUEZ, MIAMI LAKES, FL

Stuck Photos

If your photographs are stuck to each other or to a glass frame, the solution is steam. Use a steamer, a steam iron set on its highest setting, or a pan of boiling water to get steam as close as you can between the photo and whatever it's stuck to (being careful not to burn yourself). As the photo gets warmer and wetter, it should become easy to peel away. Lay out to dry, then flatten with a fat book if it has curled.

Picture Perfect

If a beloved book or photo album has gotten wet, it's not ruined yet. Try sprinkling baby or baking powder on each page, then placing it in a closed paper bag for up to a week. The powder should absorb the water while keeping your book safe.

Jar Displays

Have some beautiful clear jars, but don't know what to do with them? Try putting photos inside! Add marbles, rocks, colored sand, or other decoration at the bottom, then bend the photo ever-so-slightly so it fits the curve of the jar.

Color Matching

If you're shopping for accessories to match a color on a bedspread, couch, or piece of art, taking a photo often doesn't cut it. Especially if you print it out on your home printer, the variance in color from the photograph to the actual article can be dramatic. Instead, go to a paint store and pick up paint swatches that you think are similar in shade. Then go home and find the closest match. Mark that color, then bring the swatch to the store instead.

New Favorite

The next time someone at work asks you why you bother wearing a watch anymore, show them this neat trick: Put your watch face-up on your desk and your mouse on top of it. The reflective surface will confuse the optics inside your mouse, making your computer think the mouse is still moving. If you have a work computer that makes you log in every 5 minutes when you're not "active," you know how helpful this is!

Avoid Musty Books

If you're placing some old books in storage and don't want them to acquire a musty smell, here's the solution. Place a new sheet of fabric softener inside the pages, and that battered copy of *To Kill a Mockingbird* will stay nice and fresh until you need it again. If you fail to follow this tip or if you have books that are *already* musty, just place them in a paper grocery bag with an open box of baking soda. Fold over the bag, staple it shut, and let it sit for a week or two. Your books should smell considerably better when you take them out.

Stop Smoky Smells

Did you know that a bowl of sliced apples will remove the smell of cigarette smoke in an enclosed space? The next time you have a smoky party, cut up some apples and leave them around the house before you go to bed.

For a Great-Smelling Home

When it's too cold to open the windows, freshen your whole house fast by placing a few drops of vanilla extract on your furnace's filter. Your house's heating system will do the rest of the work for you.

Make a Room Smell Wonderful

Who hasn't wanted to make a beautiful bouquet of flowers last longer? Give your flower petals a second life by layering them with non-iodized salt in a small jar. This works best with flowers that have pulpy petals and woody stems, like roses, lavender, and honeysuckle. The salt will bring out their natural scent and help freshen your entire room. Keep a lid on the jar when you're not around to make the scent last even longer.

An Always-Fresh Bathroom

To create an automatic air freshener in the bathroom, we blot a bit of perfume or scented oil in the center of the toilet paper roll. Whenever someone uses it, the roll releases a pleasant whiff to keep the room smelling fresh.

New Favorite

If your potty-trained toddler enjoys pulling toilet paper off the roll, use this trick to keep his TP usage in line: Before putting the roll on the dispenser, squeeze the tube so that it flattens slightly. This will keep the roll from turning too easily, making the amount that comes off the roll manageable.

Smelly Shoes?

To keep your shoes smelling better, store them in the freezer! It sounds funny, but it's true: The cold temperature slows down the growth of microscopic funkiness-makers.

Even Smellier Shoes!

Here's another great tip for preventing smelly shoes. Make them a thing of the past by placing orange rinds in them. Place the inside of the rinds against the soles of your shoes and they'll absorb moisture and make them smell wonderful!

Go Sage

Go natural to get rid of stinky feet! Break up a few leaves of sage and spread them around inside your shoes. They'll kill the bacteria that causes foot odor. To cut down on how much you perspire in the first place, try drinking sage tea. Herbalists say it will take several weeks, but you'll see results!

Caring for Leather Shoes

To wear in new leather shoes without having to wear them around the block ten times, rub alcohol in at the heels and wear them while they're still wet. Soften them by rubbing them with olive or castor oil, which will also prevent cracking and drying.

Slipping Solution

Going out in new shoes? Lots of fun. Slipping as you walk past your new crush? Not so much. Use sandpaper to distress slippery leather soles and slick surfaces won't slip you up.

Instant Traction

Have you been looking for a way to make your mules stay on your feet? Spray hair spray inside to provide more traction (just be sure to let them dry before you slip them back on)!

Shoelace Trick

Having trouble keeping your (or your kids') shoe-laces tied? Shoelaces are more likely to stay tied if you dampen them with water first. Or rub a bit of Chap-stick on the spot.

Make Your Slippers Even Better

It's so simple, you'll wonder why you didn't think of it sooner. To make your slippers waterproof and there-fore safe to wear on a quick trip outdoors, simply cover the bottoms with overlapping layers of duct tape.

Reader's Tip

To protect your leather shoes from getting damaged and stained by too much rock salt in the winter months, coat them with hair conditioner and let it soak in. The conditioner will repel the salt, and help keep them supple.

—KATHY DICKERMAN-SNIVELY, OLEAN, NY

Eliminating Salt Stains

It turns out that getting salt stains on your "good leather shoes" is not the calamity you might have thought it was. You can easily get rid of stains and bring back the original luster of leather shoes and bags with shampoo. Rub it in with a soft cloth and then rinse with a damp one.

Prevent Pantyhose Runs

Weird but true: Freezing pantyhose can keep them from running. Before wearing a pair of nylons for the first time, stick them in the freezer overnight. The cold strengthens the fibers, which will keep them from running.

Catch a Run

If you notice a run in your pantyhose, don't despair. Just place a bit of clear nail polish at either end of the run and it will keep your hose from running any further.

Repel Runs

If your nylons seem prone to getting runs, try soaking them in salty water before you wash and wear them. Use a half a cup of salt for each quart of water, and let them soak for 30 minutes. Then launder as usual.

Reader's Tip

If you've ever had your skirt or slip stick to your pantyhose due to static electricity, you'll love this tip. Just spritz a little hair spray on your nylons and they'll not only be free of static, they'll be less likely to run. —FRANCIE J. SHOR

Static Cure

Slinky skirt grabbing your pantyhose and won't let go? Solve this annoyance with an unlikely household hero: a battery! Just rub the positive end of a battery over your skirt and hose. (If this happens to you a lot, you can just keep a AAA battery in your purse!) The battery releases positively charged ions that neutralize the negative ones that cause static cling. Bada-bing, no more static cling!

Two-Minute Slimdown

You don't need to purchase a shaper and certainly not a corset to make yourself look five pounds slimmer. Try leotards, tight-fitting tank tops, leggings, and spandex running pants. The trick is to layer them underneath your nice outfit so you don't get the "Are-those-pajamas-you're-wearing?" look. You'll feel firmed up and pulled-together, at least until you catch sight of your hair.

Single-Breasted Suits Us

As gravity (and middle-age) takes its toll, a layer of fat may be making its way around your midsection. We'll let you decide whether to hit the gym, but when you hit the store, stay away from double-breasted jackets. Always choose single-breasted suits, as two sets of buttons make the body appear wider.

Watch Your Wardrobe

The biggest thing people do wrong when trying to hide their weight is buying loose-fitting clothes. The truth is, baggy clothes will just make you look bigger. Instead, find an outfit that accentuates the positives (and everybody has some positives!)—whether that's your hourglass hips, great legs, or beautiful neckline. Getting clothes that are tailored, but not tight, will not only draw attention where you want it, but will let people know that you're still confident about your appearance—which is way sexier than losing a few pounds around your waist.

New Favorite

If you love the smell of air-dried clothing, but never have enough room on your clothesline, you'll love this ingenious trick: Pull the fabric off an old umbrella that has a hooked handle. Then open it up, hang it from the line, and you'll have a bunch of spokes on which to hang your laundry overflow.

Quick Fix for Long Pants

You've bought a great pair of jeans, but they're too long and you don't have time to hem them before you need to wear them. Simply fold them up and tape with duct tape. The hem will last the whole night—and maybe even through a couple of washings. This is also a great tip if you're not sure exactly where you want to hem your pants. Have a "trial run" using the duct tape, and then they're all ready to sew.

Make Mending Easier

If you're mending a hole on a sleeve or pant leg, it's easy to miss a stitch when the fabric gets all balled up. Make your job easier by rolling up a magazine and placing it inside. It will partially unroll as far as the sleeve or leg will let it, creating just enough tension to hold the fabric in place.

White Marks Got You Down?

When you let down hems on clothes such as skirts, dresses, and pants, there is often a white mark where the fabric was turned up. Vinegar can be used to get rid of this pesky stain. First warm up your iron, and then scrub the mark with an old toothbrush dipped in white vinegar that has been diluted with a small amount of water. Then press with the iron. The mark will usually come right out, but if it doesn't, repeat the process until it does.

Quick Fix for a Loose Button

After rifling through your clothes for half an hour, you've finally decided on the perfect outfit to wear—but a button is loose! If you're about to lose a button and you're already halfway out the door, use a twist tie instead. Just remove the paper covering, then twist it through the holes in the button and fasten on the other side of the cloth. Just make sure to replace with real thread later!

Knot a Problem

To prevent thread from getting knotted when sewing on a button, first run a bar of soap over the thread. The soap will prevent knots!

Reader's Tip

If your needle has grown dull, sharpen it up again by running its tip back and forth on an emery board several times.

—PATRICIA S., WEST PLAINS, MO

Easy Way to Thread a Needle

To quickly thread a needle, spray the end of the thread with a bit of hair spray. It will stiffen the thread and make it much easier to get through the eye, leaving you ready to darn all those socks.

The Zipper Fix

Got a zipper that won't stay closed? Spray it lightly and carefully with hair spray after zipping up.

Stuck Zipper?

Rub a beeswax-based candle or lip gloss on a stuck zipper and the problem is solved! You can also try rubbing the zipper with the lead from a pencil.

Let's Twist Again

If your sunglasses have gotten completely twisted, don't throw them out. Just turn a blow-dryer on high and aim it at your frames. The heat makes the plastic arms flexible enough for you to gently bend them back to their original shape.

Reader's Tip

Screw fall out of your eyeglasses? A stud earring is the perfect just-for-now replacement that will keep you from having to tape your glasses together for the trip to the optometrist. Just poke it through the hole and fasten its back.

—EMMA KERCHANKO, TORONTO, ON

Repurpose Old Mittens

Old mittens make great glasses cases! You can also use them during their "off-season" to hold summer sunglasses.

Clear Up a Contact Catastrophe

Lost a contact lens and can't seem to find it anywhere? Turn off the lights and turn on a flashlight. Sweep it over the area where you lost it and the lens will reflect the light.

Compact Storage

It's easy to take a few pills and vitamins with you on-the-go by putting them in a contact lens storage case. It's small enough to fit in your pocket, but large enough to carry everything you'd need for a day.

Goodbye Residue

To remove tape or glue residue from almost any surface, pour some vegetable oil on a rag and rub vigorously. The oil will neutralize the glue's bonds.

How to Remove Superglue

Superglue's claim to fame is that it sticks to everything —and is impossible to get off. But if you accidentally get some on your work project or even your fingers, there is one substance that can get you out of your "bind." Soak the corner of a soft cloth or paper towel in nail polish remover (make sure it contains acetone) Then hold it on the area until the glue dissolves. Be aware, however, that nail polish remover will eat away at varnish and other finishes.

New Favorite

Your excitement at remembering where you stored the masking tape came to an abrupt halt when you realized it's too old to use. But wait! There's a cure for dried-out masking tape: Simply stick the entire roll in the microwave and heat on high for 10 seconds. The adhesive on the tape will melt slightly, making it sticky once again.

The Key to Keys

You'll never fumble with the wrong key again if you color-code them with a dot of nail polish. Just apply a thick coat of a different shade to the top of each key.

Pillowcase It

Our closets are kind of a mess, but we manage never to misplace part of a sheet set. That's because after washing and folding the pieces, we put the whole set right inside one of the pillowcases, which is a convenient way to make sure everything stays in one place.

Slipcover Secret

When washing a slipcover for a couch or chair, put it back on your furniture while the cover is still damp. Not only will the slipcover be easier to get on, but it won't need to be ironed. This will help keep it from shrinking, too!

Tip for a Blustery Day

Here's a great use for old keys: Use some thread or yarn to sew them to the corners of your beach and picnic blanket. It will help it stay put once you've laid it on the ground, even on the windiest of days.

New Favorite

Baby powder is the only known substance to immediately shake sand loose from human skin! Throw a cupful in a Ziploc bag and take it on your next ocean outing. When it's time to eat, dip your hands in the bag and rub off the sand. Works on other body parts as well.

A Shoe-In

If you need extra storage space in your bathroom, one of our favorite fixes is using an over-the-door plastic shoe storage container. Available at home stores, these organizers are perfect for make-up, lotion, and even small appliances like curling irons.

Candle Holder Saver

To keep votive candles from sticking to their holders after a night of wax run-off, add a little sand or water to the bottom of the holder before you light the candle. This will keep the wax from making a mess at the bottom.

Candlestick Fit

Most taper candles are too large to fit into standard candlesticks, so you'll have to do a little work to ensure your candle fits securely. (Do not light the candle and melt wax into the base—this is messy and dangerous!) First, try placing the candle base under hot water; this softens the wax and allows it to mold to its new surroundings. If this doesn't do the trick, whittle down the wax around the base of the candle with a paring knife, checking the fit as you go. Stop when you get it narrow enough to fit the holder. Apply wax adhesive (or some sticky tack) around the base of the candle, and place it in the candlestick.

For Skinny Candles

Do your candles slide around in their holders like a kid wearing his dad's pants? Wrap the bottom with tape to get the right fit.

Reader's Tip

To light hard-to-reach wicks at the bottom of jar candles, use an uncooked strand of spaghetti. Light the end of it, then use it like a fireplace match.

—AKILAH DRAUGHTER, PETERSBURG, VA

Flower Arranging Done Easily

When arranging flowers, use transparent tape across the mouth of the vase in a grid to make an invisible guide. Then stick stems into the individual holes created by the tape. Not only will it be easier to decide where to put each flower, but they'll stay more upright with the tape to lean against.

Stop Flower Spread-Out

Ever have the problem of a beautiful bouquet spreading out too much in the vase? It ends up looking rather sad and scrawny, but here's a simple fix: Use a hair elastic to hold stems together.

Make Your Flowers Taller

Got some nice flowers whose stems are too short for the vase you want to put them in? Take a clear plastic straw and cut a segment off, then slide it over the bottom of one flower stem. Cut the straw to adjust the height of the flower inside the vase, then repeat with remaining flowers. Your floral display will now stand tall!

Vinegar for Vases

Don't put a beautiful bouquet of flowers in a cloudy vase! To make it shine like new, just pour a little white vinegar and uncooked rice inside, swish it around, and watch the clouds disappear.

> ## New Favorite
> If you've chipped a vase, stop swearing at yourself and go get your kid's biggest box of crayons. Find a crayon that matches the color of your vase and you have an easy fix! Very carefully hold a flame under the tip of the crayon, letting the melted wax drip onto the chip. Once it's cooler but not hard, smooth it out and your vase will be almost as good as new.

Keep Flowers Fresh

Florists sometimes cut flowers in the open air, which allows air into the stems and prevents the flowers from absorbing all the water they need. To ensure that your store-bought flowers stay fresh longer, submerge the stems in hot water, and trim an inch off the ends. Always cut on a diagonal to expose the most surface area to the water.

Longer-Lasting Blooms

To prolong the life of your flower bouquet, simply replace their water each day, rinsing off the bottom of their stems as you do. This will discourage the growth of bacteria while making sure they get the nutrients they need.

An Old Penny Trick

You may have heard the old household tip about extending the life of your cut flowers by adding a penny to the bottom of the vase. However, today's pennies aren't made with enough copper to effectively work as a fungicide. Pennies made before 1981 do, however, so if you find one make sure to keep it for your flowers.

Flower Food
The little bit of flat soda left in your can will revitalize and sustain fresh flowers. Pour it into the vase and let the sugar go to work keeping the flowers in bloom. Clear soda works best for a clear vase.

Get Flowers to Bloom
If you've tried cutting their stems at an angle and changing their water, but the flowers in your vase just won't bloom, try a hair dryer. Put a diffuser on it and set it to low, then point it at your bouquet and slowly sweep it back and forth for five minutes. The warmth simulates the sun, which may get your shy flowers to open up.

Reader's Tip

If you're cutting flowers from your garden, do it first thing in the morning. Flowers have more moisture then and will last longer if cut early in the day.   —HIKO LIN

Displaying Fake Flowers

Make a holding place for your fake flowers using salt. Fill your vase with salt and add just enough cold water to get the salt wet, but not submerge it. Then stick the stems of your artificial flowers inside. The salt and water mixture will turn hard, keeping your flowers exactly where you want them. When you're ready to take the flowers out, fill the vase with warm water until the salt starts to dissolve.

Stuck Ring Resort

An easy way to get a stuck ring off a swollen finger is by applying Preparation-H to the area. Wait 5–10 minutes. The swelling will go down and, with a little twisting and maybe a teeny bit of pain, the ring will slide right off.

Quick Bracelet Fastening

Having trouble getting that bracelet on? Make fastening easy by attaching the bracelet to your arm with a bit of tape. Then clasp, pull the tape off, and go!

Untangling Necklaces

Annoying tangles in thin necklace chains can seem impossible to get out, but here's a trick that may work. Place the chain on a flat surface, add a drop of vegetable or olive oil, and use a pin to tease out the knots. Then rinse in warm water. The oil will make it easier to separate out the kinks.

DIY Necklace Holders

You don't have to buy a jewelry organizer to keep your necklaces untangled. Just cut plastic straws in half, thread your necklaces through, and fasten the clasps.

New Favorite

Repurpose a plastic daily vitamin/pill container into a jewelry container that's perfect for trips. Rings, earrings, and even necklaces fit perfectly inside, and it will make sure you're accessorized for each day you're away!

Keep Necklaces Safe

Packing for a trip? Keep your necklaces safe and tangle-free by taping them to some bubble wrap. Then roll the wrap up and pack safely in your suitcase.

Jewelry Organizer as Art

This organizational tip is also a great bedroom decoration. Buy a bulletin board and lots of sturdy pushpins, then use them to hang your bracelets, necklaces, rings, and hook earrings. With all your jewelry on display, you'll be able to more quickly decide what you want to wear, and it won't be a tangled mess. You'll also get a chance to look at beautiful pieces that may not make it into your regular rotation.

Cork Earring Holder

Don't throw away the cork when you finish a bottle of wine. Repurpose it! Cork is a perfect material for storing and toting stud earrings. Cut the cork into thin slices, then poke the earrings through, put the backs back on, and toss them into your toiletry bag when traveling.

Easy Earring Finder

Protect your earrings when you're at the gym or the spa by poking them through the holes of your watchband and fastening their backs on the other side. Now you won't have to worry about losing them!

Reader's Tip

If you've lost the backs to your earrings, use a tiny sliver of an eraser instead. Just carefully cut off a piece of eraser with an X-Acto knife and stick the back of the earring through it. This replacement is even better than the original, because the eraser bits usually stay on better than earring backs!
—ALISON ORR, CA

Remove Water from Your Watch

If you've ever seen condensation under your watch face, you know how frustrating it can be! Luckily, there's a solution. Simply strap the watch to a light bulb and turn it on for a few minutes. The heat from the bulb is the perfect amount to make the water disappear.

A Pool No-No
Never wear silver jewelry in pools, because chlorine can cause pitting, small indentations in the surface. It's not a particularly good idea to wear gold jewelry in chlorinated water either, so make sure to leave your valuables at home before heading to the pool.

Pool Liners Shortcut
When pool liners tear, it can be very costly to repair them. But duct tape can do the job. Simply cover the tear, and keep an eye on it to make sure it doesn't start to peel off. Believe it or not, a single piece of duct tape can usually last underwater for an entire summer.

Pool Problems
If there is too much chlorine in your pool, don't buy expensive treatments that will just have you balancing and counter-balancing chemicals for the rest of the summer. Simply don't put the cover on your pool for several days. The sun will naturally lower the chlorine content, and after a bit of evaporation, you can add more fresh water.

Guard Outdoor Light Bulbs from Winter Wear

Before it gets too cold, consider applying a thin layer of petroleum jelly to the threads of all your outdoor light bulbs. It will prevent them from rusting and make them easier to replace when they blow out.

Safely Remove a Busted Light Bulb

To remove a broken light bulb from the socket, first turn off the electricity or unplug the lamp, and then push half of a raw potato or small apple into the broken bulb's base. Turn it to unscrew the base. Just don't eat it afterward!

Drop a Glass? Sacrifice a Sandwich

If you shatter something made out of glass on your floor, try out this crafty tip. Dampen a piece of white bread, and dab it on the glass fragments. It's much more effective than using a broom.

Picking Up After a Glass Accident

You've just shattered a vase or glass, and there are shards of glass all over the entire room. Don't panic. Put on some shoes, keep kids and pets away from the area, and then head for your newspaper bin. Wet several sheets of newsprint (usually an entire section will do) and use them to wipe up the mess. First pick up any big pieces, then wipe the newspaper on the floor. The small pieces will stick to the wet paper, making sure you get every last piece. If you get any ink streaks on the floor, just clean them up with a bit of warm water or vinegar.

New Favorite

There's a blackout, and you just realized your flashlight is out of D batteries. Even if you don't have any of these jumbo batteries around the house, there may be a solution: Place a couple of C-sized batteries inside and fill up the extra space with a ball of aluminum foil. You won't get as bright of a light, but it will help shine the way.

Stuck Glass Solution

Here's what to do if you open the cupboard and your stacked glasses are stuck together: Put a couple of ice cubes in the top glass and set the bottom one in a bowl of warm water. Remember high school chemistry? Heat expands. Cold contracts. And your glasses will unstick!

Unstick Stuck Glasses

You reach to get a glass out of a stack of glasses, only to realize they're stuck together. Reach into the cabinet again to get some vegetable oil, then pour a bit down the side of the glasses to unstick them without the risk of breaking them.

Be Creative With Ice

If you're serving punch at a party, pour some of it into ice cube trays and freeze. This way, you can keep the punch nice and cold without diluting it. This also works well with wine, iced tea, or any number of other beverages. If you want to get really exotic, mint leaves are a great thing to make ice cubes out of—just fill the ice tray with water like normal and then stuff the leaves so that they rest below the surface.

No-Spill Party Drinks

We love anything that gives us more time to talk to our company and cuts down on hosting duties during a party. One simple way to hand out drinks—use muffin trays instead of flat trays. You can easily carry two dozen glasses without breaking a sweat and even younger family members will be able to help.

New Favorite

Having a party? Put your child's inexplicable Silly Bandz obsession to good use! These rubber bands in fun shapes are perfect for putting around the stems of wine glasses so your guests can tell whose are whose.

Filtering Your Wine

Red wines that are more than eight years old tend to develop sediment. It's harmless, but it doesn't always look too nice. Get rid of sediment, and any bits of cork, by pouring your wine through a coffee filter and into a decanter before you serve it.

Fonzie's Wine Tip

The next time you attempt to open a bottle of wine only to have cork end up in the bottle, reach for a (clean) comb! Just hold the comb over the spout and pour, and it will catch any bits of cork.

Frozen Grapes

If you want to keep your wine (or other beverage) cool on hot summer days, use frozen grapes instead of ice cubes. They'll keep the drink cold and they won't dilute it or change the taste as they thaw. Just make sure you wash them before freezing!

Chill Drinks Faster

Because salt lowers the freezing point of water, your beverages will cool more quickly if you use salt in your cooler. Simply layer ice with salt, throw in the bottles and cans, and wait for them to chill.

Better than the Bathtub!

If you're having a party and have run out of space to cool beverages, don't go buy a Styrofoam cooler. Instead, fill your washing machine with ice and store bottles and cans inside. The lid will keep everything cool, and once the ice melts you can simply run the rinse cycle to get rid of all the water.

Second String

Having a party and need an extra trash bin for your guests? Just repurpose your hamper. (Your dirty clothes will be fine in a garbage bag in the closet until tomorrow.)

Pack It Up

Packing up your cooler for a day on the beach? Make sure it's at least 25 percent full of ice or cold packs. Otherwise, it won't be cold enough to keep your perishables cool.

Vanilla Ice

The easiest way to keep your cooler smelling fresh is to add a few drops of vanilla extract to a damp rag or paper towel, then wipe down the inside of the cooler before you put it away. The alcohol in the vanilla works as a disinfectant, and your cooler will smell great!

A Fresher Thermos

Put a teaspoon of salt inside your thermos before you store it to keep it fresh-smelling. For a larger cooler, try a charcoal briquette. It's surprising, but charcoal works as an air freshener.

Shake It Up

Who needs a martini shaker? Instead of buying this expensive bar tool, simply use a stainless steel thermos with a screw-in lid. If there's no way to close the sipping hole on the top, cover it with your thumb while you shake!

Reader's Tip

If you send your kids to school with a thermos or bottle of juice, a great way to keep their entire lunchbox cool is by freezing the bottle ahead of time, then allowing it to thaw while it sits in your child's locker. But because it's easy for bottles to explode due to the expansion of the ice, here's an even better option: Freeze the juice in an ice cube tray, then pop the juice "ice cubes" into the bottle. This is also a great trick for metal water bottles, which don't do well in the freezer!

—ABBEY HADDEN COLBERT

BBQ Six-Packs

Six-packs are a must-have at a barbecue—and not just for the beer. Turn an old six-pack container into a holder and carrier for condiments like ketchup, mustard, and relish. You can even stick napkins and plastic utensils inside. To make it extra strong (and waterproof), wrap it in duct tape!

Utensil Holder

An old oven mitt makes a great holder for barbecue utensils. Use its hanging loop to attach it to your grill, and it's perfect for tongs or anything else you need.

Tongs To-Do

You've figured out that putting tongs on a spoon rest often creates more mess than it saves. We got this idea from a barbecue party we went to last summer. Use a mug. So perfect and easy you're sure to have an "A-ha, why didn't I think of that?" moment.

Brighten a Backyard

You're hosting a backyard barbecue that's turned into an evening affair. Unfortunately, your outdoor accent lights aren't bright enough, but you don't want to have to turn on the glaring light by your door. Instead, fold pieces of aluminum foil in half (shiny side out) and wrap like a bowl around the bottom of the light, then attach with a few pieces of electrical tape. The foil will reflect the light in a nice, shimmering pattern.

Frisbee Reinforcement

Having a barbecue? Super-power your paper plates by placing a Frisbee underneath each one. Or, cover a Frisbee with foil and it's perfect for serving food right off the grill.

A Makeshift Fish Cage

If you have two small wire racks, you can easily cook a fish on your outdoor grill (and impress your friends). First, find toaster-oven or cooling racks and some fire-proof wire. Oil the racks, then put the fish between them and tie the racks together. Grill the fish on one side, then flip your newly constructed basket with large tongs or a spatula. This makeshift cage will keep delicate fish from breaking apart.

Find Out If You Need a New Tank

Nothing gets the summertime party going faster than firing up the backyard grill. Just make sure you keep all that smoked and grilled meat coming—it's unforgivable to run out of fuel before the last kebab is bobbed. Even without a gas gauge, there is a way to figure out how much fuel you have left. Here's what to do a day or two *before* the flip-flopped masses are set to arrive. Boil water, then pour it down the side of the tank. Place your hand on the side: The cool part has propane inside, the warm part is empty.

Sugar Does It

Can't get the charcoal going, and don't have any lighter fluid? Try using sugar. Once sugar is exposed to flame, it decomposes rapidly and releases a fire-friendly chemical that can help ignite that stubborn charcoal. Simply apply a light dusting of sugar to the coals before you light them.

New Favorite

When the coals start to die down on your grill, don't squirt them with more lighter fluid, which not only costs money, but can leave your food tasting bad (and burn the hair off your arm). Instead, blow a hair dryer on the base of the coals. The hair dryer acts as a pair of bellows, and your fire will be going again in no time.

Loosen a Tight Lid

Is the lid on your jar stuck? We have the solution. Turn the jar upside down and place it in a bowl. Fill the bowl with warm water until the water reaches a quarter of the way up the jar, then let sit for 15 minutes. The water will loosen the vacuum seal as well as soften any leaking syrup, jam, or whatever else is inside.

V-Rack Made Easy

Using a V-rack is one of the best ways to roast a chicken or turkey, but if you don't have one here's a free and easy substitution. Remove the grates from your gas stove and wrap them in foil. Poke a few holes to let juices through, then rest them against the sides of the roasting pan. Voilà: impromptu V-rack!

Getting Cutting Boards to Stay Put

Cutting boards that slip around on the counter are an obvious no-no, yet it's amazing how often we turn cutting a watermelon into an extreme sport in our house. We finally figured out that all that extra shelf liner in the pantry *could* in fact come in handy one day. We simply cut it to the right size to use as a place mat for the board, and it never slipped again.

Clean Knife Trick

We used to throw knives in the dishwasher with every-thing else. Problem is, this dulls the blades, and "gunk" (scientific word for stuck-on food left from chopping onions, raw meat, and tomatoes) would still be on the sides. Luckily, there's a neat trick for cleaning knives without dulling their edges—a cork. Simply dip one in vinegar and use it to rub off the gunk, then wash by hand with a soft cloth. No scrubbing necessary!

Remove Rust from Your Knife

If your knife is rusty, it's time to chop some onions. Believe or not, onions will remove rust from metal objects. Plunge the knife into the biggest onion you can find, let it sit for a few seconds, then pull it out. Repeat this process until the rust has dissolved, then wash as usual and dry.

Pot Pleaser

If you lose the knob to a pot lid, don't throw out the pot! Place a screw into the hole, with the thread side up, then attach a cork to it.

For a "Like New" Waffle Iron

Waffle day is so much less fun when we have to beg and plead with the waffles to come out of the iron. Here's a quick fix if the "nonstick" material on your wafflemaker has worn out: Place a sheet of wax paper in the iron, close, and heat up. Remove and now give it a try: thanks to the transferred wax, the waffles should pop out.

Seal 'Em Yourself

If your plastic bags are not resealable, you can seal them yourself with this quick trick: Fold a small piece of aluminum foil over the end you'd like to seal, and iron it so both ends of the foil close over the plastic. This will ensure that the plastic doesn't melt.

CHAPTER 2

HOME REPAIR HINTS

Get Rid of Telltale Creaks

Back when our kids were still tiny, this trick was a lifesaver. There's nothing worse than finally getting a grouchy baby to sleep and tip-toeing out of the room only to have the wooden floor in the hallway creak like the second coming. Shake talcum powder over the cracks and rub in with an old rag, and you can escape in silence!

Repair a Scratched Floor

If you've scratched your floor while doing some home repairs, it's time to ask your kid for help. No, really! Go to his box of a million different-colored crayons, and pick the one that most closely matches the color of your floor. Cut off half the crayon and place it in an old take-out container (or something else you won't mind getting crayon all over). Melt the crayon in the microwave, then spread the hot wax into the crack. Wax your floor and it will look like new.

Coffee Cure

Cover up scratches in wood furniture or floors with coffee! Just brew a very strong pot, and then use a cotton ball or rag to apply the coffee over the scratch. It works as a stain, and will have the scratch blending in with the floor in no time!

New Favorite

If you have a white mark on your wooden table and you're not sure where it came from, it may have been caused by putting a hot dish or mug onto the area. Luckily, you can easily remove this spot with a couple of household helpers. Just grab some toothpaste (as long as it's not the whitening kind) and place a dollop of it on the table along with a small amount of baking soda. Gently rub the area for a minute, then wipe clean and repeat until the mark is gone. The tiny particles of baking soda suspended in the toothpaste will rub tiny particles of wood off your table until it looks as good as new!

Wooden Dent Removal

As long as the wood hasn't broken apart underneath, you may be able to fix dents in wooden floors or furniture. Here's how: Run a rag under warm water and wring it out, then place it on top of the dent. Apply an iron set on medium heat to the rag until the rag dries out. Repeat this process until your dent is gone.

Fill a Hole in Your Vinyl Floor

If there's a small hole in your vinyl floor, here's how to patch it up without anyone noticing the spot. Find a tile that is the same color, or better yet, one that you've saved for a replacement. Make some vinyl shavings from the tile using a cheese grater, then mix them with a small amount of clear nail polish. Dab the nail polish mixture into the hole and let dry. Voilà! Your floor is like new again.

Fix Your Flooring

If your vinyl flooring is coming up, put it back where it belongs! Lay a sheet of foil on top (shiny side down), then run a hot iron over it several times until you feel the glue on the bottom of the tile starting to melt again. Place something heavy, like a stack of books, on top and leave it overnight to set.

Reader's Tip

The next time someone sends you a box full of packing peanuts, save a few and throw them in your toolbox. They're great for getting screws into stripped holes. Just stuff the packing peanut into the hole, and then turn the screw into its dense Styrofoam. Cut away any pieces of the peanut that remain outside the hole.

—RODRIGO HIDALGO, CASA GRANDE, AZ

Wall Hole Solution

Before spackling small holes in your wall caused by nails, first cut a Q-tip in half and insert in the hole, stick end first. Then spackle as you normally would. The Q-tip will completely fill the hole and ensure you won't have to go back for a second pass.

Protect Your Walls from Cracks

Before driving a nail into a plaster wall, place a small piece of tape over the spot you're working on. This simple prep step will prevent cracking in the plaster.

Patch It Up

To make a putty for quick patches, combine a tablespoon of salt with a tablespoon of cornstarch. Mix them together with just enough water to make a paste. Apply while still wet.

Finding Imperfections

Filling and sanding every hole in the wall before you paint can be enough of a pain, but sometimes it's hard to find every crack, hole, and imperfection. Make your job easier by turning off the lights in a room, then slowly running a flashlight over the entire surface of the wall. The light will cast different shadows in these areas, making them easier to see than they would have been in the daylight.

Get Rid of Excess Paint

A great way to make painting neater is to wrap a wide rubber band around your open paint can from top to bottom. The rubber band will run right over the opening of the can, and you can use it to wipe the excess paint from your brush instead of using the edge of the can. Then when you're done painting, wrap the band around the paint can the other way, at the exact level that the paint is at inside. That way, you won't have to open the can to see how much paint is left.

A Safer Basement

If you've ever accidentally skipped the last step of your basement stairs and fallen flat on your face, you'll take us up on this tip immediately. Paint the last step a bright white. Even if your basement is pitch black and your arms are full, you still won't miss it.

Step by Step

When painting steps, paint every other one as you work your way down. When those are dry, go back and paint the rest. This way, you'll still be able to use the stairs while your paint is drying (as long as you're careful!).

No More Bending for Baseboards

You've been painting baseboards for what seems like hours, thanks to the constant bending over and moving around. Make the job easier on yourself (and your back!) by borrowing your kid's skateboard. It makes a great bench on wheels!

Reader's Tip

When painting a windowsill, forget the edging tape: It's expensive, and it can pull up the paint you already have on the sill. So instead, use strips of newspaper. Dampen them and wring out as much excess moisture as you can without ruining the paper, then use them in lieu of tape. They'll stick as long as they're wet, but won't pull up any paint when you're done. —MELISSA FABIAN, VALLEY GREEN, PA

Erase a Painting Mistake

You've just painted your window trim and got a big glob of "country yellow" on the glass pane. There's no need to use a dangerous razor blade to remove the paint that spilled on the glass. Instead, remove the paint safely and easily with a pencil eraser. If the paint has dried, or is old, dab on some nail polish remover, wait a minute, then erase.

Add Marbles for Easy Painting

Before stirring paint, place a few old marbles in the can. They'll stir the paint so well you should just be able to give it a good shake to remix before its next use. To make shaking and storing even easier, first empty the paint into a plastic jug with a funnel.

Warm Your Paint

Did you know that enamel paint spreads more smoothly when it's warm? To get it up to a higher temperature, place it in a warm bath before you use it.

No Cleaning Necessary (for Now)

If you want to avoid cleaning a paint roller (for now), wrap it in foil or a plastic bag and place it in the refrigerator. The covering will keep the roller moist and usable for a few days, so you can finish where you left off later.

New Favorite

Painting doors? Avoid getting paint on the hinges by coating them lightly with petroleum jelly before you start. It's easier to protect the rounded corners than when using painter's tape, and it wipes right off!

Paint Tray Problem Solved

The easiest way to clean a paint tray after you're done rolling on paint is never to get it dirty in the first place! Instead of using plastic wrap or foil, put the paint tray in a plastic bag and pour the paint on top. Once you're done, simply turn the bag inside out and throw away.

Revitalize Paintbrushes

There's no need to throw out old paintbrushes. Just soak them in hot vinegar for 20 minutes, then wash with dish soap and warm water. They'll be close to brand-new again!

Keep Paintbrushes Like New

Even if you clean your paintbrush thoroughly, the bristles are likely to be stiff after they dry. Keep them soft and flexible with ordinary hair conditioner. Just add a tablespoon of conditioner to a pint of warm water, and after cleaning the brush, dip it in the solution for a few minutes.

Drip Guard

To catch drips while you paint, try this makeshift drip cup: Cut a tennis ball in half and slice a thin slot in the bottom bowl of one half. Then slide your brush handle through the slot so the bristles stick out of the open side. A small paper plate or cup works, too.

Remember Your Color

If you've tried saving your paint swatches in the past and can never find them when you need them, try this simple trick: Write the name and type of paint you used for each room under the light switch plate. That way, you'll know where the info is when you need it.

Reader's Tip

Putting up new wallpaper? Here's a great trick to quickly and easily get rid of the old stuff. First, score the paper with a utility knife by cutting slashes through several parts of the paper. Then, dab on a mixture of half water and half liquid fabric softener. Leave on for 10–15 minutes, then watch your old wallpaper peel right off.

—LORA BOUDINOT, WOODRIDGE, IL

Wallpaper Remover

Redoing a room with a wallpaper border? Easily remove it by blowing hot hair from a hair dryer on it. The heat will loosen the glue and it will peel right off.

Make Hanging Wallpaper Easier

Take your wallpaper out of its roll a few days before you hang it and re-roll it the opposite way. It will make it flatter and easier to hang.

Tip for the Butterfingers

How many times have you hit your fingers while hammering in a nail? Next time you're hanging pictures, put the nail between the tines of a fork before hammering. Your fingers will thank you, and your kids won't have to hear you swear.

Loosen a Rusty Nut or Bolt

To remove that pesky rusted nut or bolt, put a few drops of ammonia or hydrogen peroxide on it, and wait 30 minutes. If you're out of both, try a little bit of cola instead.

A Handy Holder for Tape

If you use tape a lot near your workbench, make the search for rolls a thing of the past. Attach a toilet paper holder or a wall-mounted paper towel holder to the wall, and you have a great storage spot for tape rolls.

A Home for Your Soldering Iron

If you regularly use a soldering iron, place several pieces of steel wool in an old coffee can. When you're done soldering, you can easily place the iron tip-down in the can to make sure you don't burn your work area.

Un-Stick a Sliding Door

If your sliding glass door is sticking, simply spray the tracks with furniture polish. It will remove dirt and give the tracks the lubrication they need to keep the door moving smoothly.

Open a Stuck Window

If humidity has sealed your window shut, here's how to get it open again: Hold a block of wood up against the frame, and tap it gently a few times with a hammer. Then move to a different place on the frame until you've tapped all around the edges. You should now be able to easily pull it up.

New Favorite
Don't tell the kids this, but scratches in the window and breakfront glass don't have to be permanent. Rub a little white toothpaste into the mark and buff. Wipe clean and coat with a solution of 1 tablespoon vinegar and ½ cup water.

Stuck Drawer?

If you've been fussing with a drawer that won't open, it's probably expanded due to humidity. Dry it out with a hair dryer set on low heat, or place a work lamp with a 60-watt bulb inside and leave for 30 minutes. The drawer will contract, and you'll be able to move it easily again. Then rub its runners or anywhere it seems to be sticking with a bar of soap or a candle. This should grease it up enough to get it moving again.

Clean Up a Spill with a Straw

You're trying to make a repair in a drawer or somewhere else with a tight corner, and you keep dripping glue that's nearly impossible to wipe up. Solve your problem by flattening a drinking straw, then folding it in half. The *v* shape is perfect for getting into tiny corners and crevices.

Drain Volcano

Most people know the old science fair project of mixing vinegar and baking soda to cause a chemical reaction worthy of a model volcano, but not many know that this powerful combination is also a great drain cleaner. Baking soda and vinegar break down fatty acids from grease, food, and soap buildup into simpler substances that can be more easily flushed down the drain. Here's how to do it: Pour 2 ounces baking soda and 5 ounces vinegar into your drain. Cover with a towel or dishrag while the solution fizzes. Wait 5–10 minutes, then flush the drain with very hot water. Repeat until your drain is clear.

Get the Most from Your Plunger

Add a little petroleum jelly to the rim of your rubber plunger. It helps achieve great suction, so the disgusting job ahead is a little bit easier.

Prevent Leaks with Floss

Instead of using expensive Teflon tape to prevent leaking between pipes and other parts that screw together, just use dental floss. Wrap the floss around the item's threads, and you'll have a tight connection.

Silence Squeaky Faucets

If the handles of your sink shriek when you turn them, try this simple fix. Unscrew the handles and rub petroleum jelly on all the threads. The jelly will keep them lubricated and (hopefully) squeak-free.

Reader's Tip

If you have an old hose you're about to throw away, here's a great second use. Cut off a two-inch section, then cut a horizontal slit all the way through it. Slide onto the handles of buckets to make them easier to carry. Reinforce with duct tape if necessary. —BREANNE RATTO MARK, ITHACA, NY

Sandpaper Your Ladder

Most stepladders are perfectly safe, of course, but if you want to amp up the nonskid surface of the rungs, there's an easy way to do it. Just paint the steps of the ladder and, before they dry, sprinkle fine-grained sand on top. The sand will stick to the steps and create a sandpaper-like surface.

Mend a Shingle

If one of your roof's shingles has fallen off, you can make a temporary replacement using duct tape. Cut a ¼-inch-thick piece of plywood to match the same size as the missing shingle. Then wrap it in duct tape (you will need several strips), and wedge it in place. Use extra duct tape to keep it there, if necessary.

A Gift for Your Gutter

Never pay to have your gutters cleaned again! To easily keep falling leaves from clogging them up, place a Slinky (yes, the child's toy) in your gutters. Stretch it out, then fasten the ends to your gutters with binder clips. The coil will allow water to get through, but keep leaves out.

Sponge Spout

Does the constant sound of your downspout dripping after a storm make you feel like someone is doing a psychological experiment to see how long it takes for the noise to make you crazy? Fix it fast with the help of a kitchen sponge. Just place the sponge at the end of the spout and it will soak up the drips while still allowing water to get through.

If you're using a flat-head screwdriver and are having trouble keeping the screw on the end, try rubbing each side of the screwdriver with a piece of chalk. The chalk will increase the friction and give you a tighter hold.

—JIM DWYER, GETTYSBURG, SD

Save Your Wall

If you do more damage than good when taking nails out of the wall by grazing with the claw, you can use a spatula as a guard, holding it between the claw and the wall each time you yank.

Brilliant Tool Replacement

You need a Phillips-head screwdriver but your search through your junk drawer was fruitless. A great replacement in a pinch is a potato peeler. The curved top edge will fit into the x-shaped groove of the screw.

Stud Finder Substitution

Looking for a stud and don't have a stud finder? Use an electric razor instead. Most razors will change slightly in tone when going over a stud in the wall.

Replacement Cap

If you lose the tiny cap to your glue or caulk tube, stick a screw in there instead! We actually prefer long screws to caps, because they'll clean out the narrow area in the tube and make sure the glue or caulk doesn't harden between uses.

New Favorite

Are the knobs to your drawers and cabinets coming loose? To fix the problem forever, remove the knob and coat the end of the screw with nail polish (use clear if you're a bit messy), then screw the knob back on before the polish dries.

Another Reason to Love Cola

When you buy a rust remover, what you're really paying for is phosphoric acid. However, phosphoric acid can also be found in something you probably have around the house—cola. Dip screws or anything else that needs de-rusting into cola and leave for several minutes. Then scrub away the black substance that remains and repeat if necessary.

Tighten Droopy Cane Chairs

A chair's caning can loosen and begin to droop. If you let it go long enough, you might even fall through the seat and hurt your bum (not to mention your ego). But, no fear! You can tighten it easily and cheaply. Apply very hot water to the underside, then dry the chair in direct sunlight.

Silence Squeaky Lawn Furniture

If your wicker seems to scream every time you sit in it, it's become too dry. Take off any cushions and spray the wicker with a hose. The water will give it enough moisture to silence the squeaks.

Wicker That Won't Age

To keep wicker from yellowing in the sun, bathe it in salt water with a wet rag when it's new.

Stow Your Wicker for the Winter

Before the first freeze arrives, bring all your wicker furniture inside to protect it from the cold. Freezing will cause the wicker to crack and split, which unfortunately, is impossible to repair.

CHAPTER 3

CAR MECHANICS' SECRETS

Two for Yourself, Two for Your Car

If your car battery has died and you don't have jumper cables, don't get a headache just yet. First, try dropping a couple of aspirin tablets into the battery. The acid in the aspirin can provide it with just enough charge to get you to the nearest service station.

Keep Your Car's Battery Lasting Longer

To prevent your car's battery from corroding, wipe down the battery posts with petroleum jelly once every couple of months.

Keyless Clues

When your car's keyless remote needs a new battery, don't head to the dealership for a replacement—depending on the kind of car you have, it can cost anywhere from $50 to $150. Instead, pry open your remote and check the size and type of battery you need. Then head to a hardware or electronics store for a much-cheaper alternative.

Don't Wait Until Empty

You should always fill up your gas tank before it dips below a quarter of a tank. Having a sufficient amount of fuel will ensure your car's fuel injection system stays healthy.

Reader's Tip

If your motorcycle is too loud (yes, there is such a thing), stick a #3-grade steel wool pad into the muffler.

—JASON SELWAY, BLACKSBURG, WV

Prevent Car Freeze-Out This Winter

If your car doors freeze shut during the frigid winter months, try this preventative measure: Rub vegetable oil on the rubber moldings around your doors. Since it's the rubber, not the metal, in your doors that freezes, lubing it with oil should do the trick.

Stop Ice Before It Starts

To keep your car's door locks safe from ice during the cold winter months, place a refrigerator magnet over the lock. You can even take an old magnet (that 2008 calendar from a local realtor, perhaps) and cut it into pieces that fit perfectly.

Winter Time-Saver

If you park your car outside during winter, you can save yourself scraping and wiping time each morning by wrapping your side mirrors and windshield wipers in old plastic bags.

Vinegar for Your Car

If you have to leave your car outside overnight in the winter, you can still keep your windshields ice- and frost-free. Mix three parts vinegar to one part water and coat the windows with this solution. (Never pour hot water on your windshield. The glass may expand from the heat and then contract as it cools, causing the windshield to crack.)

Reader's Tip

Before the winter weather hits, rub a layer of car paste onto your headlights and breaklights, then let it dry for a while before buffing off. It will help keep snow and road grime off the lights so you can see—and be seen—more easily.

—SALEENA CHAMBERLIN

Don't Get Stuck

If your car gets stuck in an icy patch and your wheels aren't getting any traction, help free it by using your car's floor mats. Take them out and place under the tires, then drive to a safe place, retrieve the mats, and be on your way.

Impromptu Shovel

Stuck in the snow (or mud) with no way to dig yourself out? A shovel may be closer than you think. Just remove your hubcap and use it instead.

Condition Your Car

After washing your car, give it a second round just like you would your head—with hair conditioner! You might think we're crazy, but applying conditioner, leaving for five minutes, and then rinsing it off will give your car a just-waxed shine. As an added bonus, it will more effectively repel water!

De-Rust Your Bumper

The best way to remove rust from your car's chrome bumper? Scrub the rusted area with a shiny piece of crumpled aluminum foil that has been dipped in cola.

Removing Bumper Stickers

We hate to break it to you, but John Kerry and John McCain lost their bids for the presidency. Get those old bumper stickers off and bring your car up-to-date. Rub cold cream on the stickers and wait 10 minutes. Then say goodbye to your former favorite candidate and peel the bumper stickers right off.

A Surefire Way to Wipe Away Window Decals

Transparent decals may be easily removed using a solution of equal parts lukewarm water and white vinegar. Place the solution on a sponge and dampen the area thoroughly for a few minutes. If this doesn't work, saturate the decal with straight vinegar and let stand for 15 minutes.

New Favorite

Got a bunch of bug guts on your windshield after a road trip? Easily remove them with a pair of old pantyhose and some vinegar. Just bunch up the hose and wet it with white vinegar, then easily scrub away.

Bug Guts to Go

Don't you hate the smashed-up insects that always seem to cover your car grille in the summer? The only thing worse than looking at them is trying to scrape them off, unless you try this trick: Before screaming down the highway, use a light coating of vegetable oil or nonstick cooking spray on your grille, and the revolting bugs will wipe off easily.

Make Dashboard Scratches Disappear

Got scuffs and scratches on your odometer? You can eliminate the marks on dashboard plastic by rubbing them with a bit of baby oil.

Steel Wool for Whitewalls

Steel-wool pads make excellent whitewall tire cleaners. It's best to use the finest steel-wool pad you can find.

Smeary Windshield Wipers

Messy wipers are a safety hazard, and they're also pretty annoying. If your wipers are smearing the windows, wipe the blades with some rubbing alcohol.

New Favorite

Misjudge how much room you had backing out of a parking spot? Just whip out a can of WD-40 and spray whichever car got left with a paint stain. Wipe with a clean cloth or tissue and the paint will come right off.

Clean Car Glass with Cornstarch

To clean dirty windows or your car's windshield, mix a tablespoon of cornstarch with about ½ gallon of warm water, apply to the windows, and dry with a soft cloth. It's amazing how quickly the dirt is removed—and no streaking, either!

Cleaning Off Brake Dust

To remove brake dust—that fine, black powder—from your car's tires, apply a bit of cooking spray or vegetable oil, let sit for 10 minutes, and wipe off. Then spray them again when you're done. The vegetable oil will reduce the collection of dust in the future, and you'll be able to wipe it off even more easily next time.

Zap the Sap!

Tree sap dripping on your car is one of the hazards of summer, but you can remove it easily with butter or margarine. Just rub the butter onto the sap with a soft cloth, and it comes right off.

Reader's Tip

When it comes to organizing your car, don't forget about all the paper that ends up in there—registration and insurance info as well as maps, scribbled directions, and more. We like to keep a small accordion file in our glove compartment to prevent those moments where we're on our hands and knees looking under the seats.

—CATRIONA BOTTER, SAN MARCOS, TX

Turn a Visor into an Organizer

Turn your car's visor into a handy place to store paper and other flat items by using rubber bands. Wrap several rubber bands snugly around the visor, then slip papers, CDs, or anything else under the rubber bands.

Organize Your Pick-Up

Sick of things rattling around your truck bed? Divide it into several compartments for storage by using spring-loaded shower curtain rods. Brace the rods against the sides of your truck bed and each other. They'll keep larger items from shifting during flight.

New Favorite

Your daughter is suddenly too cool for her Dora the Explorer backpack. It's not even worn out, but it's not really your look, either. A great way to repurpose it is to use it as storage in your car! It will easily hang on the back of one of the front seats, and keep all those odds and ends that usually litter the floor.

CHAPTER 4

SMART PET TRICKS

Rein in Pet Hair

Cleaning out your own hairbrush is bad enough, but cleaning out the one that belongs to your furry companion can be a half a day's work. Instead of getting angry next time you snag your pantyhose, give them a second life. Cut strips of hose and lay them over your pet's clean metal brush, poking the pins of the brush through. The next time your cat or dog looks like he just stepped out of a salon after a heavy brushing, all you'll have to do is remove the scraps of material, throw them out, and replace with new strips.

Reader's Tip

Does your pet hate being brushed? Make your fingers go further by buying some textured gardening gloves and slipping them on before you pet your cat or dog. The gloves will remove loose hair and any dirt from short-haired animals so well, no one will be able to tell that your furry buddy runs away every time you get out the brush.

—CASHIMERA SHOCKLEY, LA HABRA, CA

Untangle Fur

Pet owners know that matted hair can make brushing your animals a frustrating experience for you—and a painful one for them. To prevent this, rub your pet with baby powder prior to brushing. It'll be easier to remove the tangles, for which both you and your pet will be grateful.

How to Handle Pet Hair

If you don't have the heart to banish your pet from the couch, here's a solution for removing all that hair from your sofa. Just use a dry, unused dish sponge to wipe the hair into a pile with your hand. Discard the hair and then repeat the process. After you've gotten most of the hair, take a sheet of fabric softener from the laundry room and use it to pick up the rest—the hair will be naturally attracted to it. When that's done, use a vacuum cleaner to add the finishing touch.

Another Quick Pet Hair Remover

Uh oh, guests are on their way and you've just realized that your beloved cat has made a cat-fur nest all over your couch. For a quick and easy way to remove pet hair from furniture, turn to your rubber dishwashing gloves. Just slip them on, then rub the offending fur-niture with them. The hair will stick to the gloves and you can quickly throw it away.

Secret to Shiny Fur

To make your short-haired pet's fur extra-shiny, rub it down with a piece of silk, velvet, or chamois cloth.

No More Fuzzy View

If you have a cat who loves looking out the window, you know how full of cat hair the screen can get when he presses himself against it for a closer look outside. An easy fix? Just run a lint roller across the screen, or press a piece of tape against it.

Stop Scratching

Crushed red pepper shaken onto tape and affixed to furniture is an effective "Keep Out" sign for cats. The noxious smell trumps the desire to scratch. (Just remember that you may have some explaining to do to your guests!)

Scaredy Cats

All cats will run and hide if they hear a loud noise, but some cats seem particularly flighty. If your overly anxious cat runs when he hears regularly occurring noises like shut doors, loud steps, or even sound effects from the TV, here's how to help. Begin by tapping a wooden spoon very gently against a pot or pan while he is eating. Make sure the sound is loud enough that he notices, but not so loud that he gets scared. After you've done this for a couple of days, you can begin slowly increasing how loudly you tap. Once your quiet tap is a loud bang and your cat is still calm, change the surface you're tapping to wood, or try to incorporate a sound that has easily spooked him in the past—just make sure to begin quietly and work your way up again. Finally, begin introducing these sounds into your cat's daily life. Eventually he won't even notice that clap of thunder from outside.

Housebreaking Help

Housebreaking your new puppy is the hardest part about being a new dog parent, but you can make it a little easier with this tip. If your puppy has soiled newspaper, bury it just underneath the soil where you'd like him to relieve himself outside. The smell will tell him it's the right place to go.

New Favorite

If your dog has ever stepped in gum while you were out for a walk, you know how hard it can be to remove the sticky substance from between his pads. Thankfully, you can make it a little easier with some olive or vegetable oil. Rub oil all over the gum, then pull it out with your fingers or a comb. The oil will help lubricate the gum and remove it more easily. And it will even moisturize your pet's pads!

Shampoo-dle

If your dog hates taking baths, try placing a towel at the bottom of the tub before you fill it up. It will be much less slippery under your dog's paws, and that will help keep him calm.

Time for a Bath

You've finally trained your dog to be good while getting a bath in the tub, but his tiny hairs always slip through your drain's catcher and clog up your pipes. To keep this from happening, stuff some steel wool into the opening (but not too far down). It will catch every hair from even the furriest of creatures. When you're done bathing, make sure to fish the steel wool out immediately.

Build a Doggie Path

If your dog tends to track mud into the house, you can confine that mess to one area by creating an outdoor walkway for him to use before entering. The best bet is filling a path with gravel, which helps keep mud off the pooch's paws and keeps the house cleaner.

Keep Pets Safe

No need to buy a fancy nighttime collar for your furry friend. Simply cover a regular collar with reflector tape and watch Rover roam all over, even in the dark.

Butter Up Pills

If you have trouble getting your cat to swallow pills, try rubbing them in butter first. It will make them taste better to your cat, and they'll slide right down his throat.

Ease Painful Pads

If your poor pet's pads are cracked or dry, the solution is simple. Gently rub a little petroleum jelly into her pads while she's sleeping. It will moisturize the area and is completely safe if your pet decides she wants to lick it off later.

Prevent Sunburned Pets

Did you know that light-colored animals can get sunburn, too? Guard against this by dabbing a bit of SPF 15 sunscreen on your pet's nose and the tips of his ears.

Get Rid of Ear Mites

A great household remedy for ear mites is to dissolve 1 teaspoon baking soda in 1 cup warm water and rub a cotton ball soaked in that mixture on your pet's ears. Of course, if you see a pet scratching his ears, you should always take him to the vet first, just to be sure.

Reader's Tip

If your cat is nibbling on your houseplant—or worse, using its soil as a secondary litter box—here's a tip you need: Simply scatter some coffee grounds on top of the soil. Cats hate the scent and go cause trouble elsewhere! Just be careful: While coffee grounds are, for the most part, good for your plants, too much of them can cause the soil to become too acidic.   —JANICE K. MCLEOD, VERNON, FL

Beware Poisonous Plants

If your pet likes chewing on plants, beware: Some common house and garden plants are poisonous to animals. They include: tomato plants, rhododendron, daffodils, crocus, lilies, poinsettia, holly, mistletoe, lantana, laburnum, taro, yew, cyclamen, foxglove, hyacinth, hydrangea, rhubarb, narcissus, and the pits of many fruits like apricots, plums, and peaches. If you see your pet eat any of these, take him to the vet immediately! For more information about plants that may be toxic for your animals, visit ASPCA.org and go to their "Pet poison control" section.

Routine Is Key

If your pet always wakes you up precisely five minutes before your alarm goes off so she can be fed, you know that animals are creatures of routine. Changes in behavior could be a sign that something is wrong. Just to be sure, you should take her to the vet if you notice changes in appetite, thirst, frequency of urination, energy level, hiding behavior, or anything else that seems strange to you. Your pet will thank you!

Mutt Munchies

If your dog is teething, you can create a cheap chew toy by soaking an old washcloth in water, twisting it into a fun shape, and leaving it in the freezer. Give it to your pup fully frozen, and when it thaws out, simply repeat the process. Be careful doing this with tiny dogs, though, as they can get too cold if they chew on frozen toys too often.

Calm Your Canine

It seems like a silly habit of guilty "dog parents," but it's true: Leaving the TV or radio on low in the room next to your pup will keep him calm while you're away.

Christmas Cat-astrophe

Cat lovers, beware! When it's time to trim the tree at Christmastime, never use tinsel if you have a pet kitty. Cats love to play with tinsel and eat it, and it can be deadly if it gets stuck in their digestive system.

Does Your Cat Have a Weak Stomach?

If you have a cat who frequently vomits, you should (of course) take her to the vet. Unfortunately, your vet might tell you that some cats just throw up a lot. (Why do we love them so much again?) If your cat frequently vomits, it could be because she's eating too fast. If she won't overdo it with so much food available, try leaving dry food out all day, so she can eat at her own pace. But if she becomes overweight, this might not be an option. Another trick to try is pulverizing some mint with some fresh catnip and seeing if she'll eat it—mint is good for calming stomachs.

Pretty Kitty

Fat cat? Help her slim down by sprinkling a teaspoon of crushed-up wheat bran cereal on her food each day. Its low-fat, high-fiber content will keep her full. (Just make sure to check with your vet before changing your pet's diet.)

Something Fishy

If your pet is suffering from dandruff, adding some omega-3 fatty acids to his diet is a good solution. Luckily, it's easy: Buy a can of sardines in oil and chop up a few and add to his food. He'll love the taste, and his coat will love the nutrients. (Just be sure to check with your vet first.)

New Favorite

If it takes your dog awhile to go to sleep, particularly on a cold winter night, use heat to ease her into slumber. Throw a large towel into the dryer for 5–10 minutes on high, then wrap it around your dog's bedding. Dogs (especially older ones) will love the feeling of heat on their muscles and will settle down faster.

Help Pet Food Stay Put

If your pet's food dish always ends up three feet from where it started by the time he's done eating, make it skid-proof. With a glue gun, make a thin strip of glue around the bottom rim. When dry, the hardened glue will prevent the bowl from slipping so much across the floor.

Ant Answer

Do ants keep sneaking into your pet's food? Secret tip: Ants can't swim! Place the bowl of dog or cat food into a shallow bowl filled with water.

For Smelly Cats and Dogs

Sometimes, your pet is just plain stinky. If you're beginning to notice pet odor when you open your front door, it's time to take action. Add a bit of brewer's yeast (1 teaspoon for cats and small dogs and 1 tablespoon for bigger dogs) to your pet's food, and your pet will secrete fewer of those unpleasant odors. Just make sure to check with your vet before making changes to your pet's diet.

Dog Versus Lawn

Is your dog leaving brown spots on your lawn where he decides to pee? Put a few drops of vinegar into his water bowl every time you refill it and brown spots will be a thing of the past.

To Each His Own

If you have both cats and dogs, you may be tempted to feed your cat dog food. Don't do it! Besides being highly insulted if he happens to see the can, your cat needs certain nutrients that are found only in food made specifically for cats.

Potato Prescription

If your dog is having diarrhea, it's a bad day for both him and you! Luckily, you can help him get back on track by feeding him potatoes rather than his normal dog food. Potatoes contain a large amount of starch, which helps solidify stool. Just bake 2–4 potatoes and let them cool, then feed them to your dog during his normal feeding time instead of dog food. Please make sure to check with your vet before trying this or any other change in diet!

Bad Breath Bomb

If your cat or dog has horrible breath, try adding a bit of fresh chopped parsley to his food. Parsley eliminates bad breath!

Reader's Tip

You're taking your pet on the plane, but you're worried about her getting water while you travel. Instead of filling a water dish with water, which can splash out during transit, put a few ice cubes in the dish. Once your pet's cage is settled in cargo, the ice cubes will melt, giving her some much-needed refreshment. —ART GALLAGHER, BURNSIDE, CT

Scent of a Pet Owner

If you're going to be unable to pay attention to your pet for a while—such as when she's in a carrier on a long trip—put an old, worn T-shirt inside the pet carrier with her (the best are ones you've recently exercised in). Your scent will help ease your pet's worries.

Eliminating Cat Smell

If the smell from your in-heat housecat's spray has more than nine lives, try mixing 1 cup hydrogen peroxide with ½ tablespoon baking soda and 2 squirts liquid dish soap. Pour into a spray bottle and use wherever Fluffy has left her trademark. (Be sure to spot-check, as you run the risk of bleaching certain materials.)

Cat Leaving Litter?

If your cat leaves trails of litter around the house, set a sisal mat just outside her litter box, where she enters and exits the box. The fibers and grooves in the mat will catch any flyaway litter before it hits your floor.

Reader's Tip

Don't spend extra money on scented cat litter. To keep cat litter fresh-smelling, simply mix a bit of baby powder into clean litter.   —PETER AND SARAH BAILEY, FITCHBURG, MA

Free Cat Toys

Cats love toys, and they aren't picky about where they come from! Don't spend money on expensive cat toys. Instead, use a balled-up piece of paper, a cork, or anything else they can bat around the house (but that is too big to choke on). To make the toy extra enticing, throw it in a Kleenex box that has the plastic part removed. Cats will love sticking their paws inside to try to fish out the toy.

Cat Sock

If your cat loves playing with catnip toys, she'll love this homemade version: Grab some socks from your "can't find their match" pile. Put a bit of catnip at the bottom of the biggest sock, then stuff it with the rest of the socks, adding a bit more catnip as you go. Tie the end into a knot and let your cat go at it!

Easy Dog Toy

Dog toys are expensive and can be made from harmful materials. In the Colonial era, kids made their own dolls from rags. A canine version will make Fido just as happy as any designer plush toy would. All you need to do is braid together three old dish towels. Before you start, cut two strips off the side of two of them. Then use these to tie the tops and bottoms of the braid together.

How to Discipline a Cat

Unfortunately, cats rarely respond when you tell them "no." So to make sure they have a reason to not repeat bad behavior, spray them in the face with water from a spray bottle when you catch them being bad. If this doesn't work, try spraying them with air from a compressed air can (usually used to clean electronics and computer keyboards). Cats hate the feeling of air on their faces.

Furniture Scratching, Solved!

To keep your cats from scratching furniture or getting up where they don't belong, cover the area with double-sided tape or aluminum foil. They can't stand the feeling of the stuff under their paws.

New Favorite

If your cat likes chewing on electrical cords, we know you need a solution, and fast! Here it is: Unplug the electronics, then rub the cords with a wedge of lemon. Once they've dried, you can plug them back in. Cats hate the taste of lemon and will steer clear.

Come Boy, Come!

If your dog simply won't come when called, it might be time to start from scratch. Once a dog has decided that a word doesn't mean anything to him, it's much harder to make him understand that "come" means "come to me," not "do whatever you want." Pick a different word like "here" or "move," and begin your dog's training over again by standing several feet away, saying your new word, and offering treats when he obeys. Your friends at the dog park might think it's weird when you shout, "Draw nigh, Rover!" but it's way better than having him run the other way.

Fido Being Finicky?

If you've bought a new brand of food and your dog doesn't want to eat it, put a piece of beef jerky in the bag and reseal it. By the next day, the jerky smell will have rubbed off on the food, making it seem much more appetizing.

Never Pay for a Milk-Bone

When getting a "treat" for being good, most dogs are just excited about a special snack, not that it's in the shape of a bone. The truth is, doggie treats have almost the exact same ingredients as dog food, and most dogs can't tell the difference. Instead of paying extra for dog treats, keep a separate container of dog food where you normally keep the treats, then give your dog a small handful when he's done something reward-worthy.

New Favorite

In the hot summer months, you'd like to be able to give your dog a drink of water when you're out for a walk, but you haven't yet perfected how to train him to drink from a water fountain. Solve the problem by bringing a plastic shower cap with you. When you fill it with water, it will expand enough that you can hold it out as a bowl.

Easiest Way to Clean a Fish Tank

Having fish is fun, but not when you have to periodically replace the water. Make your job easy with the help of some old pantyhose and a wet/dry shop vac. Place two or three layers of pantyhose over the nozzle of the hose and secure it with a rubber band. Remove your fish to a safe location, then stick the hose in the tank and start sucking. The dirty water will find its way into the vacuum, but the rocks won't make it through the nylon.

A Bath for Your Goldfish

Before you clean out your goldfish's bowl, first prepare a salt-water bath for him. Even though goldfish are freshwater fish, salt will help your fish absorb much-needed electrolytes and kill any parasites on his fins. To get the salt water ready, run tap water into a bowl and let it sit for a day to allow the chlorine to evaporate (you should do this when filling his freshwater bowl, too). Add a teaspoon of non-iodized salt and mix until it dissolves. Then let Goldy go for a swim in the salt water for approximately 15 minutes.

A Use for Fish Tank Water!

Even old water from your aquarium can be used again. Use it to water your houseplants—they'll love the extra "fertilizer" the fish provided.

CHAPTER 5

THE SECRETS TO MAKING COOKING EASY

Pancake Perfection

For perfectly formed pancakes, use a meat baster to squeeze the batter onto the griddle. It gives you so much control you'll finally be able to make those animal-shaped pancakes your kids have been begging you for!

Pancake Pointers

Short-order cooks and chefs have a host of tricks to make the lightest pancakes. First, don't overmix the batter—you don't want the gluten in the flour to over-develop and allow the carbon dioxide that makes the little air pockets to escape. It's better to leave a couple of lumps in the batter. To further slow the development of the gluten and the leavening action, refrigerate the mixture for up to 30 minutes.

New Favorite

Don't have time to eat anything but a breakfast bar in the morning? Store it in a glasses case to make sure it doesn't get smashed in your purse or bag on the way to work.

Removing Muffins

To easily remove muffins or rolls from a pan, set the pan on a damp kitchen towel for about 30 seconds.

Repeat using a freshly moistened towel until the muffins can be eased out of the pan. Just make sure not to use your nicest towels—you can sometimes get slight scorch marks or fabric sticking.

Making Coffee More Drinkable

If you're sensitive to acidity in coffee, but love the pick-me-up in the morning, here's a way to reduce the acid level: Just add a pinch of baking soda to the drink! You can also use this tip to decrease the acidity in other high-acid drinks and foods.

Perk Up Your Coffee

It's 3 p.m., and with the day you've had, you're headed back for a second (or third) cup of coffee. Unfortunately, once you heat up some cold joe that's been sitting in the pot, you notice it looks thick and tastes a little bitter. Make stale coffee taste like it's just been brewed by adding a pinch of salt and a dollop of fresh water to your cup. Heat it up in the microwave, and you're ready to power through the rest of your workday.

Coffee Cubes

Who doesn't enjoy an iced coffee on a sultry summer day? To make sure melting ice doesn't dilute your drink, make ice cubes using the small amount of coffee left at the bottom of your coffee pot each morning. Use them in your iced coffee and it will never taste watered down. This is also a great tip for iced tea!

New Favorite

If you love iced coffee in the summer, make it even better with the help of a martini shaker or capped thermos. Pour in the coffee, milk, ice, and any flavoring, then cover and shake. The shaking will add lots of air to the mixture, making it light, frothy, and delicious.

Make Iced Tea Easier

Is there anything more refreshing than iced tea? When making a big pot of tea, here's a tip to easily add and remove your tea bags. Just wrap the strings around a chopstick, then place the chopstick over the pot.

Makin' Bacon?

Always rinse bacon under cold water before frying—it will reduce the amount the bacon shrinks when you cook it.

Mom's Omelet Secret

The best omelet you will ever eat has mustard in it. Just add ¼ teaspoon fancy mustard for each egg, and mix in when scrambling. The mustard will add a hint of mysteriously delicious flavor to the eggs, as well as making them the perfect consistency.

Fluffy Omelets

For a super fluffy omelet, add ½ teaspoon baking soda for every three eggs. Also, try adding a drop or two of water instead of milk. The water increases the volume of the eggs at least three times more than the milk does. The coagulated proteins hold in the liquid, resulting in a moist omelet.

Separating Eggs

Even if you don't have an egg separator, it's easy to divide an egg's yolk from its white. Place the smallest funnel you have over a container, then gently crack the egg into it. The white will slide into the container, while the yolk will stay behind.

New Favorite

If you've ever gotten eggshell in your bowl of cracked eggs and tried to fish it out with your finger, you know how hard it can be. A better tool than your finger, and even a spoon? An eggshell half that you were able to break cleanly. The edge cuts through the egg whites more easily than other implements.

Sunny-Side Secrets

Want to get that perfect white film over the yolks of your sunny-side-up eggs? Add a couple drops of water and cover the pan just before the eggs are done.

Hard-Boiled How-To

Who doesn't love a hard-boiled egg? These tasty treats are easy to prepare—especially if you add a teaspoon of vinegar to the boiling water. The salt will make them easier to peel, and the vinegar keeps them from cracking while they're in the pot.

Hard-Boiled Detective

It's easy to tell whether an egg has been hard-boiled: Spin it. If it wobbles, it's raw—the yolk sloshes from one end of the egg to the other. Hard-cooked eggs spin evenly, because the yolk is held in place by the cooked egg white. Reduce your risk of spinning an egg right off the counter by adding a drop or two of food coloring to the water when you boil them. It will dye the shells so you can tell the difference between the two kinds.

Peel Eggs Perfectly

For perfectly peeled hard-boiled eggs, crack the eggs slightly on your counter, then place them in a bowl of cool water. The water will seep in and loosen the egg from its shell, making sure you don't accidentally take out half the white when you're trying to peel it.

Juicer Substitution

Instead of purchasing a handheld juicer (also known as a reamer) for fruit, simply use one blade from a hand mixer instead. Halve the fruit and twist the blade into it for easy juicing.

The Juiciest Lemons

To easily extract juice from a lemon, first roll it on the counter under your hand. Heat it in the microwave for 10 seconds, then insert a toothpick. You'll be surprised how easily the juice dribbles out.

Mango Mission

If you slice open a mango and it tastes too acidic, place it in warm (not hot) water for ten minutes. This will speed up the process of its starches turning into sugars, and it will be sweet in no time! Just make sure not to leave it in the water for more than ten minutes, as it might begin to shrivel.

Chopping Dried Fruits

Raisins and other dried fruits won't stick to your knife (or anything) if you first soak them in cold water for 10 minutes.

> ## ❈ New Favorite
>
> If you're chopping nuts in a food processor, more oil is released than when you chop by hand, and you'll wind up with a sticky mess. To avoid this, simply add a bit of flour to the nuts before hitting "pulse."

For a Guacamole Emergency!

To ripe avocados more quickly, place them in a closed paper bag with an apple. But if you need ripe avocados for some guacamole now, try this tip—which isn't ideal, but will do the trick. Prick the skin of the unripe avocado in several places, then microwave it on high for 40–70 seconds, flipping it over halfway through. This won't ripen the avocado, but it will soften it enough that you'll be able to mash it with ripe avocados and your guests won't notice the difference.

Keep Fruit Looking Fresh

Even though the taste isn't affected, it's still disappointing to unveil your fruit salad only to discover a thin layer of brown oxidation all over the fruit. A common method for keeping cut fruit looking fresh is to add a bit of lemon juice. However, an even more effective method is to fill a spray bottle with water and a few dissolved vitamin C tablets (usually available in the vitamin and nutritional supplement section of your drug store). Spray this mixture on the cut fruit and not only will you stop the oxidation, you'll be getting added vitamins!

Soggy Salad Be Gone!
Avoid wet, limp salads by placing an inverted saucer in the bottom of the salad bowl before you throw in all your veggies. The excess water that is left after washing the vegetables and greens will drain under the saucer and leave the greens high and dry.

The Secret to Day-Ahead Salad
It's so much easier to prepare food a day ahead for a dinner party—but what to do about the salad? Making the salad before guests arrive usually leads to a soggy mess, but here's a tip to allow you to make the salad in advance without it going soft. Gather lettuce and any of the following ingredients: broccoli, cabbage, carrots, cauliflower, celery, cucumbers, onions, peppers, and radishes. Chop them up and place them in a large bowl. Then completely cover all your ingredients with water and keep the bowl in the refrigerator until you need it. On the day of the party, drain the ingredients

in a colander, and spin in a salad spinner. Finally, add tomatoes, croutons, and any other toppings and enjoy a crisp, delicious salad.

Sippy Cup Substitution

It's a beautiful, fresh, colorful salad until—no! Close the floodgates! Someone overdressed it and now it's barely edible. Titrate your vinaigrette with a baby sippy cup. Mix inside the cup, shake (covering the opening), and scatter over the salad with its perfectly sized spout.

Reader's Tip

If you're microwaving vegetables to eat with dinner, here's an easy way to do it: Place them in a gallon- or quart-sized Ziploc bag and cut a ½-inch slit on the side, about an inch from the top. Microwave them for 2–3 minutes on high, and they'll come out perfectly every time!   —RANDA MORLEY

Butter Your Veggies

When you scrape out the last of the margarine from the tub, don't throw the container away just yet. Throw some vegetables into the tub, microwave it for a few seconds, and voilà!—instant yummy veggies.

Plan B

Cooking dinner and your vegetables turned to mush? Simply add some herbs along with tomato sauce or cream. Then top with cheese and/or breadcrumbs and stick in the oven for 30 minutes. Your family is sure to be impressed with your new recipe for "vegetables gratin"!

Toothbrush Tool

There are many uses for an old toothbrush—you probably already use one to clean small spaces. Our favorite second-life for an old toothbrush, however, has to be in the kitchen. Use an old toothbrush to quickly and easily remove the silk from a fresh ear of corn.

Reader's Tip

The easiest way to husk corn is to cut off both ends, then roll the corn on your counter for a moment. The husk will then peel right off! —SONA GAJIWALA, CHICAGO, IL

Mushroom Maker

Mushrooms can be kept white and firm during sautéing if you add ¼ teaspoon lemon juice for every 2 tablespoons butter or olive oil.

Less Gas, More Beans

You don't have to avoid baked beans because you fear they'll make you gassy. Instead, just add a dash or two of baking soda to the beans when they're cooking, and their gas-producing properties will be dramatically reduced.

Get Rid of Bitter Onions

Rinse the bitterness away! Rinsing chopped red onions in cold water will help ease their sharp taste.

Keep Them Cold

Do you become a blubbering mess when you chop onions? Keep the tears away by leaving your onions in your refrigerator's crisper drawer. At the colder temperature, they'll release less of the chemical that makes you cry.

New Favorite

If you find the taste of onions a bit overpowering, you can still use them as a garnish or in salads with a bit less bite. Just soak the onion in cold water for 15 minutes after chopping. The water will make the onion sweeter, making it a perfect fit for your meal. When you're selecting onions at the store, go for the flat, squat kind, which will have a less bitter taste to begin with.

A Tasty Grill

To help reduce smoke and improve the flavor of food on your grill, use an onion! Cut a red onion in half, pierce it with a fork, and dip in water. Then use the onion half to wipe down the grill rack.

Beer-B-Q

If you're grilling a steak on a closed barbecue, here's a neat trick to impress your friends. Open a can of beer and place it on the hottest part of the grill. It will boil and keep the meat moist, while adding flavor, too.

Great Grilling

To get the most out of that grilled flavor everyone loves so much, add a few sprigs of your favorite herbs, such as rosemary, thyme, and savory, directly to the top of the charcoal as you grill. It will infuse whatever you're cooking with mouthwatering flavor.

Soak Your Skewers

Using wooden skewers for your veggies on the grill? Make sure to soak them first. If you don't soak them they may burn, imparting an unwanted taste to your vegetables.

A Great Use for Stale Bread

If you're broiling steaks or chops, put a few slices of stale bread in the bottom of the broiler pan to absorb fat drippings. This will eliminate smoking fat, and it should also reduce any danger of a grease fire.

Ham Too Salty?

A little salt in ham is a good thing, but if your ham slices are too salty, place them in a dish of low-fat milk for 20 minutes before heating, then rinse them off in cold water and dry them with paper towels. The ham won't pick up the taste of the milk, but will taste much less salty.

Sticky Solution

Here's a simple tip: If you wet your hands with cold water before shaping hamburger patties or meatballs, the mixture won't stick to your fingers.

Protect Yourself from Grease Splatters

Add salt to the pan when you're cooking greasy foods like ground meat and bacon, and the grease will be less likely to pop out of the pan and burn your hand.

New Favorite

Use this trick to make unfreezing a portion of ground meat easier. Place the meat in a resealable plastic bag, flatten, then score into sections (like a tic-tac-toe board) by pressing a butter knife into the bag. Seal the bag and stick it in the freezer, and when you need just a little ground meat you'll be able to easily break off a chunk.

Stop Sausage Splitting

Keep sausages from splitting when cooking them by piercing the skin in one or two places while they are cooking. Rolling them in flour before cooking will reduce shrinkage.

Better Breading

Keeping breading on foods can be a challenge, but here are a couple of tricks to try (other than using super-glue, which we don't recommend). First, make sure that the food to be breaded is very dry (pat dry with a paper towel if necessary). As for your eggs, make sure they're at room temperature, and beat them lightly. If you're using a batter, add a teaspoon of baking soda to help crumbs stick.

More Breading Tips

Breaded cutlets are less appealing when the bread-crumbs have all dropped off in the oven. Sometimes, one extra step is all you need. After coating with crumbs, let the cutlets dry on a rack for ten minutes before cooking. Better yet, let them refrigerate for 10–20 minutes. The coating will adhere better, and you'll never have to say, "sorry the breading fell off" again.

Turkey Tips

Roasting a chicken or turkey? Try basting your bird with a small amount of white zinfandel or vermouth—it will help crisp the skin, and the alcohol imparts a brown color and glaze to the outside of the meat. Or, brush the skin with reduced-sodium soy sauce during the last 30 minutes of cooking to produce a beautiful burnished color.

Poultry Pleaser

For the most tender poultry you've ever eaten, try submerging the chicken or turkey in buttermilk and refrigerating for 2–3 hours before cooking.

Stock Up

When carving a chicken or turkey, it's easy to make a stock at the same time. Place all unused parts in a pot with celery and onion (using the skins of the onion will give the stock a nice, rich color), then heat up to boiling. Reduce the heat and simmer while you make dinner. Then turn off the heat and skim the fat when cooled. Stock can be used for gravies, made into soup (naturally), and used to flavor rice, potatoes, and tomato sauce. This free and easy seasoning would have cost you up to $5 for a quart at the grocery store!

Freezing Stock

To easily freeze the delicious stock you've just made into smaller portions, line a drinking glass with a resealable plastic bag. Pour the stock into the glass until it's about three-quarters full, then seal the bag and lay flat on a baking pan. Repeat until you've used up all your stock, laying the bags on top of one another. Once they're frozen, you can move them anywhere!

Reader's Tip

When frying up fish in a pan, add a dollop of peanut butter. It won't affect the taste of the fish, but it will affect the odor—peanut butter contains a chemical that absorbs that stinky fish odor, so your whole house doesn't have to.

—MARLENA KAHN, STEUBENVILLE, OH

Cornflake Your Fish

For added crunch with fewer calories, use cornflakes instead of breadcrumbs to coat fish fillets. Not only do cornflakes contain fewer calories than breadcrumbs, they are less absorbent and give a lighter covering, so the fish will soak up less oil.

Frozen Fish Fix

Pining for fresh fish but stuck with frozen? Try this: Cover the frozen fish in milk until it thaws, then cook. It will taste fresher and your family will never know it was frozen.

The No-Fail Way to Microwave Fish

To steam fish fillets in the microwave, place them in a shallow microwavable dish (a glass pie plate is ideal) with the thinner parts overlapping at the center of the dish. Sprinkle with lemon juice or herbs, if you like, season with salt and pepper, then cover the dish with plastic wrap (making sure it doesn't touch the fish) and cook for 3 minutes per pound. If your microwave doesn't have a turntable, rotate the dish about halfway through the cooking time.

The Easy Way to Slice Meat

Cutting meat into bite-sized pieces for dishes like pastas and stir-fries is easier when it's half frozen. Place fresh meat in the freezer for two hours before you start dinner. Or, place frozen meat in the microwave and cook on the defrost setting for about five minutes (turning once if you don't have a turntable). Your knife will glide right through!

New Favorite

Wine corks (the natural kind, not plastic) contain a chemical that, when heated, will help tenderize beef stew. Just throw in three or four corks while cooking your stew, and don't tell anyone your secret!

For Tender, Tasty Chili

Marinate the meat for your chili in beer. It's a great tenderizer for tough, inexpensive cuts of beef, and it will add great flavor. All you need to do is soak the meat for an hour before cooking, or marinate it overnight in the refrigerator.

Stew's Secret Ingredient

Cooking a lamb or beef stew? Try this secret ingredient: Add a few tablespoons of black coffee and your stew will have a nice dark color and a rich taste. This tip also works well for gravies.

A Different Kind of Soup Stone

Have you ever had to throw out a batch of soup because you accidentally oversalted it? Not anymore! Potatoes contain starch, which absorbs salt, so all you need to do is peel a raw potato or two and toss it in the soup. Let the pot simmer for about 15 minutes before removing the potato, and your soup will be almost as good as new.

Boosting Spices

Want to wake up the flavor of dried herbs before using them in a recipe? Just toast them in a pan for a minute or two, and their flavors will be revived.

Infuse Your Dishes

If you're cooking with herbs that will need to be removed before eating, make them easy to remove by putting them all in a tea infuser before you add them to your dish.

Skin Garlic Easily

Here's an easy way to remove the skins from garlic! Just break the cloves off from the head and place them in a bowl or mug. Place another bowl on top and shake heartily. The skins will start to come off, making the garlic easy to peel.

Mincing Magic

Mincing garlic can be a sticky mess, but won't be if you drizzle the garlic with a few drops of olive oil beforehand. The oil will prevent the garlic from sticking on your hands or the knife.

Toothpaste Tool

You've been cooking with garlic, and now you can't get the smell off your hands! To get rid of this or any other kitchen odor, just dab your hands with a bit of tooth-paste (the white, non-gel kind works best). Then rub them together and wash off.

Reader's Tip

Don't throw away used coffee grounds—instead, keep them in a can near the sink. Rub a small amount over your hands after handling fish or chopping pungent foods like garlic and onions. The grounds will remove odors from your hands.

—AMBER M. SCHENCK

The Many Uses of a Pizza Cutter

Pizza cutters can be used for a lot more than just pizza. Use your pizza cutter to quickly slice tortillas, sand-wiches, pancakes, omelets, brownies, and even stale bread to make croutons.

Last-Minute Funnel

Need a funnel but don't have one handy? Head to the recycling bin. A soda bottle will work perfectly if you cut the bottom off and flip it upside down.

A Giant Vessel

When you started preparing the recipe, you didn't realize its contents would double in size! If you run out of space in your bowl, and you're in a pinch, simply line your entire kitchen sink with foil and throw your ingredients in there. Then serve in smaller containers.

Safety Salt

Water should never, ever be thrown on a grease fire, because it will only spread. If there's a fire caused by grease or oil in your kitchen, throw salt on it until it is extinguished. The salt will absorb the liquid causing the flames.

Reader's Tip

If your kids complain that the sandwiches you make in the morning are mushy by lunchtime, put the mayonnaise (or any condiment) in a resealable plastic bag, and stick it in the lunch box. This way, the kids can season their own sandwiches at lunchtime by turning the bag inside out and rubbing it on the bread.   —DOREEN PURTELL

Going Nuts

If you buy all-natural peanut butter, you know that it doesn't take long for the oil to separate from the rest of the spread. Solve this problem by storing your peanut butter upside-down when you first buy it. When you flip it over, the oil will be evenly distributed throughout.

Soup-er Easy

Before opening a can of soup, make sure to turn it upside down and open it from the bottom rather than the top. Then, shake in a downward motion. The soup will slip right out!

Ketchup Catch Up

Can't get the ketchup out of a stubborn bottle? Just stick a straw inside. Now when you turn it upside-down, the airflow through the straw will make the ketchup flow right out.

Cheaper Cooking Spray

Never pay for aerosol cooking sprays. Instead, buy a giant jug of vegetable oil and add it to a clean spray bottle as needed. It's the same thing and will cost a fraction of the price.

Peeled Potato Prescription

You've managed to talk your kids into helping you with tonight's scalloped potatoes, but now the potatoes are peeled long before you need them! To keep peeled potatoes from discoloring, place them in a bowl of cold water with a few drops of white vinegar, then refrigerate. Drain before cooking and add a small amount of sugar to the cooking water to revive some of the lost flavor.

Save the Skins

If your family loves mashed potatoes as much as ours does, here's a great way to use the nutritious skins in their own dish the next night. In a bowl, sprinkle the potato peelings with salt and pepper, mix with a bit of Italian dressing, and then stick them in the oven at 400° until crispy (about 20 minutes).

Quick Baked Potatoes

Halve the oven time needed for baked potatoes by placing each medium-sized potato in a muffin tin on its end. Turn over after 10 minutes, and they'll be ready in a half-hour or less.

Overdone Spaghetti?

If you forgot about your simmering pot of pasta on the stove, and your noodles are now limp and mushy, try this trick. First run them under the coldest water possible—this will stop the cooking process immediately, and make the starch inside them contract. If you're making a dish with tomato sauce, heat them back up directly in the sauce, as the acid will help them hold up even better.

New Favorite

Stop your pasta water from spilling over with this trick: Add a long metal spoon to the pot, and it will absorb the excess heat and let your pasta cook at the correct boiling point. Just be careful, because the spoon will get quite hot!

Making Pasta and Rice Less Starchy

Preparing pasta? If you put a few drops of vinegar into the water as it boils, the starch will be reduced, making the pasta less sticky. This also works with rice: For every cup of uncooked rice, add a splash of vinegar.

Unstick Your Rice

If your pasta or rice sticks together when you cook it, next time add a teaspoon of lemon juice to the water when boiling. Your sticky problem will be gone! The lemon juice will also help naturally fluff up the rice.

Rice Repair

If you burned the rice, fear not! It's white bread to the rescue. Get rid of the scorched taste by placing a slice of fresh white bread on top of the rice while it's still hot, and covering it for a few minutes.

Muffin Tin Tip

Making cupcakes or muffins but don't have enough batter to fill the tin? Before sticking the pan in the oven, fill the empty cups halfway with water. This will extend the life of the tin and ensure the cupcakes bake evenly.

Quick-Rising Solutions

It's not always a good idea to artificially cut the amount of time it takes your bread dough to rise (the flavor of the bread may not be as full), but if you're in a time crunch, it's nice to have a backup plan. To speed whole-wheat bread dough's rising time, add 1 tablespoon lemon juice to the dough as you are mixing it. For other breads, a little heat does wonders when it comes to cutting down on rising time. Set the dough (either in a bowl or a loaf pan) on a heating pad set on medium, or over the pilot light on a gas stove. You can also use the microwave to help speed the rising process by as much as one third. Set ½ cup hot water in the back corner of the microwave. Place the dough in a well-greased microwavable bowl and cover it with plastic wrap, then cover the plastic wrap with a damp towel. With the power level set at 10 percent, cook the dough for 6 minutes, and then let it rest for 4–5 minutes. Repeat the procedure if the dough has not doubled its size.

Reader's Tip

You're making cakes, cookies, or another baked good, but forgot to soften the butter. Instead of the trial-and-error involved in attempting to soften (but not melt) butter in the microwave, zap the sugar instead. Mixing butter with warm sugar will soften it in a second.

—LINDSAY HERMAN, CAMBRIDGE, MA

Soft Brown Sugar, Always

Keep your brown sugar soft and lump-free with this simple trick: Just throw a couple of marshmallows into the bag with the sugar!

Better Batter

Here's a quick tip for all you bakers. For the best-tasting cakes ever, always bring the eggs, milk, and butter to room temperature before you make your batter.

Weightless Cakes

We all know homemade cakes should not double as free weights, but what's the secret to keeping them light? A dash or two of lemon juice added to the butter and sugar mixture. That's it!

Check the Temperature Without a Thermometer

If you suspect your oven's temperature doesn't match what's on the dial, but you don't have an oven thermometer, try this simple test. Put a tablespoon of flour on a baking sheet and place it in a preheated oven for five minutes. If the flour turns light tan, the temperature is 250–325°. If the flour turns golden brown, the oven is 325–400°. If it turns dark brown, the oven is 400–450°. And an almost-black color means the oven is 450–525°. Figure out the disparity between what the temperature really is and what it reads, and make sure to set your oven accordingly in the future.

Perfect Cookies

If your cookies typically don't brown enough, bake them on a higher rack in the oven. Other tricks are substituting a tablespoon or two of corn syrup for the sugar, using egg for the liquid, and using unbleached or bread flour in the recipe.

Chilly Dough

If you're having trouble rolling out cookie dough, it may be too warm; cold dough will not stick to the rolling pin. Refrigerate it for 20 minutes for the best results.

Cookie-Dough Spoon Saver

Is your cookie dough sticking to everything? It's easy to get a spoonful of cookie dough to drop onto your baking sheet if you first dip the spoon in milk.

Bar Cookie Perfection

Want to know the secret to perfectly cut bar cookies? As soon as you remove your sweet creation from the oven, make a ¼-inch-deep incision with a knife and outline your bars. Then once they've cooled, cut all the way. This will ensure that the edges of your cookies are as smooth as can be.

Reader's Tip

The problem: You love store-bought butter spreads, but you know the trans fats inside aren't good for you. The solution? Make your own at home! Just combine a stick of butter and ¼ cup canola oil with a hand mixer. It will be soft and easy to spread! —ANNIE HONG, SAN FRANCISCO, CA

Chewy Cookies That Last

To keep your cookies tasting chewy, add a half an apple or a slice of white bread to the cookie jar. This will provide just enough moisture to keep the cookies from becoming hard.

Cookie Conundrum

Are your cookies stuck to the baking sheet? Work some dental floss between each cookie and the sheet, and you should be able to remove them easily.

Double-Decker

If you don't have an insulated or thick baking sheet, here's a simple solution: Try baking the cookies on two sheets stacked one on top of the other. This will eliminate burned bottoms caused by a too-thin pan.

An Improvised Drying Rack

If you're baking cookies or pies and don't have a cooling rack, simply line up a bunch of butter knives in alternating directions (first with the blade toward you, then with the blade away from you), and put the baking sheet on top of them. You can also use old egg cartons.

Reader's Tip

Cookies are a great, inexpensive way to show some love to neighbors, friends, and coworkers, especially during the holidays. If you're making several batches, make it easy to prepare your gifts ahead of time by wrapping them in plastic wrap before you wrap them with wrapping paper.

—AMANDA SCHNIPKE REEVES, GLENSIDE, PA

Unstick Stuck Cakes

The bad news is that your cake is stuck to the pan. The good news is that it's easy to get it out intact—you just need to heat up the bottom of the pan by submerging it in hot water. Once the pan heats back up, use a knife to easily dislodge your still-perfect cake.

Frost in Translation

Want to freeze a cake, but don't want the frosting to stick to the plastic wrap? First, put the cake in the freezer without any wrapping. Once the frosting is frozen, cover the cake with plastic wrap. The cold frosting won't stick to the wrap.

Double Frosting

You may not have time to make your own frosting, but you can blend store-bought frosting with a hand mixer to double the volume. This simple little trick saves money and calories!

Keep Icing Soft

To keep icing from hardening, just add a very small amount of white vinegar after it is whipped. You can also add a pinch of baking soda to the confectioners' sugar. This will help the icing retain some moisture, and it won't dry out as fast.

Easy Chocolate Designing

Adding a chocolate design to cakes, brownies, and other confections gives them a sophisticated touch your friends are sure to appreciate. An easy way to decorate with chocolate is to place old candy, unwrapped, in a plastic sandwich bag. Microwave for 30 seconds at a time, turning until evenly melted. Then snip off the corner and use like a pastry bag to write words and create embellishments.

New Favorite

Little kids usually end up eating cake with their hands anyway, so try this fun dessert treat: Place flat-bottomed ice cream cones in a high-sided baking pan and fill them two-thirds full with cake batter. Bake them at 325° for 30 minutes. Once they cool, you can hold your cake and eat it, too!

We Heart Cakes

A heart-shaped cake is easier to make than you might think. Simply divide your cake batter between one round pan and one square one. When the cakes are cool, cut the round cake in half. Turn the square cake so it looks like a diamond and set the half-rounds on the two top sides. Voilà!

Before "Happy Birthday"

Here's a great bakers' trick to make it easier to decorate the top of a cake: With a toothpick, trace the pattern, picture, or lettering before you pipe the icing. This guide will help you make fewer mistakes.

A Different Cake Topping

If you find icing too sweet or too rich, try this cake topping: Set a paper lace doily on the cake, then dust lightly with confectioners' sugar. Carefully lift the doily off the cake, and admire the beautiful design left behind. You can also try colored confectioners' sugar or a mixture of confectioners' sugar and cocoa powder.

Hair Dryer Magic

To give the icing on top of your cake the silky look of a professionally made one, ice it as usual and then blow a hair dryer over the top for a minute. It will melt the icing slightly, giving it the shiny appearance you're looking for.

Transporting Cakes

Here's a new twist on transporting frosted cakes. Don't just insert toothpicks and cover in plastic—the sharp ends can puncture the wrap and create a gooey mess. Instead, attach miniature marshmallows to the toothpicks before covering. You can also use strands of spaghetti instead of toothpicks.

Here's a tip that makes icing a cake much easier. To keep the cake from sliding around on the plate as you're icing it, place a dab of frosting in the middle of the plate before you place the cake on top. The icing will keep the cake in place, and by the time you've served all the slices, no one will notice the little bit of extra frosting on the bottom.

—DAWN LINNEY, FLORENCE, SC

Perfect Cake Slicing

To keep the frosting from sticking to your knife as you cut the cake, dip your knife into a glass of hot water between each cut. It will also keep cake crumbling to a minimum.

Cut Your Cake and Eat It Too

If you've got a delicate cake that will fall apart and stick to the knife when you cut it, use dental floss— yes, dental floss—to slice it. Hold the floss taut and give it a slight sawing motion as you move it down to cut through the cake.

Fun with Ice Cream

Here's a fun and unique way to serve ice cream next to cake. Buy a pint-sized container of your favorite ice cream, then slice right through it (cardboard and all) with a serrated knife, making ice cream "rounds" that are about 1-inch thick. Peel off the remaining cardboard, then use cookie cutters to make various shapes. Store them in your freezer between pieces of parchment paper until you're ready to serve. And if you don't use the entire pint, the top will still sit flush against your "short stack" to keep it fresh for later.

New Favorite

Once Christmas is over, snag a bag of tiny candy canes that are on sale and use them for these heart-shaped cupcake toppers. On a nonstick baking sheet, position two candy canes so their hooks and bottom edges are touching, forming a heart. Bake at 325° for 3–5 minutes. Pinch together to sear, then cool and remove with a spatula. They're perfect for decorating cupcakes on Valentine's Day!

CHAPTER 6

CLEANING SHORTCUTS

Squeeze Bottles Still Have Air!

Save plastic squeeze bottles, but not for storage—they make the perfect substitute for bottles of compressed air, which are used to clean out computer keyboards, electronics, and other tiny crevices. This works especially well with squeeze bottles that have small spouts, such as lemon juice dispensers. Wash them well and let them dry completely before using.

Cleaning Hard-to-Reach Places

Unless your arms are 6 feet long, dusting behind furniture or under appliances can be a real drag. Try making a dusting tool by slipping a heavy-duty sock on a yardstick and securing it with a rubber band. Spray it lightly with dusting spray (we like water and a little bit of fabric softener) and you're ready to finally grab all that dust you've been avoiding.

Quick Dusting

Instead of using a rag, wear a pair of old socks on your hands when dusting. It's efficient (you're using both hands) and cheap (remember, these are old socks), and you can wash and reuse them.

So Long, Static

You know, of course, that dryer sheets remove static cling from your laundry—but are you aware that they remove it from just about everything else too? If you wipe down your lampshades, computer screen, television, and other household items with a sheet, the static cling will disappear and the items will stay dust-free for longer.

New Favorite

Here's an all-natural way to clean your mirror that will also give it a spotless shine: Wipe the mirror with a clean cloth dipped in strong, cool tea. Buff with a dry cloth and you're done!

Lampshade Duster

If you have a pleated lampshade, you know how hard it can be to clean the dust out of those crevices. Our secret weapon? An old paintbrush. It's the perfect size for its soft bristles to get between each crease.

Your Electric Duster

Forget the feather duster. The easiest way to get loose dust off your knickknacks—and anything else in your home—is to blow it away with a hair dryer.

Burning Hair Dryer Smell?

If it's beginning to smell like fire every time you blow-dry your hair, your dryer's motor may be clogged with hair and lint. Use an old toothbrush to brush clean the back of the dryer, where it sucks in air. Now you can do your hair without someone poking a head in the bathroom to make sure everything's OK!

Reader's Tip

If you have some beautiful candles that have begun to get dusty, cleaning them is easy. Just ball up some old pantyhose and rub them down. The microfiber is perfect for picking up the dirt without harming your candle.

—GERALDINE PEEBLES

Citrus for Ceramics

To clean dust off ceramic figurines, simply rub them with the cut side of a lemon wedge. Leave the lemon juice on for 15 minutes, then polish up with a soft, dry cloth.

Another Use for Alka-Seltzer

Effervescent tablets aren't just good for curing hangovers—dissolve a tablet in warm water at the base of a vase to remove stains and leave it shiny-new.

Very Clean Vases

Even eggshells have a great use before you throw them away: getting rid of rings on hard-to-clean places in vases. Fill the vase mostly full with warm water, then add a drop of dishwashing liquid and the eggshells. They'll act as an abrasive to scrub off the stains.

Fake Flower Fix-Up

To revitalize artificial flowers, forget about using expensive cleaners. Just pour salt or rice into a paper or plastic bag, place the flowers inside petal-side-down, and shake vigorously. The salt or rice will attract the dust, leaving your flowers looking as good as the real thing!

Reader's Tip

Even after you've cleaned out your purse, it still has crumbs, grime, and little pieces of god-only-knows-what at the bottom. Quickly clean it out with a lint roller. Just roll the inside and you're done!   —JESSICA PUGH RYAN, ARVADA, CO

Cleaning Battery Leaks

If battery acid leaks inside the compartments of your appliances, there's no need to throw them away. Simply take a few spoonfuls of baking soda and add water until it's the consistency of toothpaste. Spread it on your battery terminals, let it sit 15 minutes, and wipe clean. The acid should come off easily.

Clean Up Your Keys

The easiest way to clean the gunk and dust between your computer keys is with transparent tape. Slide a 2-inch strip between the rows of your keyboard, and the adhesive will pick up any debris.

Fireplace Quick Clean

Cleaning out a fireplace is easy when you line the bottom with aluminum foil. Just wait for the ashes to cool, fold up the foil, and lay a fresh layer out.

Fireplace Cleaning Secret

Before cleaning the ashes from your fireplace, sprinkle some damp coffee grounds over them. They'll weigh the ashes down and keep dust to a minimum.

Loosening Soot

If you throw some salt in your fireplace every now and then, soot will be easier to clean from your chimney. It will also make your fire burn a cool yellow color!

Dust Repellent

To easily clean your coffee table and keep dust away for good, dampen a rag with warm water mixed with a drop or two of liquid fabric softener. Wipe down the tabletop and the fabric softener will repel future dust while getting your table sparkling clean.

Preventing Fingerprints

You just bought the coffee table of your dreams, but when it was sitting in the store you didn't realize it would attract fingerprints like bees to honey. To get rid of a persistent fingerprint problem, rub down the tabletop with cornstarch. The surface will absorb the cornstarch, which will repel prints.

No More Dings

If you have lots of dings and nicks in your coffee table, the remote for your TV (and various other accessories) may be to blame. To make sure hard plastic remotes don't dent your furniture in the future, simply wrap a rubber band around each end. The soft rubber will give your furniture a cushion, and a break from all that rough treatment.

Wax Splatters?

Removing candle wax from your table is easier than you might think: First soften the wax with a blow-dryer, then wipe with a towel soaked in vinegar and water.

New Favorite

If you have a precious oil painting in your home, it's important to keep it clean without damaging it. Our surprising cleaning tool of choice is a piece of white bread! White bread has the perfect amount of moisture to easily pick up dust, without being so wet that it will ruin your painting.

Crayon Mark Removal

If your child has drawn on your furniture or wall with crayon, run the warm air from a hair dryer over the marks. The heat will melt the waxy marks a bit, making them much easier to remove.

Not-So-Permanent Marker

If your kids (or you) get a permanent marker stain on furniture or the floor, don't despair! There may be hope in the form of rubbing alcohol. Test an inconspicuous area first to make sure it won't harm the finish, then apply directly to the stain with a rag or paper towel. Rub until it disappears, then wipe with a clean cloth moistened with water.

Groom Your Broom

If your broom has lost its shape, gather the bristles with a rubber band and leave it on for a few days so it returns to its original form. Remove the band and sweep away (if that's what you were planning on doing. Otherwise, just shove it back where it was in the pantry behind the paper towel rack.)

Minimize Broom-Swept Dust

To eliminate the trail of dust your broom leaves behind, fill a spray bottle with three parts water and one part liquid fabric softener, and spray the broom before sweeping. The spritz makes the broom strands more pliable and helps it collect dirt more efficiently.

Scoop the Loot

Picking up small parts to kids' toys is one of the most tedious chores—even and especially when the kids themselves are helping to the insipid tune of "Clean up, clean up, everybody do your part." Rather than picking stray pieces up one by one, try sweeping up the Legos and Lincoln Logs using a clean dustpan and broom.

Reader's Tip

Every time you sweep something up with a dustpan, there's that little line of grit that refuses to get swept up! Solve the problem with a bit of double-sided tape. Just tape along the edge, then replace the tape every few times you use the dustpan. The fine line of dust will stick to the tape, and you'll never do the "back up and sweep a little more" shuffle again! —MATTHEW S. PARMENTER, HAZLETON, PA

Static Cling's the Thing

Pantyhose with holes in them can't go to the office but they can still be put to work. Cut the legs off and use them as covers for your broom to make debris collection more efficient. The static charge created when you sweep the pantyhose across the floor will act as a magnet for dirt and dust. Bet you didn't know static cling is sometimes a good thing!

Two for One

You can save cash and storage space with this quick-fix cleaning alternative: Use a small, plastic garbage can as your mop bucket and you'll not only clean the can, you'll never have to buy a bucket!

Vacuum Like a Pro

When vacuuming your home, it's always annoying to find bits and pieces that are too big for your vacuum. Instead of ending up with all those icky bits in your hand, tie a plastic grocery bag to your belt loop. That way, you'll have a portable garbage can with you at all times!

Vacuum Off Odors

To rid your house of pet, cooking, or other smells, add a cotton ball soaked in vanilla or lavender oil to your vacuum cleaner bag. It's a great way to rid your home of an offensive odor by creating a nice scent instead.

For Tough Spaces

Trying to clean super-small spaces around the house? Don't buy additional vacuum equipment if your attachments are too big. Instead, grab a straw—preferably one of those giant straws from a fast-food chain—and insert part of it into the smallest attachment you have. Tape it in place, and you'll be able to suck up dirt and dust in the tiniest of spaces.

Clean Grease Like Lightning

If you've got kids, you're guaranteed to end up with a grease stain on your carpet. The big thing to remember is to not touch the stain at all—don't sop it up, wipe it, or do anything else. Instead, pour a large amount of cornstarch on top of the spot and gently stir it with your finger. Let it sit for a day, and make sure no one walks on it. The next day, use your vacuum cleaner's hose attachment (the plastic one, not the one with bristles) to suck away the cornstarch. The stain should be mostly gone, but if it's not, repeat this action until it completely disappears. You can then use the brush attachment to clear away the last remnants of cornstarch.

Salt Does the Trick on Carpet Stains

If you spill any liquid on your carpet, pour salt on the area as soon as possible and watch it absorb the liquid almost instantly. Wait until it dries, then vacuum it up. Salt tends to provide a special capillary attraction that will work for most liquids. There are a few stains that salt will actually help set, however—never sprinkle it on red wine, coffee, tea, or cola!

Patch Up Carpet Burns

Here's how to eliminate cigarette burns in your carpet: First, cut away the burn mark. Then, cut a bit of carpet from an area that's covered by a piece of furniture (such as under a couch), and glue it carefully over the burnt spot. Finally, yell at the person who caused the burn in the first place!

New Favorite

There's another way salt can help your carpet! For a cleaner, brighter carpet, sprinkle a small amount of salt before you vacuum. The salt provides a mild abrasive cleaning action that won't hurt the fibers.

Carpet Cleaning Work-Around

Finally getting around to shampooing your carpet? You don't have to remove all your furniture. Slip plastic bags over the feet of tables and chairs and secure them with rubber bands. You can clean underneath, then shift the furniture a bit and wash where its legs were. The plastic will keep the furniture from getting wet.

Paint Mishaps

If you've spilled paint on your carpet, stop cursing and head to the kitchen. Mix together 1 tablespoon vinegar, 1 tablespoon dishwashing liquid, and 1 quart warm water. Douse the area with this mixture and try rubbing it away. If that doesn't work, wait for the paint to dry and snip off the areas that have paint on them—your carpet's "hair cut" will be less noticeable than a giant paint stain.

Bottom's Up

Yet another reason we've kept baby wipes around long after our youngest finished nursery school—they work great to soak up carpet stains. We don't have to freak out when people slosh around with dark purple liquids on our handmade beige silk Persian rugs. Grape juice, red wine, fruit punch? Wobbly toddlers? Bring them on. (And if you're wondering, no, we don't actually own any silk Persian rugs! We have kids, don't we?)

A Shocking Solution

If you can't escape static electricity on your carpet, here's an easy fix. Mix 3 cups water with ½ cup liquid fabric softener, put it in a spray bottle, and apply to your carpet. Not only will the static electricity disappear, but the mixture will serve as a carpet deodorizer too.

Clothespin Your Way to Easier Cleaning

Glue one side of a sturdy clothespin to the inside of cabinet doors, the front of your washing machine, and elsewhere around your home. Hanging clothespins are great for holding plastic shopping bags, and plastic shopping bags are great for holding trash, clean rags, cleaning supplies, and more.

Clean Your Dirty Radiator

Dreading cleaning your radiator? Here's a simple way to get the job done. Hang a damp cloth or damp newspapers on the wall behind it, then use your hair dryer to blow the dust off it. The dust will stick to the wet surface behind it, and then you can simply throw away the cloth or paper.

Clean Ceiling Fans

To easily clean a ceiling fan, spray glass cleaner or a mixture of half vinegar and half water on the inside of a pillowcase. Put the pillowcase over one arm of the fan, then pull it off while applying gentle pressure toward the floor. The pillowcase will wipe the top of the blade clean.

Greasy Wallpaper

To eliminate grease on wallpaper without using chemical cleaning products, cover the area with a brown paper bag or kraft paper, then apply a warm iron. The paper will absorb the grease.

White Bread Wisdom

A great way to clean wallpaper is with white bread. You can eliminate fingerprints, light stains, and even ball-point ink by simply rubbing a piece of white bread vigorously over the spot.

Reader's Tip

Having trouble washing your dirty wall without the paint coming off too? Mix 10 parts warm water with 1 part concentrated wood cleaner like Murphy's Oil Soap, and use a sponge to wipe it over the wall. Wood cleaner is gentle enough to remove the dirt without taking all the paint with it!

—SARAH GROVER, MUNDELEIN, IL

Window Washing 101

If the sun is shining on your windows, wait until they are in the shade to wash them. When they dry too quickly, they tend to streak.

How to Clean Venetian Blinds

An easy way to clean blinds is to wrap a kitchen spatula in an old cloth and secure it with a rubber band, then dip it in rubbing alcohol or your favorite cleaner, close the blinds, and go to it!

Cleaning Aluminum Blinds

Aluminum blinds are great for keeping out light, but they can be hard to clean! The easiest way to clean smudges off aluminum blinds is with a pencil eraser. Dust will come off with a few swipes of a fabric softener sheet.

Mini Blinds Cleaning Shortcut

Give mini blinds a good clean by simply throwing them in the bathtub filled with water and a cup of white vinegar or your favorite cleanser. Shake them out well and hang them up wet. There may be a few streaks once they've air-dried, but they're nearly impossible to spot.

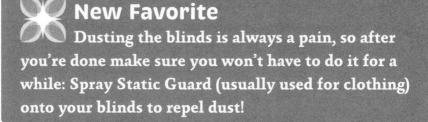

New Favorite
Dusting the blinds is always a pain, so after you're done make sure you won't have to do it for a while: Spray Static Guard (usually used for clothing) onto your blinds to repel dust!

Don't Be a Doormat

Your porch's doormat can be cleaned with a sprinkling of baking soda. Brush vigorously and then sweep away the dirt. The next time it rains, the job will be complete.

Clean a Spot with Cat Litter

If your car has leaked oil onto the floor of your garage, easily clean it up by applying some cat litter to the area (preferably the non-scoopable kind). Its super-absorbing properties will make the stain disappear in a day.

Quick Clean for Your Patio Furniture

We'll admit, we're often guilty of doing things the lazy way. The laziest way to clean plastic or resin patio furniture? Just toss it in the swimming pool before going to bed, and in the morning it'll be good as new. Meanwhile, your pool's filter will clean up the dirt.

Easy Umbrella Clean

Your patio umbrella was looking good when you packed it away last fall . . . but now it's a mildewy mess.

Here's the easiest way to clean it: Fill a bucket with warm water, then add 2 cups of white vinegar and a couple of generous squirts of dishwashing liquid. Let soak for a half an hour, then scrub with a cleaning brush. Rinse with water and let it dry in the sun. The warmth will kill whatever the vinegar and soap didn't.

New Favorite

Parents who have been through baby-proofing boot camp are trained to throw out packets of silica gel upon contact. If you don't have to worry about kids or pets getting their paws on them, however, you can put them to good use. They soak up moisture, which is handy for preserving all kinds of household metal, from gardening tools to flatware and silverware to jewelry. Just place them in any drawers or boxes you want to keep from collecting moisture.

BBQ to the Rescue

To clean digging tools easily, invest in a barbecue brush with a scraper attachment. Use the scraper to remove layers of mud from the tool as necessary as you dig, and use the brush to brush off the dried dirt before you put the tool away.

Grill-Cleaning Trick

Grilled food doesn't taste as good when the grill is dirty. Cooking spray will easily clean your grill with very little effort on your part, which is the whole point of a grill to begin with. Just cover with spray and turn on the grill for 10 minutes or so. The oil will loosen residue and safely burn it off. If you really want to impress, buff with aluminum foil once it has cooled off to make it extra shiny. Now fire it up and start searing away!

For the Foremans

Here's the easiest way we've found to clean a counter-top grill: Unplug it, then put a wet paper towel inside and close the lid for 10 minutes. The grease will be loosened up and easy to clean off.

Easy Clean for a Dishwasher

To get rid of mineral deposits and iron stains in your dishwasher, run it through an empty wash cycle using powdered lemonade mix instead of detergent. The citric acid in the mix will eliminate your problem.

Dishwasher Done!

Soap film coating your dishwasher? Run it on an empty cycle using vinegar instead of detergent. It will be sparkling clean, and your next load of dishes will be too.

Berry Clever

Those plastic baskets that berries come in are perfect for small items in your dishwasher. Just wedge in place and throw bottle tops, lids, and small utensils inside.

Silverware Saver

Never combine silver and stainless steel cutlery in the dishwasher, or the silver will turn black. Any contact with dishwasher detergent will also result in black spots. Remove silver cutlery from the dishwasher immediately after the cycle ends, and dry at once to avoid stains and pitting from salt residue.

Clean Caps, Always

When you've used all the ketchup in a plastic squeeze bottle, throw the cap in the dishwasher to remove the caked-on ketchup. Keep it handy in the kitchen, along with other condiment bottle tops. When your current bottle top gets all mucked-up, simply switch it out with a clean top and throw the dirty one in the dishwasher.

De-Gunk Your Can Opener

To clean your electric can opener, run a piece of paper towel or wax paper through it. This will pick up the grease and most of the gunk.

Replace Steel Wool

You have a pot that's in need of a good scrubbing, but you're out of steel wool. Simply reach for the aluminum foil! Roll it into a ball and use it (with some dishwashing liquid) to scrub off caked-on grease. This is also a great way to reuse foil before you recycle it.

Odor Remover

To remove odors from dishes, bottles, or plastic containers, add a teaspoon of mustard to hot water and let the item soak in it for five minutes, then wash as usual.

Splatter Saver

To lessen your clean-up time when using a food processor, protect the lid by first covering the bowl of food with a piece of plastic wrap. The lid will stay clean and you can toss the plastic wrap in the trash when you're finished.

New Favorite

We hate to throw anything away, so we love this way to repurpose used tea bags. Place them in a bowl and put them at the back of your refrigerator. They'll remove odors just as well as baking soda!

Tea Party

Here's a terrific way to make your post-dinner clean-up a breeze: Remove cooked-on food from pots and pans effortlessly by filling them with water, adding a tea bag, and simmering. The tea's acid will break up food.

Great for Graters

What's the easiest way to clean a messy cheese grater? Reach for a lemon! Just rub the pulp-side of a cut lemon across a grater and it will clean off any stuck-on cheese.

Cleaner Basting Brushes

There's nothing like a gooey, smelly basting brush to ruin your mood. Put a stop to it today! After your usual washing routine with hot water and soap, dry it off a bit by shaking. Here's the cool part, which might remind you of your eighth-grade science class. Pour coarse salt into a cup and place the brush inside. Any remaining wetness will be absorbed by the salt, leaving the bristles as clean as can be.

Preserve Pots and Pans

Make sure you let your pots and pans cool before you wash them. Drastic changes in temperature can cause them to warp, meaning they won't heat evenly and will be harder to cook with.

Mug Those Mug Stains

Get rid of really tough stains in your mugs by filling them with boiling water and adding a denture tablet. Let it sit overnight, and the stain should disappear.

Dispose of Properly

Instead of throwing baking soda away after its 30-day stint in your fridge, dump it down the garbage disposal with running water. It will keep your disposal fresh too!

Camouflage a Crack in Your China

Antique dealers use this trick to hide hairline cracks on china plates and cups. Simmer the piece in milk for 45 minutes. Casein, a milk protein, may fill in the crack, depending on its size. If your china is old or fragile, though, this could backfire—heat can cause pieces to expand and crack.

Nix the Nicks

Buff away a nick on the rim of a glass or your china with an emery board. Don't use a nail file or sandpaper; both are too coarse and will scratch the glass.

Easy Egg Clean-Up

Cleaning up after a yummy egg breakfast? Cold water cleans egg off pans and utensils better than hot water. Hot water tends to cause the protein to bind to surfaces and harden.

Stuck-On Substances

If you've given up hope of ever removing stuck-on food from your pots and pans, help is on the way—in the form of a fabric softener sheet! Just cover the stain with hot water and float a fabric softener sheet in it. Leave overnight. In the morning, the food should wipe off easily.

New Favorite

Wash your blender in less than a minute with this simple trick! Just fill it halfway with hot water, then add a drop of dishwashing liquid, cover with its lid, and hit blend for 30 seconds. Suds will fill your blender and clean it without you having to disassemble the whole contraption.

Cleaning a Melted Plastic Mess

It's happened to us tons of times, and it's probably happened to you—a bag of bread is in the wrong place at the wrong time, and you end up with melted plastic all over the counter (or toaster). To remove melted plastic from metal, glass, or other plastic, first make sure the surface is cool (that is, unplug the toaster!). Then, rub the affected area with nail polish remover until the plastic scrapes off. Wipe down the surface with a damp sponge and let it dry, and you're back in business.

Yellowed Counter?

If the enamel on your counter or tub has turned yellow, add a handful of salt to turpentine and rub onto the enamel, then wash as usual. Make sure to test in a small area of the counter first.

Keeping Trash Bins Clean

When cleaning your kitchen garbage can, sprinkle a little scouring powder at the bottom. This will soak up any liquids if your bag leaks, and will also repel mildew and keep your bin smelling fresh.

Easy Oven Cleaning

Save a lot of clean-up time by lining the bottom rack of your oven with aluminum foil when you cook something messy. But never line the bottom of your oven with foil—this can cause a fire.

The Black Bag Treatment

Make your oven racks easier to clean by coating them with cleanser, placing them in a black plastic trash bag, and setting them outside in the sun. After a few hours, they'll be ready to rinse with a hose.

Wake Up and Smell the Clean Coffee

Cut up stale bread into small pieces and run through your electric coffee grinder to clean the machine naturally. The oil and debris left from the coffee beans will be absorbed into the bread. When you're done, wipe with a rag or paper towel. Bonus points if you can think of a way to use up the oily, coffee-flavored breadcrumbs!

Bungled Beaters

If your hand mixer isn't what it used to be thanks to jiggling beaters, hardened food in its sockets may be to blame. Take out the beaters and clean out the sockets with a toothpick or bobby pin.

Cleaning Ceramic Tile

The easiest way to clean ceramic tile is with rubbing alcohol. Just pour it straight on, and mop or wipe until it dries.

Steam Out a Nasty Bathroom

If you've let the bathroom get so dirty that it now resembles a gas station restroom, turn on the hot water in the shower for 10 minutes with the door closed. The steam will loosen the buildup of mildew and mold. Then get in there and clean!

New Favorite

Trying to clean up your bathroom fast, before guests arrive? Here's how to do it in two minutes or less: Apply a touch of baby shampoo to a wet sponge and wipe down your sink, fixtures, tiles, and bathtub. It cuts through oily residue, and it smells good too.

Fabric Softener Sheets to the Rescue

To clean chrome-plated fixtures in your bathroom instantly, always keep fabric softener sheets handy. Just wipe, and the chrome will sparkle. Dryer sheets also work on shower doors or anywhere else there is soap scum!

Goodbye, Mineral Deposits

If mineral deposits have built up in your faucet, cut a lemon into quarters, then push one piece up into the faucet until it sticks. Leave for about 10 minutes, then twist the wedge out. Repeat with remaining lemon quarters until the deposits are gone.

Get Rid of Caked-On Hair Spray

If your beauty routine includes spraying your entire 'do to keep it in place, you probably have a film of hair spray on your bathroom vanity and walls. Remove it easily with a solution of two parts water and one part liquid fabric softener. Wipe on with a damp cloth, then rub off with a clean one.

Reader's Tip

If you've ever noticed streaks in your bathroom mirror the day after you clean it, you'll love this tip. When cleaning the bathroom, always wear a dark shirt. Streaks are much easier to spot when the mirror is reflecting something dark.
—SAMANTHA HITT, DESOTO, TX

Shower Curtain Savvy

Avoid leaving a shower curtain bunched up after use, especially in a small bathroom—the steam encourages mildew. Always pull it closed after bathing, and if small spots of mildew do appear, dab with baking soda on a damp cloth.

Save Your Shower Curtain

If mildew has made your shower curtain more disgusting than you'd like to admit, first wash it in hot, soapy water. Then rub a wedge of lemon on the stains and leave the curtain out in the sun. By the time it dries, the stains will be gone.

Resist Shower Curtain Mildew

If you have a pair of pinking shears (scissors with a zigzagging edge used in sewing), put them to good use in the bathroom. Use them to cut the bottom of your shower curtain liner: The uneven hem allows water to more easily slide off, making bottom-of-the-curtain mildew a thing of the past.

Say Goodbye to Soap Scum

Keep soap scum off the walls of your shower with this easy trick: Just rub wood furniture polish onto the tile and doors, and soap scum and mildew won't stick.

We're all for spending less time cleaning, especially when it comes to places company rarely sees. So here's a great new way to get rid of grout stains in your shower and tub—shaving cream! After the last shower of the day, apply shaving foam to the grout, whose stains have already started to loosen thanks to the steamy shower. After that, simply leave it on until the first shower the next day! Repeat for a day or two and your grout stains will be gone. Best of all, shaving cream doesn't contain bleach, so it's less harsh on your grout!

Rub-a-Dub-Dub

No matter how hard we scrub, we never seem to get the corners of our tub clean. Luckily, we have a clever solution! Soak cotton balls in your tub cleaner (or just some rubbing alcohol) and leave one in each corner of your tub overnight. By morning, they'll be as clear as day.

Last Resort for Grout

When the grout stains in your bathroom call for the big guns, bring on the sandpaper. The folded edge will slide into the space between tiles and around the edge. This is still a delicate job—steer clear of the tiles themselves or they'll scratch.

Grout Protector

Have a stash of broken white candles that would make for a depressing decoration but seem "too good" to throw away? It may not be the romantic image you had in mind when you bought the candles, but rubbing the wax onto your bathroom grout will help protect it from growing mold, mildew, and other stains.

Get Rid of That Ring

If your shaving cream can is leaving rusty rings on the side of your tub or sink, perform this trick right after you purchase a new container: Coat the rim around the bottom of the can with clear nail polish, then let it dry. The polish will keep out water, so the can won't rust.

Reader's Tip

This may go against years of training your boys, but in rarely used bathrooms the lid on the toilet should always be kept up. This allows air to circulate in the bowl, which will prevent mold and mildew from forming. Also, make sure to leave toilet lids up when you go on vacation!

—JENNIFER PILCHER, OLATHE, KS

PART 2

HOMEMADE WONDERS

There's no better way to save than to make products at home—and it doesn't have to be hard! It's so easy to make your own cleaners, pest repellants, plant fertilizers, stain removers, beauty supplies, and more that you probably already own everything you'll need! In this section, we'll also show you how to repurpose everyday items around your home—make multi-purpose rubber bands out of old rubber gloves (page 260), a favorite candle into an air freshener (page 247), an aromatherapy pillow out of rice (page 329), and all kinds of toys to keep your kids busy with stuff you'd otherwise throw away (pages 237–240). If you're interested in all-natural home remedies for wellness, you'll love the last chapter in this section, which shares family secrets for getting rid of colds, backache, corns, bug bites, allergies, insomnia, and more. This section also contains some of our very-favorite reader tips of all time, including using fabric softener sheets to keep bugs away (page 193), using brown sugar as a facial exfoliant (page 302), and making a tennis ball into a padlock-protector (page 248). Get ready to save money and impress your friends with these homemade wonders that are just as good as the real thing!

CHAPTER 1

MAKE-IT-YOURSELF CLEANERS

The Easiest Window Washer

You don't need expensive cleaners to wash your windows! For a cheap, effective glass cleaner, fill a spray bottle with ½ teaspoon dishwashing liquid, 3 tablespoons white vinegar, and 2 cups warm water. If you're washing something that's very dirty, use more liquid soap.

Vinegar Floor Cleaner

For mopping vinyl or ceramic floors, use ½ cup white vinegar added to 1 gallon warm water. It's cheap, effective, and completely nontoxic.

New Favorite

The secret to shiny laminated floors is baby shampoo. Just mix a spoonful of baby shampoo with a gallon of warm water and mop as usual!

Homemade Wood Cleaner

Save money on wood cleaners by making your own at home. It's simple: Just combine the juice from one lemon with 2 cups vegetable or olive oil. Use it just like you would use a store-bought cleaner!

Rings Around the Table

If you've got kids, you probably have water marks on your finished wood table. Use a little petroleum jelly to remove the white stains. Just rub the area with the jelly and let sit for several hours (or even overnight). Then rub again with a soft cloth—the stain should disappear.

Piano Key Cleaning

Don't get upset if you find your toddler wiping the piano keys with mayonnaise. It's actually a great, gentle way to get them clean. (Just make sure she doesn't move on to the sofa!)

Remove Pen Marks from Leather

If your kid has decided to write a novel on your favorite leather chair, don't panic. Just blot the stain with milk until the ink disappears, then wipe it clean with a damp sponge.

Give Your Leather a Pick-Me-Up

To revive the beauty of leather, lightly beat two egg whites and then apply to the leather with a soft sponge. Allow the egg whites to remain on the leather for 3–5 minutes, and then wipe off with a soft cloth dampened with warm water. Dry immediately and buff off any residue.

Dusting Your Plants

If your houseplants are dusty, gently wipe the leaves with a soft cloth and a damp sponge. If you want your plants' leaves to *really* shine, rub them (gently!) with a cotton ball dipped in mayonnaise. The mayo will lend a beautiful shine, and you can ditch those pricey commercial shining products.

Got Stale Milk? Use It!

If you have milk left in your glass, don't toss it out. Milk will do a great job of cleaning plant leaves. The protein in milk called "casein" has a mild cleansing effect on the plant cell walls.

Shiny Leaves

Use olive oil to keep the leaves of houseplants shiny. Just rub a little bit on each side of the leaf using a cotton ball or rag. It will get rid of dust and keep them gleaming!

Time to Clean Teddy

To clean stuffed animals, just place them in a cloth bag or pillowcase, add baking soda or cornmeal, and shake. The dirt will transfer to the powder.

New Favorite

Nothing needs a cleaning more than your child's best-loved doll. Luckily, this way to clean them is so fun your kid will want to help you! Wash the plastic faces of dolls by smearing peanut butter on them, then wiping it off. The oils in the butter seep into the plastic, removing every last bit of grime.

De-Grease Sticky Playing Cards

An oft-used deck of cards can get sticky and grimy from the oils on our hands. De-grease the cards by placing them in a plastic bag with a few blasts of baby powder. Give it a good shake before dealing the first hand.

Unclog Your Steam Iron

A great way to clean your iron is to pour equal amounts of white vinegar and water into the water holder of the iron. Turn the dial to "steam" and leave it upright for five minutes. Unplug and let the iron cool down. Any loose particles should fall out when you empty the water.

Sticky Iron?

If your iron is beginning to stick to fabrics, sprinkle some salt on a piece of waxed paper and iron it. The salt will absorb the stickiness.

Getting Rid of an Iron Disaster

If you've ever had scorched, melted polyester or vinyl on your iron, you know what a mess it can be. Wait for your iron to cool, then rub the melted muck with a rag that has been dipped in nail polish remover. Scrape off the mess with a wooden spoon (or anything else made from wood—metal can scratch). Wipe with water before ironing again.

The Key to Cleaning Keys

The easiest way to clean a computer keyboard? Simply dip a cotton swab or cotton ball in hydrogen peroxide and run it between the keys.

New Favorite

If your MP3 player has seen better days, give it a quick clean. Our favorite method? A bit of rubbing alcohol or astringent on a clean make-up sponge. Just rub it over the player and it will look as clean as new!

Dish Soap Does It

Wondering how to keep your beautiful jewelry looking like the first day you wore it? Gentle dishwashing detergent and water plus a soft cloth can clean rubies, amethysts, citrines, emeralds, sapphires, and garnets. Just make sure to wash each piece separately to avoid chipping. Diamonds can be washed similarly: Fill a small pot with a cup of water, plus a teaspoon of dishwasher detergent. Add your diamonds, bring the water to a boil, then turn off the heat and let the pot sit until it cools. Once it's cool (but not before), carefully remove your jewelry and rinse.

The Overnight Trick

The easiest way to clean emeralds, diamonds, rubies, and sapphires may be with club soda. Place your jewelry in a glass of it overnight, and it will shine like new in the morning.

Never-Wet Stones

Since turquoise, opals, and marcasite are porous stones, never immerse them in water. Instead, polish them with a soft, dry chamois and clean claws with a soft bristle brush.

Prescription for Pearls

The best way to care for a pearl (or coral) necklace is to wear it regularly—oils from your skin add a gentle luster. After wearing, wipe with a chamois to remove traces of perspiration that can damage the surface. You can also wash pearls and coral in water and very mild soap, then wipe with a soft cloth. Lay on a moist paper towel to dry.

Clean Jewelry Relief

Clean costume or inexpensive jewelry by dropping two Alka-Seltzer tablets into a glass of water. Immerse jewelry for about five minutes and pat dry with a clean towel.

Surprising Copper Cleaner

Here's an unlikely cleaning tool—ketchup. It works great on copper. Simply rub on with a soft cloth, let sit for 30–45 minutes, then rinse off with hot water and wipe dry. Who knew?

For Brass that Shines

Shining the brass hinges and knobs of your doors is easier than you think! Apply a white, nongel toothpaste (a mild abrasive) to door fittings with a soft cloth, then rub. Use a fresh cloth to wipe clean, and your brass will sparkle! To protect brass between cleanings, apply a light coating of olive or lemon oil.

Reader's Tip

Here's a great cleaner for brass or aluminum. Sprinkle cream of tartar on a wedge of lemon and rub it into the surface. Let sit for 10 minutes, then rinse and buff dry. If you don't have any cream of tartar, you can also try this trick with baking soda.   —BEVERLY NETTER, SPRINGVILLE, NY

Get Untarnished Silver

Here's an easy household solution for polishing up your old heirloom silver. Combine 1 quart whole milk with 4 tablespoons lemon juice, and let your items soak in it overnight. The next day, just rinse off your silver and dry it.

Spots on Silver

If your silver develops spots, dissolve a little salt in lemon juice, then dip a soft cloth into the mixture and rub it onto the cutlery. Rinse in warm water and finish by buffing to a shine with a chamois.

Silver Science Experiment

You can polish silver with aluminum foil, but perhaps not in the way you think. Line a pan with aluminum foil, add a tablespoon of salt, and fill with cold water. Then add your silverware to the mix and let it sit for a few minutes before removing and rinsing. The aluminum acts as a catalyst for ion exchange, a process that will make the tarnish transfer from your silver to the salt bath.

Chalking It Up

Before storing your silver, keep it tarnish free by adding in a couple of pieces of chalk wrapped in cheesecloth. The calcium carbonate in the chalk absorbs moisture from the air very slowly and prevents tarnish. For the best results, break up the chalk and expose the rough surface.

Clean Fiberglass

Cleaning fiberglass is, unfortunately, an adults-only chore. Using plastic gloves in a well-ventilated room, mix together 1 cup vinegar, ½ cup baking soda, ½ cup clear ammonia, and 1 gallon warm water. Designate a sponge just for this purpose (or use a rag) and be sure the solution doesn't touch your skin when you rub it onto the fiberglass.

A Great Future for Your Plastics

There aren't many cleaners designed especially for plastics, but it's easy to make your own. Simply mix a quart of water with 3 tablespoons of either lemon juice or white vinegar. Pour it in a spray bottle, and you've got some plastic cleaner.

Oven Cleaning Made Easy

A simple way to clean your oven is to place an oven-safe pot or bowl filled with water inside. Heat on 450° for 20 minutes, and steam will loosen the dirt and grease. Once your oven is cool, wipe off the condensation and the grease will come with it. When you're done, make a paste of water and baking soda and smear it on any enamel. The paste will dry into a protective layer that will absorb grease as you cook.

Cease Grease!

Forget about buying those expensive stove cleaners to get rid of cooked-on grease stains. Just wet the stains with vinegar and cover with baking soda. After watching the fun, foaming reaction, wipe with a damp sponge and buff with a dry, clean cloth.

Quick Fix for a Stinky Microwave

Microwave odors? Cut a lemon in quarters and put it in a bowl of water, then place in the microwave on high for 2 minutes. Wipe the inside with a soft cloth and any stains will lift easily.

Microwave Magic

To clean the smudged, greasy, food-flecked window of your microwave, use ashes from your fireplace. Rub them on the window with a wet rag, then rinse clean.

Easy Coffee Maker Cleaning

For the best-tasting coffee, make sure to clean your coffee maker regularly. Just add several tablespoons of baking soda to your pot, fill it with water, and run it as usual. Then repeat using only water. You can also use a denture-cleaning tablet instead of baking soda.

Rice Grinding

Even your coffee grinder needs a good clean every now and then, and uncooked rice can do the job. Simply mill a handful of rice as you normally do to your coffee beans. The chopped rice cleans out the stuck coffee grounds and oils, and absorbs the stale odors to boot. Afterward, throw away the rice, wipe the grinder clean . . . and grind fresh coffee!

This Cup Has Seen a Lot of Coffee!

To remove coffee or tea stains from a ceramic mug or pot, gently wipe them with a lemon sprinkled with salt.

The salt will act as an abrasive, while the acid will get rid of the tannins.

Remove Stubborn Stains

Get rid of really tough stains in your mugs by filling them with boiling water and adding a denture tablet. Let it sit overnight, and the stain should disappear.

Reader's Tip

To clean your cut crystal, mix a teaspoon of baking soda with warm water, then dab it onto the crystal with a soft rag. Rinse with water, then buff with a dry, soft cloth.

—KELLEY PINTO, ST. GEORGE, UT

Brighten Cloudy Glass

If your glasses are beginning to develop a fine film because of too many trips through the dishwasher, soak them in a bath of warm vinegar for an hour. They'll emerge sparkling clean.

Lipstick on Your Glass?

Who knew salt was the best way to remove lipstick from a glass? Rub a little over the stain to remove an imprint on the side of the glass, then wash as usual. Sticking lipstick-marked glasses in the dishwasher hardly ever works, because lipstick is made to resist water.

Stained China

Impossible-to-remove stains on your china? There may be hope yet. Apply a bit of nail polish remover to the spots with a soft cloth, then wash as usual. The spots should quickly fade.

New Favorite
To quickly disinfect a plastic cutting board, wash it thoroughly, rub half a cut lemon over it, and microwave it for a minute.

Like-New Cutting Boards

To make your cutting boards look like new, vigorously rub some salt into them. You can also treat wooden cutting boards with a very light coating of mineral oil. Be careful not to overdo it, because mineral oil may affect the potency of a number of vitamins in fruits and vegetables.

Fun Grater Trick

Cleaning a cheese grater will never be a problem if you grate a small piece of raw potato before trying to wash it out. An old toothbrush can also come in handy for this job.

Burnt Food Be Gone

Here's a great way to remove burnt food from pans. Sprinkle baking soda, salt, and dishwasher detergent over the crusty bits, then cover with water and boil for a half an hour. Even the toughest baked-on food will wipe off easily.

Cleaning Plastic Containers

To remove odors from dishes, bottles, or plastic containers, add a teaspoon of mustard to hot water and let the item soak in it for five minutes, then wash as usual.

Reader's Tip

Club soda is a terrific way to clean stainless steel sinks, dishwashers, ranges, and other appliances. The least expensive club soda works as well as the pricey brands; flat club soda is effective too. Add a little flour for really stubborn stains.   —LAUREN KEARNEY-SWOPE, SHARONVILLE, OH

Getting Rid of Counter Stains

You can remove stubborn stains from your countertop by applying a baking soda paste and rubbing with a warm, damp cloth. If the stain still remains, consider using a drop or two of bleach, but be careful—it can fade your countertop along with the stain!

Clean Dirty Kitchen Sponges

There's no need to throw out your stinky kitchen sponges. Just soak them in cold salt water for a half an hour. Rinse, and they're good to use again.

Deodorize the Disposal

A quick and easy way to deodorize your in-sink garbage disposal is to grind an orange or lemon peel inside it every so often. It will get rid of grease—and smell wonderful!

New Favorite

You've scrubbed it twice, but you can't seem to get those water spots out of your stainless steel sink! The solution? A little white vinegar. Just rub it into the spots and they'll disappear.

Toilet Bowl Cleaner

To remove hard-water deposits in your toilet bowl, pour 1 cup white vinegar into the bowl and allow it to sit for several hours or overnight before scrubbing. A fizzy denture tablet works well too!

Safe Septic Tank Cleaner

When buying your first new home, you probably thought about the backyard parties and a basement rec room. Cleaning the septic tank? Not so much. Still, the time will come when you will need to do it. Add 2 tea-spoons baker's yeast and 2 cups brown sugar to 4 cups warm water. Flush the mix and let sit overnight.

Spick-and-Span Shower Doors

Need to clean those dirty glass shower doors? You can wipe them down with leftover white wine (if you haven't finished it off!). The wine contains the perfect amount of alcohol to battle soap scum and lime. Apply with a damp sponge, leave for five minutes, then rinse off. Finish by quickly buffing with a clean, dry cloth.

DIY Scouring Powder

Make your own all-natural scouring powder by combining 1 cup salt with 1 cup baking soda. Store in a closed jar or can, and use it to scrub off hard water stains on your porcelain sinks and bathtub.

New Favorite

Believe it or not, toothpaste makes a great polish for your faucets. Just rub on and buff off with a soft cloth. The white, non-gel variety works best.

Enamel Enhancers

Remove stains from enamel with a paste of baking soda and hydrogen peroxide. This will form a gentle bleach you can rub in and leave to dry, then rinse off.

Soap-Scum Solution

Clear away shower-door soap scum effortlessly by wiping it with a used dryer sheet. It gets the job done quickly!

Power Shower Spray

Stay on top of mold and mildew by keeping this daily shower spray within easy reach of all family members. Mix one part vinegar with 10 parts water in an empty spray bottle and you're ready to go. Bonus: You don't have to worry about a toxic cleaner hitting the baby's bath toys.

For Old Copper Tubs

Removing blue-green stains caused by high copper content in your water can be challenging, even with the help of bleach. Try treating your shower or tub with a paste of equal parts cream of tartar and baking soda. Rub it into the stains, leave for half an hour, and rinse well with water. Repeat if necessary.

Freshen Your Humidifier

Humidifier smelling musty? Add 2 tablespoons lemon juice, and it will never smell fresher!

DIY Dehumidifier

You can make your own dehumidifier for your basement or other musty areas without having to spend a lot in the process. Simply fill a coffee can with charcoal briquettes and punch a few holes in the lid. Place it in a damp area, and replace the charcoal once a month as it absorbs the humidity.

Vanquish Smells with Vinegar

If you've burned dinner, welcome to the club. To get rid of the smoky scent (or any other strong kitchen odor), simply boil a cup of vinegar in 2 cups water. In 15 minutes, the smell should be gone. Or just dampen a cloth with a mixture of equal parts vinegar and water. Drape it over the cooking pot, taking care that the edges are far from the flame or intense heat.

CHAPTER 2

ALL-NATURAL PEST REPELLENTS

Repel Bugs Naturally

Don't spend money on bug sprays. Their main ingredient is usually alcohol, so save some money by simply making a mixture of one part rubbing alcohol and four parts water, then spraying it on as you would bug spray. Another natural (and great-smelling) alternative is equal parts water and pure vanilla extract.

New Favorite

Citronella candles are great for repelling insects, but they can be pricey. Get the same effect for much cheaper by mixing garlic with water and spraying it near all your outdoor light bulbs. As the bulbs heat up, they'll spread a faint garlicky scent across your yard, which will keep mosquitoes and other bugs away.

Repel with Peels

Another ingenious way to keep mosquitoes from biting you? Rub any exposed skin with orange or lemon peels. Mosquitoes hate the smell and will find someone else to attack. Ants also don't like the smell of lemon and orange peels, so grind them in your blender with some water, then spread in areas you find ants to keep them away.

Get Mosquitoes to Scram

It's a little-known fact that mosquitoes hate basil and tansy. Keep those plants in your yard and around your porch. If you're not familiar with it, tansy is a pretty yellow perennial, which has been harvested for its medicinal properties for several thousand years. In Colonial times it was used to preserve meat and keep insects away. It's a low maintenance flower, except for the odor, which irritates some people almost as much it does the bugs.

Mosquito Secret

Mosquitoes are attracted to dark blue clothing. (It's true!) If you usually have trouble with mosquito bites, trying wearing light, pastel clothes when you're out-doors. Many flying insects also like colorful clothing. Believe it or not, bugs are fooled by bright colors and floral prints on fabric. They think the prints are real flowers and end up flying too close to you or your kids.

Great Trick for Window Boxes

If you keep plants in window boxes, paint them white first. The bright, reflective surface will deter insects and reduce the risk of dry rot. It looks great, too!

If your kids squirm when you try to put bug spray on them, you'll love this tip. Keep a fabric softener sheet in each pocket to repel mosquitoes. A chemical in dryer sheets is similar to citronella, which is used in expensive bug-repelling candles. —HEATHER FRANKLIN-DANIELS, WEIGELSTOWN, PA

Getting Rid of Lice Naturally

Nothing strikes fear in the hearts of parents like the words "lice outbreak." The harsh chemicals that are used to fight lice are almost as bad as the lice themselves. Luckily, there is a cheaper, more natural alternative. Cover your child's head (or yours, if the little buggers have gotten you!) with a thick conditioner like Pantene Pro V. Put on a Disney movie to keep your kid busy, then get a wide-toothed metal comb. Dip the comb into rubbing alcohol and comb through the hair, staying close to the scalp. Between each swipe, wipe the comb on a white paper towel to make sure you're getting the lice. Dip the comb in the alcohol again and keep going. Cover the hair with baking soda, and then repeat the process with the alcohol and the comb. Wash the hair thoroughly when finished, and repeat this procedure each day for a week or until the lice are gone.

Flea Fix

You can remove pesky fleas from your pet's coat without having to pay for expensive flea collars or medications. Simply bathe your pet in salt water, and the fleas will stay away. You can also try steeping rosemary in warm water and using that as bathwater. Better yet, use a combination of the two.

A Good Night's Sleep for Your Pet

To ward off fleas from a pet's sleeping area, try sprinkling a few drops of lavender oil in the area. Fleas hate the smell of lavender oil and will find somewhere else to hide. Your pet, meanwhile, can enjoy a good night's sleep—and smell great in the morning.

Get Rid of Chiggers

There may be nothing more disgusting in this world than chiggers. You can pick them up in the woods, and they will lay eggs in the folds of your skin, causing a poison ivy–like rash. If you think you've been exposed to chiggers, take a hot bath. The heat will cause the larvae to die, making your pain (and disgust!) short-lived.

Ticks Be Gone

To easily remove ticks from you or your pet, first wet a Q-tip with rubbing alcohol. Dab it on the tick, and he'll loosen his grip. You should then be able to pull the tick straight off.

Remove Ticks with Ease

Oh no, you've got a tick! If you're having trouble prying the little bugger off, apply a large glob of petroleum jelly to the area. Wait about 20 minutes, and you should be able to wipe him off with ease.

Bees Begone

Swatting at bees who have found their way indoors is unnecessary (and never leads to anything good). Just turn out the light and open a window. The light from outside will attract them even more than your nice, juicy arm.

Picnic Pleaser

If you can't beat 'em, join 'em (kind of). At your next picnic party give stinging party crashers like bees and wasps a treat of their own—a few cans of open beer around the perimeter of your yard. They'll go for the beer and stay away from your guests. You can also try using sugar-covered grapefruit halves.

Easy Wasp Killer

If bees or moths have found their way into your home, don't panic. Fill a wide-mouthed jar with 1 cup sugar and 1½ cups water. The wasps will be attracted to the sugar and will drown in the water trying to get to it.

Reader's Tip

Is there anything worse than coming upon a swarm of wasps when you're enjoying your garden? If you find that wasps are building a nest in the same spot year after year, spray the area with white vinegar several times in the beginning of the spring and they'll find somewhere else to roost.

—DAVID JOHNS, NEW HAVEN, CT

Herbal Help

A number of herbs will ward off crawling insects. The most potent are fresh or dried bay leaves, sage, and cloves. Place any of these herbs in locations where a problem exists, and the critters will do an about-face and leave the premises. Ants, roaches, and spiders may be more difficult to get rid of. If these herbs don't work, try mixing 2 cups borax with an equal amount of sugar in a large container, and sprinkle the mixture in areas that you know the pests frequent. When crawling insects cross a fine powder, they lose the waterproof layer from their bodies, causing water loss and, ultimately, death.

Window Screen Fix-Up

To repair small holes in window screens, cover them with a few of layers of clear nail polish. It will keep the hole from becoming bigger and prevent insects from coming through.

Knock Out Roaches

Sugar and baking powder are a great one-two punch when it comes to getting rid of roaches. Mix equal parts and shake over any area where you've had a sighting or suspect entry. Clean and replace at regular intervals. Sugar attracts, baking soda (strangely) kills.

WD Roach Spray

Chasing, banging with a shoe, squishing—none of them are failsafe and they're all gross when it comes to getting rid of roaches. If you don't have bug spray on hand, here's something you may have: WD-40. Just squirt it on like you would bug spray. Just be careful because it may stain floors and carpets!

Drunk Roaches

Another great method for eliminating cockroaches is to fill a large bowl with cheap wine, then place it under the sink or wherever you see the revolting little bugs. The pests drink the wine, get drunk, and drown.

Roach Resolution

If you've tried every other solution, and those pesky roaches still want to call your house home, it's time to make roach balls. Here's how: Combine 2 cups borax, ½ cup sugar, ½ cup chopped onion, 2 tablespoons cornstarch, and 2 tablespoons water in a bowl, then roll into small balls. Place three balls into an unsealed sandwich bag and place the bags wherever your roach problem exists. Remember, though, that the roach balls are poisonous; be sure to place them where kids and pets can't reach them.

Ant Antics

Draw a line ants won't cross . . . with chalk! Ants think chalk is ash and won't cross it (because it may be a sign of fire). Use their tiny brains against them by drawing a thick line of chalk along windowsills, cabinets, or anywhere else they enter your home. You can even draw a line on your picnic table!

New Favorite

Flour mixed with cayenne pepper makes a great barrier to ants in your cabinets. You can also sprinkle outside wherever ants are infesting your garden or yard. Ants will run for shelter and you can sweep up the powder. Try ½ tablespoon pepper together with ½ cup white flour (sifted makes it easier).

Ant Answers

If your yard or garden is infested with pesky ants, sprinkle artificial sweetener (anything with aspartame) over the affected areas. Or try oats, cornmeal, instant grits, or cream of wheat. The ants will eat the dry cereal, which will then absorb all the moisture in their bodies and kill them.

Get Rid of Ant Hills

To get rid of ants for good, sprinkle cornmeal near ant-hills. They'll eat it, but they can't digest it, and they'll begin to die out. Wait a couple of weeks and see if your ant problem improves.

Avoid an Ant Infestation

Never use decorative paving stones near your home. Certain ants love to make their homes underneath them! Use them away from your house to be certain ants won't decide to come in for a visit.

A Not-So-Happy Ending for Carpenter Ants

Get rid of carpenter ants naturally with this formula: Mix one packet dry yeast with ½ cup molasses and ½ cup sugar, and spread on a piece of cardboard. Leave this sticky trap wherever you see the ants; they will come in droves to the sweet smell. Unfortunately for them, they'll also get stuck. Wait until your molasses mixture is covered with the creepy pests, then throw away.

Free a Bug; Don't Smack It

If a flying insect is in the car with you, do *not* swat at it! Instead, pull your car off to the side of the road, open all the windows or doors, and let the critter fly out. When you're driving, it's hard to tell what kind of bug it is, and it may have a stinger.

Fruit Fly Fix
Fruit flies are always a pain, because they usually hover around fruit baskets and other areas you don't want to spray poisonous bug spray. Instead, spray a little rubbing alcohol on them. They'll fall to the floor and you can scoop them up and throw them away.

Impromptu Bug Spray
If flies or bees have invaded your home and you want to get them away from you fast, squirt a little hairspray into the air. They hate the stuff and will go elsewhere.

Give Flies the Brush-Off
If you prefer not to use chemicals to get rid of flies, and you're not the most accurate fly swatter, invest in a strong fan. Scientists say that flies' wings are unable to

operate in a breeze above nine m.p.h, so open the windows, turn the fan to full power, and they'll soon buzz off. This is also a great trick for an outdoor party—just aim a few fans at the center of the action instead of spraying down your yard with awful-smelling repellent.

Keep Flies Away from Your Pool

There's nothing more irritating than having flies and other bugs swarm around you while you're trying to take a dip in the pool. We've had some luck keeping bugs away by applying a liberal amount of vinegar around the perimeter of the pool with a sponge.

Reader's Tip

Heading on a picnic and hate the thought of all the flies that will be dive-bombing your al fresco feast? Keep them away with an easy addition to your picnic basket. Just poke some whole cloves into several lemon wedges, then place them around the edges of your picnic blanket. The flies can't stand the scent and will stay away.　　—DANA FEHLHABER

Mealworm Menace

Keep a few sticks of wrapped spearmint chewing gum near any open packages of pasta, and they'll never get infested with mealworms.

Save Us from Silverfish

Silverfish like to hang around damp places, but they'll slither away if you decorate with spiced sachets. Try combining sage, bay leaves, and apple pie spices in fabric bags and hanging them in the kitchen, bathroom, basement, and other moist areas. You can also scatter whole cloves around.

Get a Leg Up on Centipedes

Borax works for repelling centipedes and millipedes. Sprinkle around areas where you've spotted them making a run for it. (Also works for the less offensive crickets.) Borax is an inexpensive cleaner than can be found at larger supermarkets, home stores, and discount retailers. Unfortunately, it isn't pet- or kid-safe, so sprinkle wisely.

For Crawling Critters

Sometimes, getting rid of insects is as easy as making it hard for them to get where they're going. Smear petroleum jelly around the base of plant stems, and ants and other crawling insects will slide right off, protecting your plants.

Debug a Plant

To get rid of bugs that are harming your houseplant, place the entire plant (pot and all) in a clear, plastic dry cleaning bag. Throw several mothballs in with it, and tie a knot at the top. The sun will still get through, but the bugs will die after a week in seclusion with the mothballs.

Clear Out Slugs with Cabbage

If you're having problems with slugs eating your flowers, and nothing seems to work, your solution might be in the form of distraction. Slugs love cabbage, so planting a few in your garden will ensure they stay away from your flowers and go for the cabbage instead.

Solve a Snail or Slug Problem

Need to get rid of snails or slugs in your garden? Find the cheapest beer you can, then pour it into several shallow containers (shoeboxes lined with aluminum foil work well). Dig a few shallow holes in your garden and place the containers inside so that they are at ground level. Leave overnight, and the next morning, you'll find dozens of dead (or drunk) snails and slugs inside. These critters are attracted to beer (who isn't?), but it has a diuretic effect on them, causing them to lose vital liquids and die.

Reader's Tip

Do you have a sprouting head of garlic? It's best not to use in cooking, because it will have lost much of its potency. But you can have a brand new head of garlic in no time, and keep bugs out of your garden at the same time. Put the whole bulb (sprout/pointy end up) in your garden and cover with an inch of soil. It will continue to send up shoots, and in a few months, a whole new bulb of garlic will have grown under the soil's surface. Meanwhile, the smell of the garlic underground will keep many insects away from your other plants. —MARTHA STANLEY, NEON, TN

How to Kill Spider Mites

Do you have trees that are infested with spider mites? You can make a mixture to get rid of them using ingredients already in your kitchen. Take a pound of flour, five gallons of water, and a cup of buttermilk, mix it all together in a large bucket, and put it in a plastic spray bottle. Use it on your trees once a week, and it should keep the mite population under control.

The Japanese Beetle Invasion

Keep your rosebush the pride of your garden by getting rid of those icky Japanese beetles. Pour a bowl of self-rising flour and go outside, sprinkling it over the whole bush like it's some kind of magic potion (which, in this case, it is).

No More Gnats

If you suspect that one of your plants has a gnat problem, here's how to find out for sure. Slice off one-third of an uncooked potato and place it face down (peel side up) on top of the soil. Leave it for a week to 10 days, and if the potato is still clean, you've got no gnats to worry about. If gnats are present, however, there will be larvae on the underside of the potato slice. To rescue your plant, kill the gnats with vodka. (Yes, vodka.) Mix one part vodka to three parts water, pour it into a spray bottle, and spray away. Do this for a week, and the pests will be long gone.

Aphid Answers

Are aphids invading your garden? Here's an easy, organic way to keep them out. Chop up an onion, place it in a cup of water, and puree it until it's liquid. Pour the concoction into a plastic spray bottle and use it to mist the plants aphids are attracted to. For best results, try it at dawn before the sun starts blazing.

New Favorite

If aphids are infesting your plants, here's an easy solution. Cover a tennis ball with petroleum jelly and leave it nearby. The bugs will be attracted to its bright color, and then get stuck on its side.

Save Your Plants

If you want to keep bugs off your plants, try spraying their leaves with a solution of 10 parts weak tea and one part ammonia. Try it first on a few leaves to test for damage, and make sure pets and children don't try to eat or lick the leaves (hey, they've done weirder things!).

Keep Plants Pest-Free

When watering outdoor plants, place a few drops of dishwashing liquid into the water, and make sure it gets on your plants' leaves. The detergent will keep bugs away, making sure your plants remain healthy and beautiful.

Worms in Your Plants?

If your plant is plagued by worms, the problem is easily solved. Just stick half a dozen unlit matches into the soil, coated end facing down. The sulfur content in the matches will keep the worms away.

Moth Trap

Trap moths by mixing one part molasses with two parts white vinegar and placing the mixture in a bright yellow container. The moths will be attracted to the color and the smell, then drown inside.

Not Your Mother's Mothballs

Mothballs have that telltale old attic smell, and even worse, they contain a carcinogen. Use a pretty-smelling natural potpourri made of rosemary, mint, thyme, ginseng, and cloves for the same effect. You want about eight times as many cloves as the other ingredients, since they are what actually keeps the moths away. You can also add lemon peel and tansy. Store in little sachets, which you can buy in a craft store, or tie up in old rags. If you have moths on an item of clothing, put it in your freezer for two days and then clean as usual.

Freeze Your Wool

Placing your woolen clothes in a well-sealed bag isn't always enough to keep moths away, as any eggs laid in them beforehand will hatch—and the new moths will have a field day. To make sure all the eggs die before you put your clothes in storage, place the airtight bag of clothes in the freezer for 24 hours.

Mice Hate Mint

If you're suffering from a mouse infestation and can see the mouse holes, smear a bit of mint toothpaste nearby and the smell will deter them. You can also rub toothpaste along the bottom of your baseboards and anywhere else mice may get into your home.

Not Even a Mouse

As cute as they are, you don't want mice in the house, and certainly not around the kitchen. Shake baking soda around their hiding spots, and they'll stay away. It's safe for pets and kids, and easy to clean up with a broom or vacuum.

Best Bait for Mice

If you've seen a lot of Disney movies, you probably think mice live for cheese. But when you're baiting a mousetrap, a better bet is peanut butter. Since it's sticky, you can be sure the mouse won't grab it and run, and scientists say they love its sweet scent even more than your best piece of Cheddar.

A (Dead) Mouse House

If you're squeamish about having to pick up the remains of a rodent you've set a trap for, place the baited trap inside a brown paper lunch bag. Rodents like exploring small spaces, and once the trap has done its trick, you can scoop it right up and throw it away.

New Favorite

If pigeons or other birds won't leave your patio alone, try sprinkling baking soda anywhere they like to perch. They don't like the feeling of it under their toes! You can also try sticky-side-up tape.

Foil Birds with Foil

If birds or other critters are nibbling at your fruit trees, try hanging long strips of aluminum foil from the branches. They'll be attracted to its shiny surface, but once they bite it, they'll fly away.

Keep Bugs Away from the Birds' Bath

Keep bugs away from a birdbath! Just a few drops of canola or vegetable oil will keep mosquitoes from laying eggs in the water in your birdbath, won't hurt the intended residents, and will save you from lots of itchy bites.

Give Squirrels the Slip

This idea may conjure up a cartoon chase scene, but here's a safe, natural way to feed the birds and not the squirrels: Simply rub vegetable shortening or oil on the pole leading up to your feeder to keep the uninvited guests from letting themselves in.

Reader's Tip

If squirrels are making a nuisance of themselves around your home, keep them away with a homemade pepper spray. Take a cup of your favorite hot sauce, add a spoonful of cayenne pepper and a capful of Murphy's Oil Soap, and mix together. Spray the mixture in whatever areas you want the squirrels to steer clear of. —MEGAN RYE, WASHINGTON, DC

Deter Pests in Your Garden

If you've ever bitten into a shred of foil that had gotten stuck to a piece of candy, you know how unpleasant the sensation is. Rodents hate the feeling of foil between their teeth, too, so placing strips of foil in your garden mulch will help deter rodents and some bugs. If rodents are eating the bark of your tree, you can also wrap the trunk in foil.

Say Goodbye to Moles
Moles are pretty cute, until they're wreaking havoc on your yard. Use this all-natural solution to get rid of them: Just soak some old rags in olive oil, then stuff them in all the holes you can find. Moles hate the smell and will stay away.

Deer Repellent
If deer are getting to your flower garden, throw a few mothballs on the ground. Deer hate the smell of mothballs. (Who doesn't?)

Buh-Bye, Bambi!
Hanging small pieces of a deodorant bar soap on trees will keep deer from munching on them. Or, try a piece of your clothing that you've worn for several days—deer don't like the smell of humans.

Protect Your Grill
Make sure rabbits, mice, and other critters don't chew through the rubber pipeline that connects your propane tank with your grill—reinforce the entire thing with duct tape. This is a good idea for anything else in your yard made out of rubber, as this is a favorite chew toy of rodents!

Keeping Neighborhood Cats Away

If your neighbors' cats are causing havoc in your yard, don't even try to go talk to their owners—once the cats are let out there really is nothing they can do to keep them fenced in. Instead, sprinkle the edge of your yard with orange peels and coffee grounds. Cats don't like the smell, and the scraps will eventually create great compost for your lawn.

Reclaiming Your Yard from Raccoons

Have the raccoons grown rather bold around your backyard and trashcans? Try this equivalent of a phony "Beware of Dog" sign by distributing dog hair around your property. You can also try planting cucumbers, which both skunks and raccoons avoid like the plague.

CHAPTER 3

HOME-GROWN FERTILIZERS AND GARDEN SUPPLIES

A Seed Sponge

Here's an inventive seed-starter: a sponge. Place a few seeds in the crevices of a wet sponge, and wait for them to sprout! Not only will it keep the seeds nice and moist, you can then plant the entire sponge in your garden.

More Seed Starters

Plastic take-out containers make great makeshift holders to jumpstart seed growing. Put seeds in soil, layer about halfway, water, and close the lid. Seeds should sprout in no time when the container is left in the sun.

Freezing Seeds

If you have more seeds than you can use this spring, store them in a sealed container in your freezer. The cold will keep them fresh until next year.

Reader's Tip

Here's a fast and easy way to sow seeds while still making sure they're perfectly spaced. Fill an old salt or spice shaker with the seeds and some sand, then sprinkle the mixture into the dirt when it's time to plant. —PAM EEKHOFF, CHARITON, IA

Make Your Own Bonemeal

As you may know, bonemeal is an excellent source of nutrients for your plants. But instead of spending $8–$10 on a bag at your local gardening store, make your own! Bonemeal is just bones, after all. Save bones from chicken, turkey, steaks, and stews, then dry them out by roasting them in a 425°F oven for a half an hour or microwaving them on high for 1–6 minutes (depending on how many bones you have). Then place them in a plastic or paper bag and grind them up by hitting them with a hammer, then rolling them with a rolling pin. Mix the resulting powder into your soil for a life-producing treat for your plants. And you didn't spend a cent!

Food for Your Geraniums

Who knew geraniums love potatoes? They contain all the nutrients a growing geranium plant needs and can also make it easier for you to transplant these beautiful flowers. Simply carve out a hole in a raw potato using the end of a vegetable peeler, insert the stem of a geranium, and plant the entire thing in its new pot or in your garden.

Plants Like Beer, Too

If you host a big party at your house, don't throw away all the beer from those half-empty bottles. Instead, pour it into a bucket, let it sit for a day or two until the beer gets flat, then pour into your garden or on your potted plants. The nutrients from the beer will give the plants an extra boost. Wait a minute, wasn't this in *Little Shop of Horrors*?

A Must-Have for Growing Carrots

The best thing you can give your carrot seeds is also what keeps you going during the day—coffee! Mix carrot seeds with coffee grounds before you plant them. Having some extra bulk to plant will ensure they don't end up all lumped together, and the coffee will provide your growing plants with much-needed nutrients. Don't drink coffee? Many Starbucks give away used grounds as part of their "Grounds for Your Garden" program. Just ask at your local Starbucks.

Healthy Pepper Patch

This advice definitely sounds like an urban legend, but it's such an easy way to grow fantastic sweet peppers that you have to try it. A matchbook buried with each pepper plant will transmit sulfur, a great fertilizer for them. In addition, to give these nutrient-seeking plants the magnesium they need, add 2 tablespoons Epsom salts to ½ gallon water and soak the plants with the mixture when you see the first blossoms of the year.

Revive a Fern

If you have a fern that's seen better days, and appears to be light in color, perk it up with this simple solution: Mix a tablespoon of Epsom salts into ½ gallon of water. Water it with this mixture twice a year for best results.

Houseplant Favorite

Forget expensive food for your houseplants. Just feed them flat club soda periodically and they should thrive. The minerals in club soda are beneficial to plants.

Plants Love Starch

Your houseplants need nourishment, particularly in the dead of winter when the sunlight is limited, yet there's no need to buy expensive plant food. Just remember to save the water in which you boil potatoes or pasta, let it cool, and use it to water your plants. They love the starchy water.

A Little Fat on Your Roses

Want to give your roses an extra dose of fuel? A small amount of fat drippings placed at the base of a rose bush will keep it healthier and make it bloom more frequently.

Reader's Tip

Mix dried banana peels in with the soil next time you plant something new; you'll give it the potassium and phosphorous it needs to grow beautifully. —EVAN STOOKE, RED LION, PA

Composting Made Easy

If you've been putting off having a compost pile because of the hassle of always having to traipse to the other side of the yard, simply keep scraps in your freezer until you're ready to compost. Banana peels, apple cores, eggshells, coffee grinds, and other scraps can all go right into a plastic container.

Increase Soil Acidity

If you live in a hard water area, add 1 cup vinegar to 1 gallon water, then use it to water plants that love acidic soil, such as rhododendrons, heather, and azaleas. The vinegar will release iron in the soil for the plants to use.

You Say Tomato, I Say Grow Faster!

If the end of the growing season is nigh, and you'd like your tomatoes to ripen on the vine more quickly, there are a few things you can try. Remove damaged, dead, or diseased leaves, and cut off all new flowers. Keep a daily eye on the tomatoes, and pick them as soon as they're ripe, so the plant can devote its effort to ripening the rest of the fruit. Harvest the tomatoes when they're red, but still firm. Believe it or not, watering the plant less will ripen the tomatoes more quickly!

Cheap Lawn Fertilizer

Did you know Epsom salts are one of the best natural lawn fertilizers around? They're composed of magnesium and sulfur, both of which are highly beneficial to grass. Magnesium kick-starts seed germination and is also a player in manufacturing chlorophyll, the substance that plants create from sunlight in order to feed themselves. Sulfur, meanwhile, also helps with chlorophyll, while simultaneously enhancing the effects of other fertilizer ingredients such as nitrogen, phosphorus, and potassium. It also deters certain pests such as ground worms. With all these benefits, it's no wonder that savvy lawn care specialists have been using Epsom salts for years. You can either sprinkle them on your lawn using a spreader or make a liquid solution out of them by adding some water and putting the mixture in a spray bottle.

A Second Life for Shells

You may not have time to build a compost bin (or the stomach for a bucket full of worms), but you can easily crush shells from last night's seafood dinner and scatter them over your lawn. The calcium helps the grass grow.

Keep Your Plants Covered

If you have smaller outdoor plants, you don't necessarily need to bring them inside to keep them protected from frost. Simply cover them at night with small plastic garbage bags (the kind that have pull handles), and tie the handles snugly around the pots. Don't forget to remove the bags in the morning, though, so the plants can soak up the sun.

Perk Up Houseplants

If your houseplants aren't getting enough sun, maximize the amount of light they *are* getting by placing them on top of a table covered in foil (shiny side up). The foil will reflect the light, and your plants will thank you.

Reviving Plants

This may sound like a cure from the Middle Ages, but garlic does a fine job of reviving diseased plants. Grate 2 cloves into 4 cups water and use as much as you need to quench the thirst of your struggling plants. Given the myriad health benefits garlic offers to humans, it's not surprising it can help the immobile organisms that share your home (and we don't mean your spouse and kids).

Protecting Your Plants from Mildew

Here's an old treatment to prevent plants from suffering from mildew or black spots. Mix together ½ tablespoon baking soda with a drop of vegetable oil and 2 cups soapy water. Spray on both sides of the leaves of plants that are affected. Complete this treatment in the evening and never in full sunlight; otherwise the leaves may scorch. While the soap helps to spread the mixture and the vegetable oil causes it to stick, the baking soda makes the surfaces of the leaves alkaline, which will inhibit the fungal spores. The biggest advantage of this method is that there will be no adverse environmental impact, thanks to the all-natural ingredients.

Daily News Keeps Weeds Away

Here's the most inventive weed-prevention technique we've heard: Wet newspapers and layer them around the plants (then cover with dirt and mulch so your yard doesn't look like a trash heap).

Weed Buster

Bull and Russian thistle sound powerful, but they're no match for WD-40. When you need to get these weeds out of your way, give them a spray with some house-hold oil to kill them in a day or two.

Get Rid of Poison Ivy

When it comes to poison ivy, an ounce of prevention really is worth a pound of cure. So if you've got a patch of this pernicious vine on your property, kill it. Mix ½ gallon soapy water with 1½ pounds salt, spray the plant, and run in the other direction.

Keep Gloves Handy

In our family, we're never all ready to go at the same time. Since we love to garden, we keep a few pairs of garden gloves by the door so the early birds can pull out a few weeds while they're waiting for the slowpokes. It prevents having to take the time to pull the weeds later—and keeps a certain someone from yelling at everyone else to hurry up!

Reader's Tip

Let your lawn grow to starve weeds! Try to keep your lawn about 3 inches high. The higher the grass, the less direct sunlight is available for pesky weeds to grow.

—RICHARD DOMBROWSKI

Sidewalk Cleanup

Want to get rid of the grass growing in the cracks of your sidewalk or patio? Make a mixture of salt and baking soda, sprinkle it into the cracks, and the problem should be solved.

Make Pots Like New

Remove the stains in clay and plastic flowerpots with vinegar. Just fill the kitchen sink with two-thirds water and one-third vinegar, and soak the pots. In an hour, they'll be good as new! Make sure to wash with soap and water before re-using.

Safe Transport for Your Plants

When transplanting, always use lightly moistened soil and peat moss to help retain moisture in the roots. If the soil is dry, it won't hold together well during the transplant, which might result in a messy move at best and a plant casualty at worst.

Reader's Tip

If you break a terra-cotta pot, don't toss it out—use it to help your garden drain more easily! Break into tiny pieces, then mix with your soil to promote drainage. If they could, we're sure your plants would thank you!

—DARLENE MULLINS, MARSHFIELD, MO

Tea for Plants

If you have any doubt that tea really is a panacea, here's one more amazing use for it: nurturing your plants and keeping them moist. Place a lining of tea bags along the bottom of a plant container, then pot and water as usual.

Reuse Packing Peanuts

Packing peanuts will take several decades to decompose, so you can make better use of them than throwing them away. Place them at the bottom of flowerpots before covering with soil and planting flowers and other plants. They'll keep the pot well-drained and much lighter than if you had used rocks.

There Really Is a Use for Dryer Lint!

Use dryer lint to prevent dirt from falling out of your potted houseplants when you water them: Place some dryer lint in the pots so it covers the holes. The water will drain out, but the dirt will stay in!

New Favorite

When you break out the charcoal for grilling season, save a few briquettes for your garden. Crush them into pieces about 1-inch wide and sprinkle them on top of the soil. Not only is the carbon in the charcoal great for plants, but the charcoal absorbs water and then slowly releases it, meaning that your plants' roots will stay moister for longer.

Early Bird Gets the Water

Early morning is the best time to water your lawn or garden because you'll minimize evaporation. The absolute worst time to do it is during the bright sun of the afternoon.

Protect Your Soil (and Your Shirt!)

To keep mud from spattering when you water plants in window boxes, top the soil with a half-inch layer of gravel. Do the same for outdoor plants to prevent mud bombs during heavy rainfalls.

Plants Like It Warm

If you have a water softener, water from your sink may not be the best for your plants. Instead, use water from your outside tap, which doesn't go through the softener. If necessary, bring the water in and let it warm up a bit. Cold water can chill plants' roots.

Pencil Test

Wondering if your plant has had enough water? Here's the equivalent to sticking a fork in a pan of brownies to see if they're done: Poke a pencil into the dirt and pull it back out. Clean means it's time to water. Soil on the pencil means the plant is okay for now.

Plant IDs

Here's a cheap, easy idea for labeling plants—especially herbs, veggies, anything you might consume. Use white or beige plastic knives, the kind you may have stashed from fast-food restaurants. Simply write the name of the plant on the knife with a permanent marker and stick into the ground. They're waterproof, and last forever.

For Easy-to-Raise Plants

At PlantNative.org, you can find lists of flowers, shrubs, trees, vines, and grasses that are native to your area. This means they'll not only be less expensive to buy, they'll also hold up well in your garden.

Fun Yard Project

We always thought moss looked quaint in between cracks in our sidewalk, so we learned how to grow our own. Pull up some common lawn moss and blend it with active-culture yogurt. Find a cool spot with lots of shade and paint it into nooks and crannies, stone walls, and flower pots.

How Far Down?

When you plant seeds, you want to make sure you bury them at the correct depth. Save time and energy by marking 1-inch measurements on the handles of your tools instead of using a ruler.

New Favorite

Is your hose full of holes? If you have an old hose you're no longer able to use (or an extra one lying around) repurpose it as a soaker hose. It's easy: Just poke holes along its length with a straight pen, then place in your garden to slowly water your plants.

Watch That Hose!

When watering your garden with a hose, take care not to drag the hose over your plants. Place a few short, heavy stakes in your garden to create an alleyway for the hose, restraining it from rolling around and distressing the delicate plants. If you don't have stakes, simply cut a wire hanger into six-inch pieces, bend them into arches, and use them to guide your hose.

Store Your Hose to Its Max

Your garden hose will last twice as long if you store it coiled, rather than folded. Try coiling it around a bucket. Note that the hose will be easiest to work with when it's neither very cold nor very hot outside.

Fun Hose Fix

It may drive you crazy to hear your kids chomping away on chewing gum, but when it comes to fixing a small leak in your hose, the gum will actually serve you. To minimize the "ick" factor you may want to chew on a new piece yourself, but either way use it to cover the hole and massage it outward so it extends roughly ½ inch in any direction. It will harden by the next morning.

Save Your Grass

Don't worry about collecting clippings when you mow your lawn. It's a waste of landfill space, and you'll deprive your lawn of nutrients it can use through natural composting. Instead, take off the bag and leave the clippings in the grass. You'll be surprised how quickly they work their way between the blades and disappear.

For Grass that Won't Stick

The rain stopped just in time for your outdoor party, but not in enough time for the grass to dry before you want to mow it. To solve this problem, simply spray the blades of your lawnmower with vegetable oil or non-stick cooking spray, and the grass won't stick!

Ramp Up Your Mowing Game

Save yourself the boring task of poking holes in your soil to aerate it. Instead multitask the easy way by wearing spiked golf shoes or soccer cleats to aerate while you mow your lawn.

New Favorite

When you're clearing out leaves this fall, make a sturdy leaf bag with this smart trick: Cut out the bottom of a hard plastic laundry basket, and stick the bottomless basket into your leaf bag. It'll hold the bag in place so you can dump leaves into it without worrying about spills. Just remove the basket when the bag is ready for the trash.

Prune Plants Safely

Take care when pruning your roses and other thorny plants in the garden—you don't want to prick your fingers. Try holding the branches with a pair of kitchen tongs while you snip.

Pruning Solution

Use a solution of bleach and water to disinfect pruning shears after you're done so you don't spread diseases between plants. Rinse with tepid water until the bleach is gone.

Tough Love for Trees

Treating your fruit trees like they're bad will yield a good crop. Smack the trunks with a rolled-up newspaper to get the sap moving more efficiently through the branches, which, in turn, helps the tree produce more fruit. Think of it like a massage to increase blood flow. And be prepared for strange looks from passersby.

Tree Sculpting

Pruning will be less of a chore if you keep your eye on the goal of a strong and healthy tree. If it's more of a motivator, though, remember you don't want to get sued if a weak branch falls on a neighbor. On pruning day, follow a simple plan: first get rid of any branches that are clearly dead, dying, or infested. Then home in on the ones that are too long, crisscrossing each other, or growing weak. Step back and admire your work.

New Favorite

If you still have old, unused cassette tapes lying around, pull out the film and use it to tie up any trees or plants that need to be held to stakes. Better yet, old panty hose also makes an effective tie: Just cut the nylons into narrow strips. It works better than plastic ties because the panty hose expands as the plant grows.

Rust-Free Tools

Make sure your garden shears never rust with a little car wax. Just rub a little paste over the shears (including the hinge) to prevent them from ever getting stuck again.

Garden Club

Not sure what to do with that old golf club bag? Don't throw it away or stick it in the garage sale pile just yet. It's perfect for carting garden tools around your yard!

Attract Beautiful Birds

Want to make your birdbath a hotspot for your feathered friends? Simply add some colorful marbles or pebbles to attract neighborhood birds. The brighter the color, the better!

Reader's Tip

There's a chemical in lavender that inhibits the growth of algae. Make a bundle of lavender flowers and daylily leaves for your birdbath to keep it free and clear. Change every few weeks.
—TINA CAUDILL, POUND, VA

CHAPTER 4

EASY DO-IT-YOURSELF SOLUTIONS

Never Buy a Baby Wipe Again

If you have a baby, you know that one costly item that's impossible to use less of is baby wipes. When we had babies, we saved hundreds per year by making our own diaper wipes! They are easy to make and can be kept in an old baby wipes container, a plastic storage bin with a lid, or a resealable plastic bag. Here's how to do it: combine 2 tablespoons each of baby oil and baby shampoo (or baby wash) with 2 cups boiled and cooled water and one or two drops of your favorite essential oil for scent (optional). Remove the cardboard roll from a package of paper towels, then cut the entire roll in half (you can also tear off sheets by hand and stack them in a pile). Put some of the liquid mixture at the bottom of your container, then place the half-roll in the container. Pour the rest of the liquid over your paper towels and voilà—homemade baby wipes! Let the wipes sit for about an hour to absorb all the liquid, and your baby will never know the difference.

Diaper Rash Remedy

When your baby gets diaper rash, nix those pricey ointments and try a homemade remedy instead. Make a paste with about ¼ cup petroleum jelly and 1 table-spoon cornstarch, then spread it along your baby's irritated skin.

Dryer Lint Dough

Make a Play-Doh substitute for your kids with an unlikely ingredient: dryer lint! First save up 3 cups of
dryer lint, then stick it into a pot with 2 cups water,
1 cup flour, 6–10 drops food coloring, and ½ teaspoon
vegetable or canola oil. Cook, stirring constantly, over
low heat until the mixture is smooth. Then pour onto
a sheet of wax paper to cool.

Colossal Blocks

Make towers you can tumble without upsetting your
downstairs neighbors! Cereal boxes can easily be con-
verted into oversized blocks for undersized humans.
Make sure to shake out any excess Raisin Bran and then
tape shut the top with packing tape. Add shoeboxes to
the collection, along with boxes from cookies, crackers,
and even ice cream sandwiches, for a variety of sizes and

shapes. You can cover with wrapping paper or magazine pages if you like, or use contact paper over the original packaging to infuse an Andy Warhol–inspired bit of pop art into playtime. Keep adding to the collection instead of the recycling bin.

Paper Log Cabins

If you collect enough paper towel tubes you can make your own jumbo "Lincoln Logs." Separate half the tubes and cut out 1½-inch squares at either end. Take the uncut rolls and stack them perpendicularly by sliding the end into the openings you cut.

Make It Fit

Save dress-up time from turning into meltdown time by keep clothespins on hand for oversized costumes. Grandpa's shirt tripping up your toddler? Simply gather in the back and clip. Is the tutu falling down every time she (or he) attempts a pirouette? Make it pint-size by clipping it at the waist and letting the excess material gather at the side. Clothespins can grab hold of much more material than safety pins and they're safer, too.

Save Your Bottles

If you're looking for a cheap and practical toy for kids, thoroughly wash old ketchup, salad dressing, and shampoo bottles and let the kids use them to play in the swimming pool or bathtub. They're also a good way to wash shampoo out of hair at bath time.

Here's a simple toy to occupy your fussy baby for a good five minutes or so. On a strong piece of cardboard (you can always cut one side of a box) trace the circle at the end of a toilet paper tube four times, then cut out the circles so they're just slightly bigger than the shape you traced. Your baby will enjoy pushing toilet paper tubes through the holes from one side to the other.

—FAWNNE PEMBERTON, BON AIR, VA

Crazy for Bubbles

Warm weather means bubble season for young kids, but you don't have to pay for store-bought bubbles. Here's our inexpensive homemade solution for bubble greatness: Mix 1 tablespoon glycerin with 2 tablespoons powdered laundry detergent in 1 cup warm water. (Glycerin, often called "vegetable glycerin," can be found online and at many health-food and vitamin shops.) If it's safe for your kids, any unpainted piece of metal wire (like a hanger) can be turned into a bubble wand: Just shape one end of the wire into a circle. Blowing into the mixture with a straw will make smaller bubbles float into the air. For colored bubbles, add food coloring.

Ramp It Up

Use a poster mailing tube as a ramp for toy cars. Hold it level while your child slides a car in, then raise the end you're holding so the car whizzes down and out the other side. You can also use multiple cars and collect them at one end in a bucket or pan for a pleasing clacking sound as they zip out of the tube and join the heap. When they're all in a pile, dump them out and start again.

Smock Frock

Your kids may not want to be ghosts for Halloween (for the third time) this year, but they can still make good use of old pillowcases—for smocks. Cut out holes for the head and arms, slide them over your kids' heads, and start painting away. The best part is, the more paint-splattered the smock gets, the closer it will resemble a Jackson Pollack original, and the more inspiration it will offer the little painters next time.

Plug the Socket

If you don't make it a practice to travel with your entire baby-proofing kit including gates, grates, and banister shields (shame on you!), use Band-Aids in hotel rooms to cover open outlets. You'll still need to keep an eye on babies and toddlers playing nearby. Band-Aids take an eternity to remove from human skin but a second for a baby to remove from any other location—but it's better than leaving the outlet completely bare.

Reader's Tip

Use a shower curtain ring to keep a toddler out of your cabinets. Just run the ring through two handles that are close by and latch. —RANDY RODRIGUEZ, WAXAHACHIE, TX

Another Curtain Ring Use

You *could* pay 50¢ a pop for links that secure your child's toys to his stroller. But for a less expensive substitute, try using shower curtain rings, which are available in 12-packs for less than $2.

Drip Dry

Hang a meshed potato bag from a hook on your shower organizer to store your child's bath toys. The air will get at them and you'll keep mildew at bay.

Pick a Card

Pudding boxes are the perfect size for storing decks of cards. Glue three together to make a little playing-card shelf.

Converted Bumper

For safety's sake, pediatricians don't recommend using bumpers in a baby's crib anymore, but if one's been given to you at a shower or passed along as a hand-me-down, put it to good use baby proofing your coffee table or other pointy or hard surfaces. We used ours to wrap the edges of a metal daybed in the family room. (Of course the downside is it cuts down on the number of reasons you have at the ready for why kids can't do cartwheels inside the house.)

Reader's Tip

It's hard to say goodbye to those adorable frog or ducky rain boots when your kids outgrow them or burst a hole through the toe. Turns out you don't have to. Put a small bag filled with rice or beans inside each boot and you've got yourself two cute bookends for your child's library.

—CYNTHIA HUSTER, SOLO, AK

Knife Holders

Your cutlery will stay sharp and safely away from poking other items in your kitchen drawers if you glue two corks together length-wise and use them as simple knife-holders. The sharp side of the knife lies where the corks join.

This Solution's a Corker

Avoid slamming kitchen cabinets by putting homemade silencers on them. Just save the cork from your next bottle of wine, slice it into skinny pieces, and glue them onto each inside corner of your cabinet. Problem solved!

A Cheaper Cushion

You've probably seen those little cushions with the sticky material on the back that can be placed on the bottom of furniture or the backs of picture frames to keep them from scratching. Rather than spending the money for these expensive items, buy cushions for corns and bunions instead! As long as they aren't medicated, they're the exact same thing, and usually much cheaper.

Reader's Tip

When sliding heavy furniture across a wooden floor, put socks on the legs. It will make for a much smoother ride and you won't scratch the floors. —AMANDA KREHBIEL

Cheap Clips

Instead of buying those clips for fastening cereal and chip bags, simply buy a box of large binder clips from an office supply store. They're the exact same thing at less than half the cost.

Make Your Own Bowl Scraper

Have you ever seen those bowl scrapers in kitchen stores that sell for $3 to $10? These circular, plastic tools are easy to make at home. Simply take the lid of a round take-out container, cut it in half, then remove the rim. Instant savings!

Shaken, Not Stirred

Who needs a martini shaker? Instead of buying this expensive bar tool, simply use a stainless steel thermos with a screw-in lid. If there's no way to close the sipping hole on the top, cover it with your thumb while you shake!

Shabby Chic Trivets

Hardware and home improvement stores have lots of ceramic tiles that can be adapted as mix 'n' match trivets. Choose from a variety of designs and colors to add unique accents to your table setting. Add some extra protection by attaching some felt circles to the corners of each tile.

Shelve the Contact Paper

Instead of using contact paper on your kitchen shelves,
use some peel-and-stick vinyl floor tiles instead (cut
to size if necessary). They're super easy to clean, and
they're usually cheaper, too—some stores will even
give you a free sample.

Starting Over

Telling your ninth grader "You can always erase it"
when you're helping him with his math homework
doesn't work if his pencil eraser has been hardened
over! File the stubborn eraser with an emery board until you take the coating off, and be glad pencils are—in
rare cases—still employed by the under-20 set.

Cereal for Serials

Are magazines piling up around your home? Make
some colorful and functional magazine holders by
cutting cereal boxes at angles and covering them with

wrapping paper. Cover with some craft lacquer for a durable finish.

New Favorite

Parents who have been through baby-proofing boot camp are trained to throw out packets of silica gel upon contact. If you don't have to worry about kids or pets getting their paws on them, however, you can put them to good use. They soak up moisture, which is handy for preserving all kinds of household metal, from tools to flatware and silverware, to jewelry. Just place them in any drawers or boxes you want to keep from collecting moisture.

Milk It for All It's Worth

With three kids, empty cardboard milk cartons pile up on a daily basis in our kitchen. Not all cities accept them in recycling, but we discovered they can be reused as handy mailers for CDs or DVDs rather than adding to the landfill. Rinse out an empty carton, let it dry, then cut both ends. Push to flatten and trim into a square that will fit the CD or DVD. Wrap the sides with duct tape, cover with wrapping paper or a paper grocery bag, add a label, and it's ready to go anywhere the US postal service delivers.

In the Bag

Cereal boxes are easy enough to divert to the arts and crafts table or recycle. But what about those sturdy wax bags inside that usually land in the trash? Use them in place of Ziploc bags or wax paper. When the cereal's gone, shake out the crumbs, rinse, and prop up to dry in the drainer. They're especially useful for cakes or muffins you want to freeze for another day.

Chalk It Up

Chalk is good for more than writing! If your kids have outgrown sidewalk chalk or you happen to have some around, place it in the damp areas of your home (like your basement) to absorb excess moisture and repel mildew. Use a container that allows air to get through it, like a mesh bag, a coffee can, or a paper bag with holes poked in it.

Heaven Scent

Even if your favorite scented candle is almost completely gone, it's easy to keep the smell with you! Carefully cut or break the remaining candle into pieces, then put them in an old sock or nylon and hang in your closet. The enclosed space will be filled with your candle's scent every time you open the closet door.

New Way to Scare Crows

Scarecrows have been around for over three millennia. Here's a modern take on them: Instead of throwing away CDs or DVDs you no longer want, hang them in and around your garden. The flashes of reflected light will scare birds and squirrels enough to keep them at bay.

Make Your Own Watering Can

Don't spend money on a watering can unless it's for decorating purposes—it's much easier to make your own. Simply wash out an old gallon milk jug, then poke or drill very small holes below the spout on the side opposite the handle. Fill it with water, screw the top back on, and you have a homemade device to water your plants!

Plant Sitter

Now there's one less thing to worry about when you're on vacation. Water your plants yourself *in absentia* with this handy trick. An ordinary plastic drink bottle filled with water just needs a little hole toward the bottom to serve as a continual drip for your plants. Turn it on its side and place on the soil near the plant stem. Now go enjoy your trip and know you won't come home to a bunch of withering geraniums.

Keep Plant Moisture In

Place a few corks in your plant pots before adding soil. They'll hold moisture in for those hectic days when you don't have time to attend to the plants. Corks also make nice tags for your plants. Write one name on each cork and poke a toothpick into one end of the cork. Stick the other end in the dirt.

Reader's Tip

Here's a surefire way (no pun intended) to get your fire started without spending money on expensive specialty kindling. Keep a sealed jar of rubbing alcohol, and when you finish a bottle of wine place the cork inside (natural, not plastic, corks only). When you're ready to get a fire going, all you'll need is one cork under a few sticks. For safety reasons, make sure to keep the jar away from your fireplace.

—CARA GEISS, GARDEN CITY, KS

Lemon Peels for Kindling

The best thing to use as kindling in your fireplace isn't newspaper (or printed-out emails from your ex). It's citrus peels! Lemon and orange peels smell delicious when they burn, and they contain oils that not only make them burn longer, but help ignite the wood around them. Finally, they produce less creosote than paper, which will help keep your chimney clean.

Surprise Kindling

Instead of throwing away lint you've cleaned out of your dryer's screen, use it as kindling for your fireplace. It lights quickly and can be stuffed places paper can't.

Put Out a Fire

You're ready to go to bed, but the fire you started a few hours ago is still awake, glowing with its last few embers. Instead of making a mess with water, throw some salt over anything that's still burning. It will snuff out the flame and you'll end up with less soot than if you let it smolder.

Shopping Bag Holder

An empty tissue box is great for holding plastic shopping bags that are waiting for their chance at a second life. As you place each bag in the box, make sure its handles are poking up through the hole. Then thread each new bag through the previous bag's handles. That way, when you pull a bag out of the box, the next one will pop right up.

Silence Squeaky Hinges

Who needs WD-40 when you have vegetable oil? Simply rub it on squeaky hinges with a cloth, letting the oil run down the sides of each hinge. Or just spritz nonstick cooking spray right on them.

Penny Wise

A penny won't get you much these days, not even when it comes to penny candy, but it may help to turn a screw. When you don't have a screwdriver on hand, try using a penny if the slot is wide enough.

Aluminum Answers

If your household scissors are getting dull, sharpen them back up by cutting through several layers of aluminum foil at one time. It's that easy!

Sewing Machine Saver

There's no need to replace your sewing machine needle if it's become dull. Simply stitch through a piece of sandpaper a few times and it will be sharp again.

New Favorite

If you have a boat and spend a lot of time on board, prevent drowned keys by sticking a few corks onto your key chain. Should they fall into the water, you'll find the corks bobbing along the surface.

Stop a Goggle Boondoggle

Goggles are necessary when swimming laps, but it's annoying when they fog over. Luckily, the solution is simple. Just coat the inside and outside of each lens with a layer of shaving cream. Leave on for a couple of minutes, then wipe away. The shaving cream leaves an imperceptible film that repels fog.

Toothpaste Trick

Most optometrists will try to sell you an expensive cleaner when you buy your glasses. Instead of buying theirs, simply use a tiny dab of white toothpaste (not a gel) on both sides of the lenses to polish them and keep them from fogging up.

Dress Up a Bedroom

If you love the look of lace, add some to your bedroom or guest room with this inexpensive trick. Buy a rectangular lace tablecloth that is 70-by-90 inches, and you can place it directly on top of your existing comforter. You'll have friends asking how you could afford to dress up your bed with lace!

Do-It-Yourself Headboard

To perk up your bedroom with a splash of color, get crafty with a DIY faux-headboard. Find a colorful sheet that complements the décor of your room; any fabric will work, so consider cotton, linen, velvet, and even fur! First, consider the width of your bed; a headboard should be slightly wider than your mattress. Then decide what style of headboard you like best, and cut your fabric to the right size and shape. Either wrap your fabric around a foam base and hang it on the wall, or hang it up on its own.

Just-Do-It Dust Ruffle

Have a dust ruffle for a double bed but your mattress is twin? Just bunch the ruffle up on whatever side of the bed touches the wall, and safety-pin it to the box spring to keep it in place. No one will ever know!

Kitchen Decorating Idea

A fun and vintage-looking decoration for a kitchen is framed seed packets. Dig through whatever is available at your gardening store, then carefully slit the top to let the seeds loose. Center the empty pack on a matte or solid-color background, then glue with rubber cement or white glue. Frame, then hang on the wall for a perfectly themed picture.

The Art of Hanging

To hang lightweight artwork that's not in a heavy frame, there's no need to buy picture wire. Dental floss will do the trick.

Hang Pictures Easily

To get rid of the guesswork that comes with putting a nail in the wall to hang a picture, try this easy trick. Place a dab of toothpaste on the back of the frame on the hook or string (whatever will touch the nail). Then hold the frame up to the wall, position it carefully, and press it against the wall. The toothpaste will leave a mark that you can hammer a nail through, then wipe away.

Just as Good as Sticky Tack

A terrific way to hang posters in your kid's room without leaving holes or stains is with white, non-gel toothpaste. Just put a generous drop on the back of each corner, press to the wall, and watch it stick.

New Favorite

You'll love this way to keep all the cords to your various electronic devices organized on your desk. Clasp several binder clips to the side of your desk, then slide the cord through the arms and let the plug be held by the narrower end of the binder clip. Instant organization!

Organize Bunches of Cords

Don't throw away empty toilet paper or paper towel rolls! Use them to store the millions of cords running behind your entertainment center. The rolls keep the cords untangled, and if you also write which appliances the cords belong to on the roll, you just might be the most organized person in your neighborhood.

Keep 'Em Separated

No more digging around swearing underneath the desk with a weak flashlight! The plastic tags on bags of bread are handy for labeling the various cords in your house. Use a permanent marker to identify whether it's the lamp, radio, or phone, and hook it onto the corresponding cord.

Upward Spiral

It may be hard to watch your child's notes on the conservation of matter go into the recycling bin, but when it comes time to part with school notebooks, save the spirals. They work great to collect stray cords and wires. Attach the spiral horizontally to a strip of wood using a hot-glue gun. Place it behind your computer and "thread" your cables through the rings. They'll stay separate and it will keep them from falling to the floor when not in use.

New Favorite

Wrapping paper is cheaper than drawer liners and works just as well! Just spray some wrapping paper with your favorite air or fabric freshener and place at the bottom of a clean drawer. Double-stick tape will keep it in place if it's sliding around though it's not recommended for your Aunt Betty's fine oak drawers. In that case you'll just have to make do with a little shuffling around. (She always did.)

Thrifty Drawer Organizer

Sure, you can spend half your paycheck on drawer organizers, or, since no one but you will see them anyway, you can make your own with shoeboxes instead. Make dividers out of the lid if you want separate compartments. For example, depending on your collection, socks could take up two-thirds of the box, tights and leggings another third.

Pantyhose Problems?

Are pantyhose overrunning your sock drawer? Place each pair in its own resealable sandwich bag. Write any pertinent information (like the size, or whether or not it's control top) on the outside. If they're still taking up too much space, place them in a plastic storage bin under your dresser or somewhere else out of the way.

The Perfect Tie Holder

Don't throw away the little z-shaped hooks that come with dress socks—use them as tie holders! Slip them onto a hanger, and they are perfect for hanging the tie that accompanies that particular suit.

Straighten Up Unruly Drawers

If your bathroom drawers are a jumbled mess, invest in an inexpensive plastic silverware tray. It's a great way to organize the little things you've got rattling around in there.

Pillowcase It

Our closets are kind of a mess, but we manage never to misplace part of a sheet set. That's because after washing and folding the pieces, we put the whole set right inside one of the pillowcases, which is a convenient way to make sure everything stays in one place.

Bed Pillow Know-How

Here's an easy way to start your spring-cleaning: begin with your bed pillows. To make them fluffy and fresh, just place them in the clothes dryer with a dryer sheet and two clean tennis balls for a few minutes.

Quick Fix for a Saggy Mattress

To keep your mattress from sagging, it's a good idea to reverse it once a month. If it dips in the middle, place a few folded sheets under the center to even it out.

Medicine Cabinet Magnet

If you have a metal medicine cabinet, mount a magnet inside it, and you'll be able to place nail clippers, tweezers, safety pins, or other handy items at your fingertips. And if your cabinet is not made of metal, just glue the magnet inside.

Reader's Tip

Minimize the damage caused by muddy shoes inside your front door with a dish rack placed over a baking tray. It will make a handy caddy for wet, dirty shoes by letting the air get at them so they'll dry (and clean up more easily when the sun comes out). Then get as much mud as you can off the dish rack and tray and stick in your dishwasher.

—SHANNON WHITNEY, WHISKEY CREEK, FL

Shoe Mats

If you have a "no shoes" area in your home, grab some old plastic placements that are no longer suitable for the table. They're perfect for lining the wall next to your entryway to protect the floor. Everyone in your family can even have his or her own placemat!

Shoe Covers

When you get plastic shower caps at hotels, save them for your suitcase. They make the perfect covers for dirty shoes!

Reboot Your Boots

Keep your boots looking their best by storing them with empty wine or soda bottles inside. They'll stay upright and maintain their shape.

Purse Stuffer

When storing pursues, use scrunched-up plastic bags to help them keep their shape. If you have an extra pocket, keep a plastic bag balled up inside even when you're using the purse. You'll be amazed how often it comes in handy (or how many times you'll wish you had a plastic bag with you when you don't).

New Favorite

When you're ready to throw them out, cut rubber gloves into strips with an extra sharp scissors to make rubber bands! The fingers will provide you with small bands and the palm section will give you giant rubber bands with tons of household uses. We find them handy for kindling wood and keeping sports equipment together.

Get a Handle on File Boxes

Pretty rectangle file boxes are tempting to buy, but often not as useful as one might hope when perched high on a shelf and rather inaccessible. Make them easier to handle by adding a handle. There are many pretty knobs available—usually for cabinet doors—but you can attach them to the file boxes, too. Picture piercing an ear—you want to make a hole with an X-Acto knife, small, but big enough to put the knob through. On the other end use a screw and nut to keep the knob in place.

Dry-Erase Mirror

Rather than purchase a bulletin board or whiteboard for your home, write messages to your family members on the mirror in your bathroom with dry-erase markers. The bathroom gets heavy foot traffic, so it's a great place to keep notes and reminders for everyone in your family.

Bountiful Bathroom Storage

Those three-tiered baskets that you usually find holding fruit in the kitchen are also perfect for bathrooms. Store brushes, hair gel, Band-Aids, or whatever else is taking up too much space in your medicine cabinet. If placed out of reach of your kids, it's also a great place to store shaving supplies.

God's Gift to Organization

Clear plastic storage bins may be the greatest thing we have going for us. If you feel like your house is constantly cluttered, go to your nearest organizational store, superstore, or even dollar store, and stock up immediately. But before you go, take a look around your house to find empty areas for some covert storage. Buy long, flat bins for under the couch and you can store board games, video games, and DVDs. Buy tall, stackable ones for keeping items in a closet. And buy whatever fits best under your bed to maximize this perfect space for storing off-season clothes. Make sure to keep at least one in easy reach—we have one that's simply for all the *stuff* we find in our living room that needs to be put back elsewhere in the house.

Bag It!

One of our favorite organizational tools is a hanging shoe organizer. These canvas contraptions are made to allow you to store your shoes on the back of a door, but their individualized compartments make them perfect for storing anything. Keep one in the bathroom for bobby pins, make-up, and lotion; one in your kitchen for spices; and one in the TV room for rarely used remotes and video game controllers. We also keep one in each of our children's rooms, so that when we yell, "Clean up your room!" they have a handy place to stow toy cars, action figures, and the million other little things that find their way onto their floors.

CHAPTER 5

REMOVE ANY STAIN! AND OTHER LAUNDRY SECRETS

Diaper Must-Do

When you purchase new cloth diapers, make sure to wash them 8–10 times before using. This will not only increase their absorbency by puffing the fabric up a bit, but it will make sure all the chemicals used in their production and packaging have been washed out.

Reader's Tip

There are special bags on the market for separating delicate items in your laundry, but most can be adequately protected in a pillowcase tied in a knot. Place tights, bras, delicate lingerie, stuffed animals, and anything that might be damaged inside, knot the top, and throw into the washing machine with the rest of your load. You can also use a pillowcase for all the mini socks in your wash, which never come back as a complete set. The water and soap will still reach everything but they'll come out without the usual wear and tear.

—ERIN HABERMANN, JAY, ME

Delicate Situation

You don't need to spend money on detergents just for delicates. Instead, use this homemade solution: 1 cup baking soda mixed with a basin of warm water. The baking soda will clean your clothes without harming their delicate fibers.

Vinegar As a Fabric Softener

Never buy fabric softener again! Instead, simply use white vinegar. Use the same proportions as you would for a liquid fabric softener—you'll never notice the difference.

Eco Fabric Sheets

Save on laundry products while you're saving the environment. Instead of buying fabric softener sheets, pick up a bottle of the liquid kind. Mix a solution of one-half fabric softener and one-half water, and put it into a spray bottle. For every laundry load, spritz onto a cloth and toss it in the dryer. A small amount (several sprays) will go a long way.

Keep Jeans from Shrinking

Jeans are usually tight enough as it is! To minimize shrinking, wash them in cold water, dry them on medium heat for only 10 minutes, and then air dry them the rest of the way.

New Favorite

New jeans are great, except for how stiff they are when you first put them on. Break them in without having to do some strange squats by throwing them into your dryer with a few tennis balls. After 15 minutes on low they'll be as good as . . . worn!

Stain Quickie

Here's a great use for a cleaned-out plastic bottle (of the ketchup or salad dressing variety). Keep a mixture of water and laundry detergent, or your favorite stain remover, inside, and use it to quickly pre-treat stains on your clothing.

Rub Out Stains

An old toothbrush is useful for gently rubbing stain remover into an item of clothing. Just be sure the toothbrush itself is relatively clean. As with all stains, early treatment is best, even if the item sits for a few days before it goes into the wash.

Setting Stains

Don't let a stain "set" even if you are running out the door. Instead, spray with stain remover or soak in water and store in a resealable plastic bag until you have time to deal with it. Once a stain dries, it's much harder to remove. You should also never rub a fresh stain with a bar of soap. Many stains can set further when treated with soap.

New Favorite

Hand sanitizer can fight germs *and* clothes stains—we always keep it on hand in case of spills. If you've dropped something on your clothes, immediately rub a generous amount of sanitizer on the spot; blot with a soft cloth or tissue, and reapply as necessary. The alcohol in the sanitizer will quickly get to work breaking up the stain.

Stain Know-How

Whether you're using a commercial stain remover or one of the stain remedies in this chapter, you may have to apply a stain-remover more than once for tough stains. Don't give up if it doesn't come out the first time! If all else fails, just keep the garment near your washing machine and wash it over and over (applying the stain-remover each time) until the spot is gone. Just make sure the stain is gone before you dry the fabric in the dryer. The heat from your dryer can further set the stain.

How to Wash Lace

Even if you hand-wash it, lace can get easily tangled and torn when cleaning. To prevent this from happening, safety-pin the lace to a sheet or smaller cloth. Wash gently as usual, then unpin when dry.

Why the Sour Face for Lace?

If you own a lace tablecloth or doily that is beginning to turn yellow, let it soak in a bucket of sour milk for a few hours to return it to its former brilliant white. Just make sure to hand-wash it in mild detergent afterward!

Whiten Yellowed Items

Weird but true: Discolored socks or other whites will return to their original color if you boil them in a pot of water with a few slices of lemon.

New Favorite

There's one problem just about every parent is faced with at one time or another: a giant dried mud stain. Who knew it could be conquered with a potato? Just cut any kind of potato in half and rub the cut end on the stain. Let sit for 5 minutes, then soak the garment in cool water for an hour. After it's done soaking, throw it in with the rest of your laundry and the item will be ready to wear (and get mud on) again!

Cosmetics Cure

If you've stained a towel or other fabric with some make-up, dampen the stain with rubbing alcohol, then apply some of your regular laundry detergent directly to the spot before laundering.

Lipstick Stain?

Lipstick prints on silk seem like disaster, but it's almost as easy to lift them off as it is to get them on there. Use transparent or masking tape to pull off the stain. Any remnants can be sprinkled with talcum powder and shaken off.

Shoe Polish Mishap?

If you got shoe polish on your clothes, all is not lost. Try applying a mixture of one part rubbing alcohol and two parts water for colored fabrics and only straight alcohol for whites. Sponge on, then launder.

Reader's Tip

To remove a lipstick stain from fabric, cover it with petroleum jelly for five minutes, then wash as usual. The glycerin in the jelly will break down the oils in the lipstick, making it easy to wash away.   —FRANCINE PEREZ, DEXTER, NM

The Answer to Ink Stains

To remove ink from clothing, rub the area with a cut, raw onion, letting the onion juice soak in. Let sit for two to three hours before laundering.

Stop Grease Stains in Their Tracks

If you're cooking over the stove and grease splatters onto your clothes, think fast. Grab some baking soda from the cupboard and rub it into the spot to absorb as much grease as possible. This will make it harder for the stain to set and will soak up most of the grease before it works its way into the fibers of your clothes.

Act Fast for Paint Spills

Treat a paint stain while it is still wet; latex, acrylic, and water-based paints cannot be removed once dried. While the paint is wet, rinse in warm water to flush the paint out, then launder. Oil-based paints can be removed with a solvent; your best bet will be to use one recommended on the paint can.

Paint Last Resort

Got dried paint on your clothes? Unfortunately, it's often impossible to remove. Before you give up completely, however, try saturating the stain in one part ammonia and one part turpentine, then washing as usual.

Getting Out Gum

Rub gum stuck on clothes with ice until the gum hardens, then carefully remove it with a dull knife before laundering. If that doesn't work, you can also try placing a piece of wax paper on the affected area, then ironing the wax paper. The gum should transfer from the cloth to the paper.

Get Rid of Grass Stains
You can get rid of grass stains with toothpaste. Scrub it into the fabric with a toothbrush (naturally) before washing. The white (non-gel) kind works best.

Tired of Tar Stains?
If you have a tar stain on your clothes, try petroleum jelly—just rub it in until the tar is gone. The jelly itself might stain the fabric, but it's easy to remove with a spray-and-wash stain remover.

Get Rid of Gas
Nothing stinks on your clothes like gasoline! To remove the odor, place the offending clothes in a bucket

of cold water, and add a can of cola and a cup of baking soda. Soak overnight, then line dry outside if possible. If there is still any odor left, just wash as usual and it should be gone.

Tomato Product Stain Secret

Ketchup catastrophe? Remove excess ketchup from clothes with a dull knife, then dab with a damp, warm sponge. Apply a bit of shaving cream to the stain, then launder as usual after letting set for several minutes.

New Favorite

The best way to remove stains from cooking oil (olive, vegetable, canola, etc.) is with regular shampoo. Just make sure it doesn't have a built-in conditioner.

Fix a Wine Blunder

We've got you covered when it comes to wine stains. Blot a wine stain with a mixture of one part dishwashing liquid and two parts hydrogen peroxide. If this doesn't work, apply a paste made from water and cream of tartar and let sit.

Care for Coffee Stains

To remove coffee stains, stretch the garment over a bowl, cover the stain with salt, and pour boiling water over the stain from a height of one to two feet. (The gravity helps.) Of course, always test first that the garment can withstand hot water (unlike, say, cashmere). Repeat a couple of times if necessary, but some of the stain (especially if it's not fresh) may remain. If so, treat with your usual spray-and-wash stain remover and then launder.

Lemon for Tea Stains

Tea and lemon are best friends—even in the laundry room. Rub a tea stain with equal parts lemon juice and water. Just make sure the mixture only gets on the stain, using a Q-tip or eyedropper if necessary.

Berry Stains?

Berries sure are delicious, but the stains from their juice can be hard to remove. If you got berries on your clothes, soak the stain overnight in equal parts milk and white vinegar. Then launder as usual.

Because Stains Are the Pits

If you're sick of the yellow stains on the armpits of your white shirts, use this pretreatment to stop them before they start. Turn the shirt inside out and sprinkle the pits with baking soda, then press with an iron on medium heat for 3 seconds. The pressed-on powder will absorb sweat and keep the fabric clean. If your shirt is already stained, mix 2 tablespoons salt with 2 cups hot water and use a little elbow grease to rub the stain out.

Nail Polish News

Unfortunately, the only thing that can remove nail polish is nail-polish remover. If the fabric can withstand this harsh chemical, work it in from the inside of the fabric by pressing it in gently with a paper towel.

Too Much Suntan Oil?

You had a great time at the beach, but you accidentally got suntan lotion all over your cover-up. To remove this stubborn stain, cover with liquid dish detergent and rub in. Then turn your kitchen sink on at full blast and run under cold water.

Out, Blood Spots!

To get out blood stains, soak the stained area in club soda before laundering. If the blood is fresh (ouch!), make a paste of water and talcum powder, cornstarch, cornmeal, or meat tenderizer and apply it to the stain. Let it dry, and then brush it off.

Suede Stains

Your emery board that you normally use on your nails can remove small stains from suede. Gently rub the file across the stain a few times to remove the mess.

Give Your Leather a Pick-Me-Up

To revive the beauty of leather, lightly beat two egg whites and then apply to the leather with a soft sponge. Allow the egg whites to remain on the leather for 3–5 minutes, and then wipe off with a soft cloth dampened with warm water. Dry immediately and buff off any residue.

Baseball Cap Cleanse

Wash a baseball cap on the top rack of your dishwasher, and remove while still wet. Then, place the cap over a bowl to regain its shape, and dry it away from direct sunlight.

New Favorite

Keep your straw hat looking like new with hair spray. Spray evenly over the entire hat, then rub your hand gently over it to push in any fraying ends. The hair spray will keep them all in place, and your hat will look shinier than ever before!

Off the Cuff

What's the secret to wrinkle-free pants? When hanging up your pants to dry, make sure to hang them by the cuffs at the bottom. (Either use a pants hanger with clips, or just add clothespins to a hanger.) Thanks to gravity, they'll dry with few to no creases!

Crease Prevention

Don't buy special pants hangers; you can avoid creases in suit pants with this clever tip: Cover the bottom of a hanger with a paper towel tube which you've cut lengthwise, and gently lay the pants over it.

When to Air Dry

Make your clothes last longer by taking your cotton and denim clothing out of the dryer 20 minutes before the cycle is about to end and letting them air dry the rest of the way. Excess dryer heat can break down the fibers in your clothes prematurely.

Drying Without a Line

Line drying your clothes is energy efficient and great for them. Not only is air-drying less harsh, you'll also love the smell of real sun-dried linens. If you don't have a clothesline, hang shirts and pants on hangers from tree limbs! Just make sure not to put brights in the sun, as they may fade.

New Favorite

If you have a toddler or pet safety gate that you no longer need, give it a new life in the laundry room! Lean it against the side of your washer or the wall and it will make the perfect drying rack for delicates and sweaters.

Refresh Drapes

The easiest way to freshen draperies is to place them in your dryer with a damp towel, on the delicate cycle, for one half hour. For extra freshness, hang them outside afterward if the weather allows.

Keep Drapes Fresh

Try this nifty trick to make sure your new or recently cleaned drapes stay crisp and fresh: Spray them with a few light coats of unscented hairspray before hanging them up.

Wrinkle-Free Sheets

Though we like wrinkle-free linens as much as the next person, we simply don't have the time to iron bed sheets like our mothers used to. Still, there are a few things you can do to stop wrinkles before they start. Believe it or not, drying your sheets in the dryer can actually increase and set wrinkles. Instead, fold the sheet into quarters or eighths, snapping it and smoothing it out after each fold. Then place the last fold over a clothesline. The fabric is so light, it will easily dry, with only a few wrinkles still intact.

For Sweaty Summers

On sticky summer nights, cool down by sprinkling a little baby powder between your sheets before retiring for the night.

Add Scented Salts for Beautiful Linens

Salt is a miracle worker when it comes to removing linen stains; and if you use scented salts in your laundry, you'll get the extra bonus of lovely-smelling sheets. Add ¼ cup scented bath salts during your washing machine's rinse cycle. Not only will your sheets smell great, but the salt will act like a starch to keep them extra crisp. Just make sure not to use bath salts with dyes.

Reader's Tip

If you have a white linen tablecloth or other cotton item that has turned yellow over time, bring it back to its original brightness with baking soda and salt. Just bring a gallon of water to a boil, remove from the heat, stir in ¼ cup each baking soda and salt, and add the fabric. Let it soak for at least one hour. Then rinse and launder as usual. —MONA RUGGIERI

Storing Tablecloths

Why fold linen tablecloths, which will only mean having to iron them again to get the creases out? Instead hang them over a curtain rod. It's easy enough to nail a rod inside a closet against the side or back wall. Then you'll always know where to find them, or, better yet, be able to direct someone else so that you can attend to whatever's burning on the stove.

Wax Splatters

Nothing is more disheartening than discovering hot wax has just dripped onto your tablecloth. But there may be a way to fix it. Place a brown paper bag on top of the wax, then iron the bag with an iron set on medium heat. The wax should transfer to the bag, and you can peel it right up.

Good Gravy!

Did your clumsy uncle spill gravy all over your best tablecloth? Not to worry! Just blot up what you can with a paper towel, then sprinkle artificial sweetener or flour over what remains on the tablecloth. After dinner, soak the tablecloth in the washer with your regular detergent for half an hour, then wash as usual.

For Tablecloth Blunders

If you spill wine on a tablecloth, blot up as much as you can as soon as you can with a cloth, then sponge with cool water. Wash immediately. If the fabric is not machine washable, cover the stain with a small cloth dampened with a solution of detergent, water, and vinegar, then rinse. Get the cloth to the dry cleaner as soon as you can.

For the Best Potholders

Your potholders don't have to look stained and dirty. Wash them frequently, and after each wash, spray them with starch. Spray starch repels grease, so your potholders will stay unblemished.

For the Spray Starchers

If you use spray starch while ironing, you may notice that it sometimes leaves a film on your iron. To remove this film and clean any other dirt on your iron, let the iron cool and then wipe the area with a cloth dampened with white vinegar. To keep the starch off in the first place, simply let it soak in for several seconds before ironing.

White Sneakers That Stay White

After purchasing new white canvas sneakers, spray them with spray starch to help them resist stains. The starch will repel grease and dirt, keeping them whiter!

Keep Leather Looking New

Shining your leather shoes? Forget the shoe polish. First, dampen a cloth and wipe away any dirt, then put a few drops of vegetable or olive oil on a clean, soft cloth and rub into your shoes. The oil will remove the scuff marks, and they'll shine like new.

New Favorite

Here's an unlikely tool for polishing your shoes: a banana. Just rub the banana peel over your shoes, moist side down. Then buff with a soft cloth.

The Magic of Lemon Juice

For a brighter shoeshine, place a few drops of lemon juice on your shoes when you are polishing them.

Get Rid of Salt Stains

If your shoes or boots are stained with salt from trudging through winter streets, simply dip a cloth or an old T-shirt into white vinegar and wipe away the stain. It's that easy!

Remove Scuff Marks from Shoes

Just about any scuff mark can be removed with the help of some nail polish remover. Wet a rag with some, then rub on the scuff mark lightly but quickly. You may need to give your shoes the once-over with a damp cloth afterwards.

Restore Shoes

Are your white shoes suffering from scuff marks? Rub a little baking soda into the offending areas and the marks will practically disappear.

Reader's Tip

One all-natural way to treat scuffs on light-colored shoes is by wiping them with the cut edge of a raw potato, then buffing with a soft cloth.   —PATRICIA LEVENTHAL, DELTA, CO

CHAPTER 6

MAKE YOUR OWN BEAUTY SUPPLIES

New Favorite

Give your skin a rejuvenating treat with an inexpensive item: an orange! Just dip a cotton ball into some freshly squeezed orange juice, then wipe over your face. Leave on for 5–10 delicious-smelling minutes, then rinse with cool water. The citric acid and vitamin C in the OJ clean and tighten your skin, clean out your pores, and help prevent pimples in the future.

Milk Is Magnificent

Looking for a fabulous age-defying skin treatment? Check your fridge! Milk is nutritious for your insides *and* your outsides: Lactic acid works as an exfoliant, and milk's amino acids and proteins have a calming effect on red skin. Stick to fat-free milk for the best results.

Luxury with a Pore-pose

Here's a great addition to your nighttime beauty regime that is simple to do, and feels luxurious! Before washing your face, simply wet a washcloth with hot water, then wring out and place over your face for up to 30 minutes, refreshing with more hot water as needed. The warmth will help open up your pores, allowing your cleanser to reach the deepest bits of dirt, and making your face feel even cleaner.

Cure for Oily Skin

If your skin is feeling oily and needs a refresher, try this amazing homemade facial treatment: Combine 2 tablespoons each of plain yogurt and cornmeal with 2 teaspoons lemon juice, then apply to your face and rinse off after 10 minutes. The lemon juice will wake up your face while the cornmeal and yogurt will soften skin and keep it blemish-free.

New Favorite

Get a chemical peel without spending a cent! Just crush a few green grapes with 1 teaspoon of the finest sugar you have. Massage onto your face and leave on for 10–15 minutes before washing off. Do this a couple of times a week and you'll see the same results as an expensive glycolic acid peel, thanks to the alpha-hydroxy acids in the sugar and grapes.

Wrinkle Cure and Face Massage in One

When you're feeling too lazy to hit the gym, work out your face instead! Doing facial exercises can help keep your skin looking fresh and young. Begin with this exercise for tired eyes: Simply look up and down with your eyes closed. Then move on to massaging your temples, which not only feels nice, but also helps relieve headache tension and can help prevent wrinkles. Pulling your skin from the eyebrows outward is also a good wrinkle-preventer. Exercise your cheeks by rubbing them in circles, chewing gum, and blowing on an instrument or into a straw.

Puff-Proof

If you often wake up with puffy eyes, there's an easy remedy. Drink a glass of water before you go to bed, and make sure your head is elevated while you sleep. This will make sure you're not retaining fluid in the area.

Relief for Swollen Eyes

If you suffer from dark under-eye circles that don't seem to go away, the culprit could be the sun, which can harm the delicate skin there. Luckily, the solution is simple. Simply place a thin slice of raw cucumber over each eye and relax for up to 20 minutes. The enzymes in the cucumbers lighten skin while the cool feeling of them over your eyes will constrict blood vessels slightly, making puffiness a thing of the past.

Trick for Puffy Eyes

Fix a puffy under-eye area by rubbing egg whites on it. As the egg whites dry, you'll feel the skin get tighter. Leave on for a few minutes after it dries, then rinse off with cool water.

Powerful Pimple Paste

A topical paste made out of water and crushed-up aspirin will help get rid of pimples. Wash your face with warm water first, apply paste, then rinse off with cool water after 10 minutes. This treatment should not be used more than five days in a row as it can dry out your skin.

Stop a Zit in Its Tracks

If a giant pimple sprouts up at work, here's a way to make it less noticeable without applying a face mask at your desk: Place an ice cube on it for 30–60 seconds, then place a few eye drops onto a tissue and hold it on the spot for 3 minutes. This will cause the blood vessels below your skin to contract, making the pimple less red and easing some of the irritation.

Natural Acne Fighter

Sprouting pimples like they're going out of style? Try this neat trick to clear up your face. Cut a raw potato in half and rub the flat end over your face. Leave the juice on for 20 minutes before rinsing off. The starch in the potato will help dry out your oily skin.

Perfect Toner

Here's an all-natural toner that shrinks pores and leaves your skin clean and smooth: Mix ¼ cup tomato juice and ¼ cup watermelon juice. You can store it for roughly three days in the fridge.

Reader's Tip

Honey is a great-tasting makeshift lip balm. (You'll notice it listed in the ingredients of many store-bought varieties.) Just dab a bit on moist lips and rub around with your finger!

—ESTELLE TRUMP, LANSING, MI

Set Your Lipstick

Keep your lipstick from smudging or setting with this simple trick: Just rub an ice cube over your lips after applying lipstick! It will last longer than ever before.

Lip Tip

To avoid getting lipstick on your teeth, after you apply, close your mouth over your finger and slowly pull it out. This will save you time and time again!

Farewell, Rough Lips

Get rid of dead skin on your lips with an all-natural exfoliating rub made from ingredients in your own kitchen. Mix a drop of sesame or olive oil with brown sugar, then rub the delicious mixture gently over lips to remove flaky skin. Finish by applying petroleum jelly.

Reader's Tip

Break your addiction to lip balm with this remedy for chapped lips. Buy a child's toothbrush with a really soft head, dip it in Vaseline, and scrub the heck out of your lips. It will get rid of rough patches while moisturizing the rest.

—AMY FORSTADT, HIGHLAND PARK, IL

Cheap Make-Up Remover

For an inexpensive way to remove mascara, eye liner, and shadow, try baby shampoo. It contains many of the same ingredients as eye-make-up remover, and works just as well. Dispense a small amount on a tissue or cotton ball, rub over closed eyes, and rinse with water.

Hair Loss Help

Here's another defense of caffeine: It helps your hair grow in thicker. One day, a topically applied shampoo containing caffeine may cure hair loss. For now, go for the kind you drink, especially coffee or black or green tea, and pour it over your hair before shampooing.

Save on Shampoo

Here's a quick and easy way to halve the amount you spend on your shampoo: Just use half the shampoo! Fill a bottle with half water and half shampoo and you'll have plenty of suds to get the job done at half the cost.

Hold the Mayo

If you're suffering from summer-damaged hair, use this easy, homemade treatment to revitalize and deeply condition it. Simply apply mayonnaise to your scalp, then work it into your hair from the roots down. Leave on for 15 minutes (and don't let your family laugh at you!), then rinse.

Luxurious Locks

Don't toss out that last bit of hair conditioner with the bottle! Instead, make it into a luxurious leave-in conditioner by adding 3 tablespoons of water and shaking. Put into a spray bottle to spray over wet hair after showering, and your locks will never be shinier!

Give Hair a Lift

Oily buildup in your hair can make it dull and flat. Use 1 tablespoon baking soda mixed with your usual shampoo to give it bounce and body. Besides its myriad applications in everything from cleaning and cooking to first aid and teeth whitener, this sodium bicarbonate wonder-substance will also absorb the extra oil in your hair and give it great volume.

Don't Dare to Neglect Hair Care

If you want to strengthen your hair, make sure to brush or comb it thoroughly each night. This will increase circulation in your scalp, loosen dry skin, and help moisturize your hair with your body's natural oils.

Summer Scalp

Hot summer sunshine can increase sweat production and make your scalp look and feel much greasier. To counteract this problem, try more frequent washings with a small amount of shampoo, and use a much lighter conditioner than you use in the winter.

New Favorite

We usually wouldn't recommend pouring a glass of champagne on your head to someone trying to save money, but it's so great for your hair we have to mention it . . . you know, in case your night gets really wild! The antioxidants found in champagne strip product buildup from your hair and leave it looking shinier than ever before. Just apply some to clean, wet hair and let it dry! You can even use it after it's gone flat.

Handy for Hair

A dryer sheet can freshen up your hair when it's full of smoke or when you haven't had time to wash it. Keep one tucked into your purse at all times, and rub on your hair when needed. (As a bonus, it will help tame frizzy, dry hair.)

Flake Fighter

Did you know that bacteria clogging up your hair follicles cause dandruff? You can fight these bacteria with a little lemon juice! Squeeze the juice from one lemon and add ½ cup warm water, then pour over your scalp and let sit for five minutes before shampooing as usual.

Natural Dandruff Remedy

Instead of buying dandruff shampoo, use apple cider vinegar to regulate the acid level on your scalp and clear out the dry skin flakes. Maximize the benefits by adding fresh mint! To make an organic solution at home, heat ¼ cup apple cider vinegar with ½ cup water and a few leaves of fresh mint. Once the mixture is warm, remove it from the heat and let it sit for fifteen minutes to cool off before you chill it in the fridge overnight. Tomorrow use it to cover your scalp—massaging the mixture into your hair—and wait a half hour before you shampoo it out.

Blondes (Usually) Have More Fun

Ever heard the one about blonde hair turning green in a swimming pool? We've seen it happen. Thankfully, there is a solution: our 40th President's favorite "vegetable." Coat your hair with tomato ketchup and let it sit for a half an hour or so before you rinse it off. Then follow with your regular hair washing and conditioning routine. Remember to use up those packets stockpiled from fast-food places!

New Favorite

Uh-oh, you just tried dyeing your hair a new color, and it looks bad enough that you don't want to leave the house without a hat. What to do? Just wash it three or four times using an anti-dandruff shampoo that contains zinc pyrithione. This chemical diminishes dye quickly without damaging your hair.

The Power of Powder

Has your perfect day at the beach left you with a ton of sand in your hair? Before shampooing, massage a tablespoon of baby powder into your roots, and brush thoroughly. The powder helps loosen the sand, so shampooing will now be easy!

Hot Oil Treatment at Home

Instead of paying a salon to do it, give yourself a hot oil treatment at home for cheap. Rinse your hair completely with very hot water, then rub a tablespoon of olive oil (or mineral oil) into the hair—for longer hair, use more oil. Put your hair in a towel and wait at least 30 minutes; then wash as usual to get the oil out.

Help Dry Hair

Suffering from dry hair? Here's a surefire way to make your hair supple again. Mash a banana and mix with a teaspoon of almond or olive oil. Rub the mixture into your hair and scalp, and let sit for 20 minutes. Rinse off and shampoo and condition as usual. You'll be surprised at the results!

Too Much Tanner?

Uh-oh, you got a little carried away with the fake tanner, and you need a quick fix! If unevenness of color is the problem, try gently rubbing the area with baking soda on a damp sponge. If you simply used too much tanner, wet a cotton ball with alcohol and rub it over your skin. You can also try using bleach made for body hair.

Ladies Only

Men, look away while we tell the ladies this secret cleavage tip. To instantly make your chest look more youthful, mix up this treatment and apply to your visible cleavage area: 1 egg white, 1 tablespoon each of honey and plain yogurt, and 1 teaspoon olive oil. Rinse off after 10 minutes. It will brighten, tighten, and make you feel 10 years younger!

Reader's Tip

Deodorants and antiperspirants are full of harsh chemicals, so here is an all-natural (and inexpensive) version you can make yourself: Just combine ¼ cup baking soda with 7 drops of essential oil in any scent. Leave in a jar and apply to underarms once or twice daily. —SPENCER BURTIS

Wax On, Wax Off

If you're waxing off hair, you know it's not going to feel pleasant. But you can take a little of the "ouch" out of the job with some baby powder. Sprinkle it on your skin before you wax, and it will form a barrier that protects your skin and makes the hair adhere to the wax better.

Waxing Saver

When you get your eyebrows waxed, bring some eye drops with you. Applying a bit of the eye drops onto sensitive areas will reduce redness, allowing you to go to your waxing appointment and then back to the office!

> ## ❀ New Favorite
> This amazing cellulite treatment is no joke! Just add olive oil to coffee grounds until you make a paste, then rub into the problem areas (like your upper thighs) for 1–2 minutes and wash off. The grounds will dehydrate fat cells, reducing that dimpled-skin look.

Save Money on Hand Soap

These days, most dishwashing liquids have moisturizers in them to keep your hands smooth even after doing the dishes. They work so well, you can use dishwashing liquid as a stand-in for hand soap! Just fill an old soap dispenser with 2 tablespoons dishwashing liquid and top off with water. Shake to combine and you'll have hand soap at a fraction of the cost.

Gimme Some Sugar

If you have ink stains on your hands from a marker or pen, try this: Just add a bit of sugar to your hands when washing with regular soap, and the granules will act as a gentle abrasive to help wash the ink away.

Oat Scrub

Are your hands super dirty from working in the garden? Keep some dry oatmeal handy to help, and add to your soaped-up hands. The oats' abrasive action will get your hands cleaner quicker.

Make Your Own Hand Cream

Buy a small container of pure beeswax online or at a health-food store and you can make the very same luxury hand creams you always pine over (for a fraction of the cost). Just combine 1 teaspoon beeswax with 3 tablespoons water, 2 tablespoons olive oil, and 1 tablespoon vegetable shortening or shea butter. Add 2 drops essential oil (which can also be found online and at heath-food stores) for a lovely scent!

Reader's Tip

Here's a trick to give you that salon look when painting your own nails: Dip a bobby pin into nail polish remover and dab along the edge of your cuticle for a cleaner line.

—PATTY DEGIORNO, TOTTENVILLE, NY

For the Softest Cuticles

Keeping your cuticles moisturized ensures your nails stay healthy and grow long. Make your own cuticle cream by thoroughly mixing 2 tablespoons each of olive oil and petroleum jelly along with the zest of half an orange. Store in the refrigerator when you're not using it, and apply at bedtime.

Another Cuticle Trick

To keep the cuticles of your nails super soft, pour mayonnaise into a small bowl and keep your fingers submerged in it for five minutes. Keep the bowl covered in the fridge and take it out three or four times a week to repeat this admittedly strange beauty routine.

Fast Dry for Nail Polish

You have just enough time to touch-up your nails before you leave—but not enough time to dry them. Make your nail polish dry more quickly by spraying your final coat with cooking spray. The oil will help them dry faster, and moisturize your cuticles, too!

New Favorite

Ever wondered if there's a way to clean dirty emery boards? Just press transparent tape onto them, smooth over a bit, and peel off. Metal files can be cleaned with soap and water.

Brighten Your Nails

If your fingernails have become stained by wearing dark nail polish, here's a quick fix: Plop a denture-cleaning tablet into a glass of water and soak your nails for a couple of minutes. The stain will come right off.

Brighten Skin Naturally

Rubbing a slice of pineapple or papaya onto your skin will help remove dead cells. Leave for five minutes, then rinse off with water. For a more exfoliating action, use olive oil mixed with salt.

Flyaway Eyebrows

To smooth out your eyebrows, rub them with a little petroleum jelly applied to an old toothbrush. (There's a limit to just how much the petroleum jelly can do: If your eyebrows could double for bangs, you'll need something more drastic to rein them in.)

Homemade Exfoliant

For a super-smoothing skin exfoliant, mix a handful of Epsom salts with a tablespoon of olive oil and rub over wet skin to cleanse, exfoliate, and soften the rough spots. Rinse off well for a polished finish. If you don't have Epsom salts, use the coarsest table salt you can find.

Get Rid of Dead Skin

Another way to slough off dead skin easily is by applying mayonnaise over any dry, rough patches. Let sit for 10 minutes, then wipe away with a washcloth that has been dampened with warm water.

Twisting Your Elbow

Is the skin on your elbows looking a bit rough? Here's an easy treatment: Cut a lemon or lime in half, then sprinkle it with brown sugar. Bend your elbow and shove it right into the citrus, then twist the fruit back and forth. The fruit's acid will slough off dead skin with the help of the sugar.

Too Much Perfume?

Oops! You accidentally put on way too much perfume, and you're afraid the restaurant you're going to will smell like someone just let off a flower-scented bomb!

To make your perfume less strong but still a little fragrant, dab a cotton ball moistened with a bit of rubbing alcohol wherever you applied the scent. Your friends will thank you!

Fight Spider Veins

Here's an easy way to help prevent those annoying spider veins on your legs. Several times a day, roll onto the balls of your feet and then your tiptoes from a standing position. Hold for a few seconds and repeat a few times. This will keep the blood flowing in your legs and prevent spider veins from forming.

New Favorite

You may have never used witch hazel, but this astringent made from the bark and leaves of the witch hazel plant has been used for hundreds of years for medicinal purposes like soothing cuts, sore muscles, and insect bites. But our favorite uses for this all-purpose wonder are beauty-related. Soak a washcloth or cotton ball in witch hazel, then let sit on razor bumps or even varicose veins to get them to fade. If you can't find witch hazel at your local drugstore, check out vitamin shops and health food stores.

Refreshing Foot Soak

Walking all day? You'll love this invigorating foot soak. Fill a basin with cold water, then slice up a lemon and add the slices along with several sprigs of mint. The oils in the lemon and mint will help revive your skin while leaving it smelling fresh.

Another Foot Bath Formula

If you need a good soak in a foot bath, here's a soothing recipe. Pour a gallon of water into whatever container you use for foot soaking, and then add 1 cup lemon juice, 1 tablespoon olive oil, and ¼ cup milk. Mix thoroughly, stick your feet in, and relax!

Dancin' Feet

Feet tend to swell. So after a long day of work, when you're getting ready to go out dancing with the girls, it can be a real tight squeeze to get into your favorite pumps. The solution? Rub your favorite lotion on your feet to help you slide in with ease.

At-Home Pedicure

Feet getting rough? You'll love the way they feel after this treatment: In a blender, combine 2 small cucumbers, the juice of 1 lemon, and 3 tablespoons olive oil. Divide between two large plastic freezer bags, then place your feet inside and secure around your ankles with rubber bands. Let sit for 5–10 minutes, rinse off, and pocket the money you would have spent on a pedicure.

Citrus A-Peel

Give yourself a luxurious bath treat without spending a cent. Just save the peels to citrus fruits like lemons, limes, and oranges in a container in your fridge. When it's time for a bath, throw them in the warm water. They'll not only release a lovely scent, they'll also help slough off dead skin cells.

Tea-Rific

Here's an easy way to have a relaxing soak in a bath without having to buy bath salts. Just place one or two green tea bags under the faucet as you fill up your bath. The antioxidants in the tea will leave your skin feeling fresh.

Helping Oatmeal Help You

Have you ever noticed that oatmeal is often a main ingredient of bath products? Well, guess what—you have that very same oatmeal in your kitchen! Unfortunately, it's not as easy as just throwing some into a hot bath. First, grind the oatmeal down in a blender or coffee grinder to expose its inner skin-soothing qualities. Then place it in a piece of cheesecloth with a few drops of your favorite scented oil. While you're running your bath, hold it under the faucet, or tie it with a bit of string. You'll have a luxurious oatmeal bath, and even a little sachet you can use as a washcloth to help you exfoliate your skin.

Stop Suitcase Spills

When you're packing for a trip, keep some plastic wrap nearby. Before you pack shampoo, sunscreen, or other toiletries, take off the caps, place a layer of plastic wrap over the mouth of the container, and twist the cap back on. The plastic wrap will give you double the protection against suitcase spills.

CHAPTER 7

NATURAL REMEDIES AND FIRST AID

Soothing Back Pain

If you have chronic back pain or other sore muscles, try adding yellow mustard to a hot bath. Add a few tablespoons for mild pain, and up to a whole eight-ounce bottle if the pain is severe. The bathwater may look strange, but your aching back will thank you.

Back Pain? Check Your Wallet

If you're a man who suffers from back pain, your wallet may be to blame. Sitting on a bulky wallet can cause your spine to become misaligned and your muscles to compensate. Try carrying your wallet in a front pocket (where it's also safer from pick-pockets), or make sure it's as thin as possible.

Reader's Tip

If you can't afford a back massage (and haven't had any luck recruiting the unemployed minor who lives in your house), take matters into your own hands by using two tennis balls in a tube sock. Drop the balls in, tie it shut, take a hold of each end, and roll away. You can also use your body weight to get more pressure by lying on top of the balls.

—DANIKA RICHARDS, MEMPHIS, TN

The Answer for Aches

If you're suffering from aching muscles (either from illness or too much exercise), try this homemade cure. Mix 1 tablespoon horseradish with 1 cup olive oil. Let sit for 30 minutes, then apply it to aching areas.

Aid Arthritis with Oatmeal

Believe it or not, you can help relieve arthritis pain with oatmeal. Just mix 2 cups oatmeal with 1 cup water, warm the mixture in the microwave, and apply to the affected area.

Binder Clips to Build Strength

If you suffer from arthritis, try this trick to make it easier to open jars and perform other daily tasks. Take a medium-sized binder clip and push back the wings with your thumb and index finger. Hold for 5–10 seconds, then move on to each finger of each hand. Do this a few times a day and it should help your grip.

Sunburn Relief

You had a great day at the beach, but now you're suffering from a terrible sunburn. Help ease the pain by rubbing shaving cream over any sunburned areas. The soothing ingredients will make your skin feel better, while the foam won't trap heat near your skin like lotions and gels.

Suffering from Sunburn?

Nothing's worse than a bad sunburn. The good news is you don't need an expensive lotion to soothe your burnt skin. Just cut an apple in half, remove the core, and rub over the affected area for 3–4 minutes. Apples will keep your skin from blistering or peeling.

Red Face?

This face mask is perfect for sunburned or irritated skin. Combine ¼ cup full-fat yogurt with 2 tablespoons oatmeal. Mix vigorously for one minute, then apply to your face. Leave on for at least 10 minutes, then wash off with warm water.

Vinegar Again!

To help ease the pain of a sunburn, rub white or apple cider vinegar on the affected area with a cotton ball or soft cloth. You may smell a bit like salad dressing, but your skin will immediately feel cooler.

After-Sun Soother

Lots of people swear by aloe lotion for treating sunburns, but green tea is a cheaper option and just as effective. Use a cooled, tea-soaked washcloth as a compress on your tender skin. (Some people say topically applied green tea may even protect against skin cancer.) This is also a great way to ease a sunburned scalp. After washing and rinsing your hair as usual, pour the cooled tea over your scalp. Your poor skin will thank you!

Reader's Tip

If you sustain a minor burn in the kitchen, reach for some ginger. Cut off the end and press the exposed area against your burn. Many say ginger works even better than a piece of aloe plant at soothing burns. —ICHIRO SATO

Toothpaste Toolbox

Who knew toothpaste could do just about anything? If you've sustained a minor burn, cover it with white, non-gel toothpaste to ease the pain and help it heal.

Got Milk?

Ow! If you or your child bites into a piece of pizza that's too hot to eat, reach for a glass of milk. Drinking milk will soothe the roof of your mouth better than drinking cold water will, because the protein in milk will create a protective film over any burns. Now let the pizza cool a bit before you take another bite!

Try Honey, Honey

The ancient Egyptians relied on honey for cuts and burns long before antibiotics were around. Besides offering a soothing protective layer over minor wounds, the honey provides a natural antibiotic. Put a layer of pure honey on before a bandage.

Sanitize a Cut

You just got a nasty cut on your hand, but don't have anything to clean it out with before you put the bandage on. Luckily, there's something in your medicine cabinet that you may not have thought of—mouthwash. The alcohol-based formula for mouthwash was originally used as an antiseptic during surgeries, so it will definitely work for your cut, too.

New Favorite
Splinters used to be major events at our house until we discovered this trick: Vegetable oil softens the skin and helps the offending piece of wood slide back out.

Surefire Splinter Removal

The easiest way to remove a splinter? Just put a drop of white glue over the offending piece of wood in your finger, let it dry, and then peel off the dried glue. The splinter will stick to the glue and come right out.

Paper Cut Relief

Instantly ease the sting of a paper cut with a bit of white glue. Just dab a small amount onto the area. Once it dries, it creates a liquid-bandage barrier that will seal out germs and make it hurt less.

Keeping Finger Bandages Dry

You put a Band-Aid on your finger to cover up a scratch, but you still have to go through your day full of hand-washing, child-bathing, and dishes-doing. To keep the bandage dry while you work, cover it with a non-inflated balloon—any color will do!

Vanquish Ingrown Hairs

Suffering from ingrown hairs? This all-natural solution will ease the itch and pain. Combine 1 cup sugar, the juice from half a lemon, 2 teaspoons apple cider vinegar, and ¼ cup honey. Blend together until smooth, then heat in the microwave until warm (about 15–20 seconds). Let it sit on the affected area for 20 minutes.

New Favorite

Ouch! Your razor was a bit dull and now you have razor burn. Cure the redness and pain instantly by applying a layer of plain yogurt to the area. Let it sit for five minutes, then rinse off and pat dry. The lactic acid in the yogurt will calm your irritated skin.

Relief for Shaving Nicks

Anything that helps keep the bathroom line moving in the morning is a welcome addition in our house. Let the post-puberty males in your house know that shaving cuts can be treated with a little lip balm to stop bleeding without any sting.

Overnight Hydration

During the night, the skin rests and repairs itself after the stresses of the day, so nothing's worse than waking up to dry skin in the winter. Use a humidifier or place a damp towel over your radiator at night to replenish moisture in the air and keep your skin hydrated. This helps to humidify the air around you and reduce excessive water loss from your skin.

Bruise Eraser

White vinegar can help heal bruises. Soak a cotton ball in vinegar, then apply it to the bruise for an hour. It will reduce the blueness of the bruise and speed up the healing process.

Slippery Solution

Soothe and help heal minor bruises and scrapes by using the inside of a banana peel to gently rub the injury. Treat as fast as possible to reduce bruising.

Reader's Tip

If you have a rash, you can still help ease the pain even if you're not sure what's causing it. Simply add a cup of baking soda to a warm bath and soak for 15 minutes.

—PAM HAMILTON

A Tip Worth Its Salt

A soak in hot saltwater does wonders for those suffering from poison ivy rashes. Try a basinful if it's just one area. If you fell into a patch of the itchy stuff, treat yourself to a nice, hot, salty bath.

Canker Sore Cure

If you have a canker sore, hold a damp tea bag over the area. Tea bags are filled with healthful tannins. Cool the tea bag for even more relief.

Hydrogen Peroxide Can Help

Hydrogen peroxide may help reduce and relieve canker sores. Simply mix one part peroxide with one part water, then dab on any affected areas several times a day or swish around in your mouth for as long as possible.

New Favorite

Don't let a cold sore get you down. We've got a simple fix for you that barely costs a cent! Add a drop or two of water to baking soda until you form a paste. Then apply the paste to the cold sore and let sit for 10 minutes. After several days, your cold sore will be gone!

Corn Removal

To get rid of corns, soak a Band-Aid in apple cider vinegar, and apply it to the corn for a day or two. You can also try soaking your feet in a shallow pan of warm water with half a cup of vinegar. Either way, finish by rubbing the corn with a clean pumice stone.

Foot Bath for Health

If you find you're susceptible to athlete's foot, here's a trick to keep that nasty fungus at bay. Once or twice a week, soak your feet in a hot bath mixed with two cloves of crushed garlic. The garlic will kill athlete's foot before it starts, and you won't be afraid to walk around in sandals. To treat a case of athlete's foot that has already begun, try soaking your toes in mouthwash. It may sting a little, but the fungus will be gone in just a few days.

Yellow Toenail Buster

Battling toenail fungus? Soak your toes in the darkest beer you can find. The yeast in the beer attracts the fungus out from underneath your nails. (Unfortunately, it's important that you don't *drink* any beer during this treatment! It will up the yeast content in your body, making the toenail fungus more likely to stick around.)

Duct Tape for Warts

It's long been stated as fact—then disputed—that duct tape can help cure warts. It may seem strange, but medical studies have concluded that when patients cover their warts with duct tape every day for a month, 85 percent of them will see a reduction in the wart. That's compared to only a 60 percent reduction in patients who used cryotherapy (having the wart frozen off by a dermatologist). It's hard to believe, but many people swear by the treatment! Our opinion? Especially if you don't have health insurance, it's worth a shot.

Bug Bite?

A great way to stop mosquito bites from itching is with a dab of diluted ammonia. In fact, ammonia is the main ingredient in many of the itch-relief products currently on the market. Just mix four parts water for every one part ammonia. You can also use rubbing alcohol in place of the ammonia.

Try a Little Tenderness

If you've just come back from a long weekend camping, you'll love this tip. Use meat tenderizer to treat insect bites! Moisten a teaspoon of tenderizer with a little water and rub it immediately into the skin. Commercial meat tenderizers contain papain, an enzyme from papaya. Papain's protein-digestive properties will help decompose the insect venom.

Relief from Chigger Bites

Chigger bites? Aspirin helps—but not in the way you might think. Make a thick paste by crushing several aspirin tablets and then mixing in a bit of water. Rub the paste on any bites, and it will ease the pain and itching.

Itch Relief

We love this quick fix for an insect bite! Just rub antiperspirant or deodorant over the spot and the itch will go away.

> ## New Favorite
> Bitten by a bug? Just apply some polysaccharides to the area and you'll feel almost immediate relief. They might sound complicated, but they're easy to find in the form of banana peels! Just place a banana peel on the bite, yellow side up, and it will relieve itching.

Ease Wasp Stings

Stung by a wasp? Apply apple cider vinegar to the area with a cotton ball and the sting will subside.

When Bees Strike

When you're stung by a bee, carefully grasp the stinger and pull it out as fast as you can. The less venom that enters your body, the smaller and less painful the resulting welt will be. Ice the area immediately to reduce the swelling. If it still hurts, try cutting an onion in half and applying the fleshy side to the sting. It should help ease the pain.

Soothe Stings

If you're stung by a wasp, hornet, or bee, reach for a lemon. Make sure the stinger is gone, and quickly rub the area with some lemon juice to neutralize the venom.

Blister Resister

If you've ever used a Band-Aid to cover a blister, you know that it isn't quite enough protection when it gets touched or bumped. Our preferred way to keep a blister safe is with a cotton ball. Just tape it on with a bit of medical tape.

New Favorite

Suffering from itchy, flaky feet? The culprit may be athlete's foot, which is easy to contract in gyms and other areas where you may be barefoot. Before you try expensive creams, try this old-fashioned remedy: Submerge your feet in a solution of two parts water and one part white vinegar for 10–15 minutes. The acidic nature of the vinegar bath will kill off the athlete's foot if you use it every night for a week or two. This treatment will also work for toenail fungus!

Headache Help

If you tend to get headaches in the late mornings, late afternoons, and after a long nap, they might be due to low blood sugar, also known as hypoglycemia. These headaches can be helped by eating foods that release sugar slowly, such as bananas, whole grains, and oats.

Are Your Eyes Causing Headaches?

Less-than-perfect eyesight can trigger headaches because the muscles around the eyes squeeze in order to focus. If your headaches come on after reading or working at a computer, make sure you give your eyes a rest every 15 minutes by focusing on a distant object for at least a minute. You may also want to get your eyes examined to see if you need glasses.

Drink Up for Headaches

Many headaches are caused by dehydration. Before you reach for the pain reliever, try drinking two or three glasses of water or an energy drink like Gatorade. You may find you're back to normal in no time.

Water, Water, Everywhere

How much water is enough water? Divide your body weight in half. The number you come up with is how many ounces of water you should be drinking daily. For example, if you weigh 150 pounds, you should consume 75 ounces of water each day.

Sore Throat Reliever

Aspirin does more than just relieve headaches! If you have a sore throat, dissolve two non-coated tablets in a glass of water and gargle. Just be sure to note that this only works with aspirin—don't try it with other pain relievers like ibuprofen.

Better Than a Bloody Mary

In the peak of sore throat season, get a reprieve by gargling with this spicy mix: 1/3 cup tomato juice, 1/2 cup hot water, 5 drops pepper sauce. Gargle. It works even better if you gargle with lukewarm saltwater first.

Soothing a Sore Throat

Relieve your sore throat with a time-tested home remedy. Slice off two-thirds of a lemon and place it on a shish kebab skewer or barbecue fork. Set your gas stove to high and roast the lemon over the open flame until the peel acquires a golden brown color. (This works on electric stoves, too, although not quite as well.) Let the lemon cool off for a moment, then squeeze the juice into a small cup. Add one teaspoon of honey, mix well, and swallow.

Rx, Vinegar

White vinegar stops nosebleeds. Just dampen a cotton ball and plug the nostril. The acetic acid in the vinegar cauterizes the wound. Who knew?

Reader's Tip

If you have a pollen allergy, try to keep sneeze-inducing allergens out of your home. Take a shower immediately after doing any yard work to get rid of pollens you may have carried in on your hair and skin, and throw your clothes in the laundry basket. Animals can carry in pollen, too. After taking your dog for a walk or letting your cat out, wipe him or her down with a wet rag or baby wipe. Showering at night can also reduce pollen on your hair and skin and help you sleep better.   —JOANNA HUYCK, MADISONVILLE, KY

Warming Socks

If you have a cold that's been hanging around forever, try this remedy to rid yourself of congestion once and for all. Get a pair of cotton socks damp, but not dripping, with cold water. You can even put them in the freezer for a couple minutes to make them extra cold. Put them on, and then put a pair of dry wool socks on over them. Go to bed immediately. As you sleep, the heat from your upper body will be drawn down to your feet, allowing the inflammation to reduce. You'll be stunned to find that your feet are warm and dry by morning.

Steam Away a Cold

Steam is a wonderful household remedy for colds, especially with some aromatherapy oils mixed in. Try pouring hot water into a bowl and breathing in as you lean over it. Stick your tongue out as you do it—this will open the throat and allow more steam through, which prevents membranes from drying out. Add aromatherapy oils to the water that are especially known to alleviate the symptoms of congestion, such as black pepper, eucalyptus, hyssop, pine, and sweet thyme.

Cold Cure

Stuffy nose? Don't spend money on decongestant—head to your fridge instead. Cut the "root" end of two scallions and carefully insert the white ends into your nose (being cautious not to shove them too high!). You may look silly, but your nose will start to clear in a couple of minutes.

If you've ever experienced pressure in your ears during an airplane ride, you may have chewed gum to relieve it. If you have a cold or sinus pressure, this trick will help your ears in a similar way, and is especially great for kids. Just blow up a few balloons, which will increase the pressure in your sinuses and help unblock your ears.

Onion Ear Muffs

Oil found in raw onion is antimicrobial, which makes onions great cures for upper respiratory ailments. If you have a minor earache, onion may help. Slice a fresh onion and heat it in the microwave on high for one minute. Wrap it in cheesecloth or another thin cloth so that it doesn't burn your skin, and then hold it against the ailing ear for 20–30 minutes. See a doctor if the pain gets worse or continues for longer than 24 hours.

Get Your Ducts in a Row

If you find yourself getting headaches or sinus trouble more often than you used to, it might be that your home's ducts simply need a good cleaning. Whenever air conditioning or heating is on, tiny particles that have accumulated inside the ducts blow out, too, including mold, mouse droppings, and plain old dust. If you have severe allergies, a professional duct cleaning may be just what the doctor ordered.

Get Rid of Swimmer's Ear

If your children are prone to swimmer's ear, a bacterial infection of the ear canal, take this precaution when they've been in the pool: Dab a solution of one part vinegar and five parts warm water into each ear three times a day. The vinegar will ward off bacteria and keep your kids' ears pain-free.

Reader's Tip

To treat dry ears and eliminate earwax buildup, use a glass dropper and put five drops of olive oil into each ear, then put cotton balls in your ears for five minutes to allow the oil to soak in. It will nourish the skin and reduce your body's need to produce wax.　　—ALECIA SAUNDERS-ROSS, GARNER, NC

Alleviate Neck Tension

Been leaning over your work too long? Try this to help a hurting neck. Inhale and raise your shoulders up to your ears, pulling them as high as they will go. Then let go with an "ahhh" and drop them slowly back down. Repeat several times to release muscle tension.

Insomnia Cure

When you're having trouble sleeping, try taking a deep breath. Take five, as a matter of fact. Start in your belly—envision blowing up a balloon there—and move to your chest, filling your lungs to their capacity. Exhale slowly. This will signal to your nervous system that it's time to relax, and help you nod off naturally.

Salt Will Soothe You

If you're experiencing insomnia, you will love this salty tip: At bedtime, drink a glass of water, then let a pinch of salt dissolve on your tongue, making sure it doesn't touch the roof of your mouth. Studies have shown that the combination of salt and water can induce a deep sleep.

Rub Away the Bloat

Feeling bloated? It could just be trapped gas. Encourage it to move by gently stroking from your right hip up towards your ribs, then across the bottom of your ribcage and down towards your left hip. Repeat several times.

Reader's Tip

If you've got an upset stomach due to indigestion or a hangover, try drinking a glass of club soda with a dash of bitters. It should help ease your pain.   —ALI RAINEY, ASH GROVE, MO

Mitigate Motion Sickness

If you get nauseated every time you ride in a car, boat, or train, take some lemon wedges with you. Suck on them as you ride to relieve nausea. You can also try sucking on a piece of ginger or drinking ginger tea.

Relieve Nausea Naturally

Nothing's worse than a bad bout of nausea. Try this simple trick to help relieve your discomfort: Drink a little ginger ale, then chew a handful of crushed ice, and finally sniff a piece of black-and-white newspaper. It may seem like an old wives' tale, but it works!

Root Out Morning Sickness

Ginger root, taken as a powder or in tea, works directly in the gastrointestinal tract by interfering with the feedback mechanisms that send sickness messages to the brain. Take some when you're feeling nauseated to help alleviate your symptoms.

Original Hiccup Cure

When "Boo!", drinking upside down, and holding your breath don't work, try this to get rid of your hiccups. Insert a Q-tip into your mouth and gently dab the back of the throat under the soft palate. You're trying to hit the uvula, which requires good aim, a diagram, or both! If this doesn't work, try putting sugar under the tongue and letting it dissolve, or swallowing a tablespoon of lemon juice.

Instant Hand Sanitizer

To avoid spending money on expensive hand sanitizers, make your own at home with these ingredients: 2 cups aloe vera gel, 2 teaspoons rubbing alcohol, 4 teaspoons vegetable glycerin, and 15 drops eucalyptus oil. Mix the ingredients well and you should be able to use it the same way you'd use the commercially made version.

Homemade Heating Pad

Don't spend your money on an aromatherapy pillow! Instead, add uncooked, long-grain rice to a sock and tie it shut. Whenever you need a little heat after a long day, stick it in the microwave on high for 1–2 minutes, and you'll have soothing warmth. To add a little scent to the pillow, put a few drops of your favorite essential oil into the rice.

Impromptu Hot Packs

In an emergency, a one-liter plastic soda bottle can make an excellent hot-water bottle. Just make sure that you wrap it in a hand towel before placing it against your skin.

A Different Kind of Ice Pack

If you're a vodka drinker, you're well aware that it doesn't solidify in the freezer. For this reason, it's also a great tool for making your own homemade gel ice pack to use on aches or injuries. Just pour two cups of water, one-third cup of vodka, and a few drops of green or yellow food coloring (so everyone will know not to eat the contents) into a heavy-duty Ziploc freezer bag. Put it in the freezer for a while, and you've got an instant ice pack. If you don't keep vodka around, you can simulate the same effect with liquid dishwasher detergent. (If you do use detergent, though, make absolutely certain to label the bag so nobody ingests it.)

Tiny Ice Packs

Get rid of the hundreds of condiment packets in your junk drawer and help ease the pain of smaller bruises, scrapes, and burns by keeping the packets in your freezer, then taping them to ouches with scotch or medical tape.

Sock Pack

If you don't have an ice pack on hand, simply fill a sock with ice cubes and tie it closed. Refill as needed. Run it under the faucet if you're not feeling much (other than the blinding pain of your injury, that is).

Contrast Showers

You'll love the feeling of this simple routine that will help boost your immune and circulatory systems and even relieve stress. Toward the end of your shower, turn the water up as hot as you can stand it and allow it to warm your body for three minutes. Then turn it down so the water is cool, and let it run over your body for 30–60 seconds. Repeat as many times as you like, ending on cold. When you get out of the shower, rub yourself vigorously with a towel to encourage circulation. Do not continue the contrasting temperatures, however, if you feel dizzy, nauseated, or excessively chilled.

Pinch to Relieve Stress

Many people hold stress in the area between their eyebrows, and in time, vertical stress lines will develop here. When you feel your brow knit together with concentration or stress, take a moment to pinch the muscle there, working from the center of the brow along the brow-line in each direction with a thumb and bent forefinger. Not only will it make you feel better, it will prevent wrinkles, too!

New Favorite

If you're a chocolate junkie but are trying to lose weight, you may be interested to hear that your favorite food may actually *help* you take off the pounds. Chocolate increases serotonin levels, so it can help lessen depression, stress, and other reasons why you may find yourself wanting to consume more food. The trick? You can only eat 1.4 ounces per day, preferably in the morning. (But hey, that's better than nothing!) Doctors recommend 70 percent dark chocolate for the biggest weight-loss effects.

Pepper Your Dishes

Lose weight without lifting a pound! Derived from the plant *Capsicum annuum*, cayenne pepper has been reported to not only make you lose weight by elevating body temperature, but also to improve circulation and to lower cholesterol. As it's a mild stimulant, it can also be added to hot water with lemon juice as an alternative to coffee.

Satisfy a Sweet Tooth
Trying to lose weight but keep craving something sweet? Keep a bunch of grapes in your fridge and grab a handful when the hunger hits. Grapes release sugar quickly, so they are great for satisfying your sweet tooth. If you don't feel like the grapes are hitting the spot, wait 10 minutes and see how you feel before reaching for the candy!

Avoid Insulin Surge
Caffeine on an empty stomach stimulates insulin surge, which leads to unbalanced blood sugar and weight gain, in addition to taxing your adrenal glands. Instead of drinking coffee first thing in the morning, try having it with your afternoon snack—or at least after you've had breakfast.

Detox with Lemon
Lemon juice not only smells great, it tastes delicious, too. Mix it with hot water and try it as an alternative to hot tea and coffee. You may find it wakes you up just as well, and your body will thank you.

A Breath of Fresh Air

This is simple advice we've all heard before, but how often do we put it into practice? When you're feeling anxious or overwhelmed, take a deep breath. If you're really stressed, try doing some cartwheels, standing on your head, or doing a few exercises. By changing what you're doing, you can often change the way you view what's going on around you. For many people, the majority of their stress comes from work. Make sure the daily grind isn't getting to you by talking a walk during your lunch break (some offices have even started yoga or exercise groups!). Make a date with a friend to walk each day so you'll commit to doing it. And don't forget to breath deeply while you're taking in some sun!

Pet Therapy

Playing with or petting your pet is known to reduce blood pressure and stress, as well as improve your mood. It has been proven to work with all kinds of pets: dogs, cats, hamsters—every type but dust bunnies.

Exercise the Easy Way

Oftentimes, surveying the latest home exercise equipment or worrying about which gym to join are just excuses for putting off actually getting in shape. Start exercising *today* by using your stairs (if you have them) and cans of food as hand weights. You can march in place anywhere, do squats while waiting for the pasta to cook, and rotate your arms while talking on the phone with a headset. If you do have some equipment, but want access to more, try circuit training with a neighbor—you have a bike and treadmill, she has a weight machine and rower. Trade every other day. Even without any machines you can create your own little circuit, setting up stations to do sit-ups, push-ups, jumping jacks, and even a few yoga poses if you're feeling adventurous.

Simple Homemade Weights

If you can't afford a set of weights, but you'd like to do some weight training, just take some empty plastic milk jugs and fill them with dry beans. Problem solved!

New Favorite

If you find you're often stiff after exercising, you probably just need more water. Dehydration is a major cause of post-exercise muscle soreness. Drinking water regularly while you work out should keep water levels high enough to combat pain.

PART 3

SAVING
MONEY
EVERY DAY

Knowing household solutions is fun, but if you're feeling the pinch, what's really important to you is saving money. This section gives you hundreds of easy ways to save money in your daily life without sacrificing a thing. Better yet, we'll tell you easy ways to *make* money online—like selling your old cell phone, MP3 players, and other gadgets (pages 344-345); taking surveys (pages 371-372); and trying out websites before they're launched (page 353). The first chapter also gives you the best places to find free stuff online, including shampoo, jewelry, books, patterns, stickers, résumé help, classes, medicine, and more. Saving money every day doesn't have to be difficult—sometimes it's just a matter of knowing the best places to park (page 370), what days it's cheapest to fly (page 385), and that batteries last longer if you keep them in the refrigerator (page 437). And of course, we have even more reader tips in store. We hope you find some fun ways to save in the final chapter of the book we made just for you!

CHAPTER 1

FINDING GREAT DEALS, FREE MONEY, AND MORE ONLINE

Visit WhoKnewTips.com!

We don't mind doing a bit of shameless self-promotion for our site, WhoKnewTips.com, because we know you're sure to find some great freebies and money-saving ideas when you visit. Not only will you see the most recent freebies and discounts we've found around the web, you can also submit your own tips to be featured in our next book. And of course, you'll find out more about Who Knew? products and see our most recent shows. You can also follow us on Facebook and Twitter by going to Facebook.com/whoknewtips or Twitter.com/whoknewtips.

Learn to Cook

Love to cook or wish you knew more? Take free cooking classes at your local Williams-Sonoma store. They offer technique classes and product demonstrations that range from making your own soda to cooking steak to dinner-worthy sandwiches. To locate your nearest Williams-Sonoma and to see their events calendar, go to Williams-Sonoma.com and click on "Store locator." Then keep an eye out for the "Store events" section.

Crafty Classes

Did you know that, in addition to selling craft supplies at great prices, Michael's also offers free classes on making crafts? Free classes often center around a holiday (such as Mother's Day, Fourth of July, or Thanksgiving), and will teach you how to make something you can bring home as a present or decoration. Michael's also offers more general classes on beading, painting, and other crafts for a small fee or free with purchase. To find out what your local Michael's is offering, go to Michaels.com and click on "Find a store." Once you've located your nearest Michael's, click on "This store's events" to see what kind of crafts you can learn for free.

Reader's Tip

If you want to learn online, OpenCulture.com is a great resource for free textbooks, courses, films, language lessons, and more.   —PAT LEVIN, LIVONIA, MI

For Do-It-Yourself Kids

At The Home Depot's Kids Workshops, you and your child can build fun projects like toolboxes, fire trucks, mail organizers, birdhouses, and bug containers. The workshops are free, designed for kids 5–12, and occur the first Saturday of each month in all Home Depot stores. These fantastic classes not only give you a fun activity to share with your kid (adult participation is required), they teach safety and skills. In addition to the newly constructed project, each child receives a kid-sized Home Depot apron and an achievement pin. Details can be found at HomeDepot.com. Once there, just enter "Kids workshops" in their search bar.

Lowe's How-To Clinics for Kids

Lowe's is another good source for DIY kids' projects. Bring the entire brood into any Lowe's store and build a free wooden project. Each participant also receives a free apron, goggles, a project-themed patch, and a certification of merit upon completion of the project. Clinics are offered every other Saturday from 10 a.m. to 11 a.m., and all building materials and tools are provided. Get the details at LowesBuildAndGrow.com.

Free, First-Class Education

Massachusetts Institute of Technology—one of the United States' most preeminent technological universities—offers free course materials online. Get reading lists, homework assignments, and audio and/or video lectures for a mind-boggling variety of classes including SCUBA diving, written language for Chinese speakers, TV theory, and 1,895 more. Want to really impress your friends? Try some classes on calculus, brain structure, bioengineering, or even "Wheelchair Design in Developing Countries." If you're willing to put in the time to learn, these classes will definitely teach you things you never knew. Visit the site at OCW.MIT.edu to get started.

Language Lessons

Take lessons in Spanish, French, Italian, and German
absolutely free at BBC.co.uk/languages and you can
travel internationally more easily (or just impress your
friends). The site also offers quickie lessons in Chinese,
Japanese, and even more exotic languages like Kudu.

Free Business Classes

The US Small Business Association is dedicated to helping your small business succeed. At their site, SBA.gov,
you'll not only find free tools and resources for small
business owners, but free classes as well! These online
courses are each about 30 minutes long and will teach
you about financing your business, marketing and advertising, obtaining government contracts, and more.
Just go to SBA.gov and click on "Counseling and
Training."

Small Business Help

The Association for Enterprise Opportunity is an association of organizations committed to small businesses. On their site, MicroEnterpriseWorks.org, you'll find plenty of information about the grants and other resources that are available for the budding entrepreneur.

Résumé Help

Get all kinds of free, professional advice on your career (or desired career) at CareerOneStop.com (or call 1-877-348-0502), which will give you tutorials on résumés and cover letters, give you salary information, help you find free classes in your area, and more.

New Favorite

If you're working on your résumé, check out ResumeCompanion.com. Indicate what position you're applying for, and it will give you the perfect phrases to describe the type of work you've done at previous employers.

Applying for a Government Job?

If you're applying for a government job, you probably need to take a civil service exam. But don't spend money on expensive test prep books or software. Instead, go to PSE-net.com/library.htm. This site, run by the Public Service Employees Network, gives you links to buy books about each of the exams, but also provides links to free resources offered by various states and other organizations. Just click on the type of test you will be taking, and see what they have on offer.

Free Faxes

Never pay for a fax again! Instead, go to FaxZero.com, where they'll let you either enter text to be faxed or upload a PDF or Word document. Pay an extra $2 and they won't put their ad on the cover page.

Why Pay for Microsoft?

"Great Software . . . Easy to Use . . . and it's Free!" That's the claim at OpenOffice.org, and it's true. Check out their free word processing and spreadsheet programs that are similar to programs that Microsoft offers. Another good site for these types of programs is Google Docs: Docs.Google.com. At Google Docs you can open Microsoft Word and other files, then share them over the internet with others.

Cash for Your Gadgets

Now you can keep your old electronics out of the landfill and possibly get some free cash in exchange! Services such as BuyMyTronics.com and Gazelle.com recycle or refurbish your old cast-offs and send you a check in return. Just fill out the easy forms on their websites.

They'll make you an offer and, if you accept, send you a box with postage to ship your gizmo to them. They take cameras, cell phones, MP3 players, game consoles, personal computers, and more.

Reader's Tip

Go to Apple.com/recycling to find out if your old computer (Mac or PC) is worth anything! If Apple can use the parts, they'll pay you in the form of an Apple gift card. You can also get 10 percent off an iPod by bringing your old one into an Apple store. —DARREN COLE, SOLVANG, CA

Educate Yourself Before You Buy

After gas, one of the biggest costs associated with having a car is the interest you pay on the loan. Before you go buy a car, get a loan in place first—the financing the car dealership will offer most likely won't be as competitive. Know your credit rating, and check with your employer's credit union or look online for deals on car loans. A good place to begin is a page that lets you compare rates and find out information on car loans. One site we like is BankRate.com. Click on "Auto" from the homepage.

Go for the Gold

With the value of gold so high these days, now is the time to get rid of your old gold! Take a look through your jewelry box for broken pieces and items you no longer wear. As long as they're 10 karats or higher, you can get big money for them. Just make sure you're dealing with a reputable gold broker. Never mail in your scrap gold—make sure to talk to someone in person at a jewelry or coin store. Use the online calculator at Dendritics.com/scales/metal-calc.asp to find out how much your gold is worth, and expect to get about 75–85 percent of that amount from a broker.

Get Money for Ink

Got empty cartridges for a printer, copier, or fax machine? TonerBuyer.com will buy them from you, and even pay the shipping! Fill out their online form to find out how much your cartridges are worth, then print out the prepaid mailing form and wait for your check in the mail. You can also bring empty printer cartridges into Staples stores, which will get you a $2 credit (up to 10 a month).

Online Painting Tool

If you've ever painted an entire room and wished you could change the color with a snap of your fingers, then this site is for you. Visit Behr.com and register with their site to use their "Paint Your Place" program for free. It will allow you to upload a picture of a room in your home, then change the wall color without having to buy a bucket of paint (and spend all day painting).

New Favorite
Getting married? Many stores now offer freebies and rewards just for having gifts purchased on your registry! Check out Kohls.com, Macys.com, and JCPenney.com for more information.

Rebates from Ebates

Get cash back just for shopping online at Ebates.com. Before you shop at your favorite sites (including HomeDepot.com, BN.com, Khols.com, Target.com, and more), just log in at Ebates.com first. Then click through to your desired website. You get a certain percentage of cash back on each site, and a check will be mailed to you every three months. It's that easy! A similar site we love is FatWallet.com.

Get Some Swag

"It's like a frequent flyer mile for using the web," Swagbucks.com says about their internet rewards program. Swagbucks can be redeemed in their online store for video games, free MP3 downloads, toys, posters, office supplies, gift cards from major retailers, magazine subscriptions, and more. To earn Swagbucks, simply search the web from Search.Swagbucks.com and click on your point rewards when they pop up! You can also earn points by subscribing to their newsletter, following them on Facebook and Twitter, and taking surveys and polls. If you're interested in earning freebies easily online, this is the program for you.

Free from P&G

To get free samples of Proctor & Gamble products, including everything from body wash to laundry detergent to toothpaste, go to PGEverydaySolutions.com and click on "Register today." You'll also receive their excellent email newsletter, which has household tips and tricks as well as a wide variety of coupons.

Savings, Right at Home

RightAtHome.com is a savings site by Johnson & Johnson. In addition to promoting their household products, they also have lots of great tips for organizing, crafting, cooking, and cleaning. The best part, of course, is their "Special offers" section, which has big coupons and free samples for products like Ziploc bags, Scrubbing Bubbles cleaner, Glade air fresheners, Windex window-washing kits, Drano drain declogger, and more.

Extra Money for Photographers

If you have a gift for taking beautiful photographs, there may be a side career for you in photography. Advertise your services to become a wedding and special events photographer, and make some extra dough on the weekends—just make sure you have a sophisticated website where people can view your work. You can also make money selling your images to publishers and creative professionals who are looking for stock photography. Go to ShutterPoint.com, Dreamstime.com, or iStockPhoto.com to find out more about selling your images online.

New Favorite

If you usually print out your digital photos using an online service, you know that there are a lot of them, and they often have promotions and sales. To help you figure out which one can give you the best deal right now, check out PrintRates.com. You tell it the number of prints and sizes you need, and it will tell you where to find the best deal.

Free Jewelry!

Believe it or not, you can get free jewelry with no catches—all you have to do is pay the $6 shipping fee! SilverJewelryClub.com allows you to pick the necklaces, earrings, and other jewelry you want, then ships it to you for only $6. The amazing thing about this site is that the pieces really are quality items made from sterling silver and real gemstones, and they have so many pretty options, you'll want them all! Luckily, the site not only allows you to pick as many free items as you want, you can come back again for more! In return, all they ask is that you consider shopping at their full (not free) site, Peora.com.

Thanks, Walmart!

Not only is Walmart one of the best stores to find discounts, but they also give away free samples on their website! Once you get to Walmart.com, though, they're sometimes hard to find. Look for their "In stores now" section, then click on "Free samples." They have several freebie offers each week, but you'll have to answer a short survey and may not receive the sample if you don't qualify. For example, if you're applying for a free sample of Purina One cat food, but admit you don't have cats, you may not be freebie-worthy!

Facebook for Freebies

Facebook is one of the best ways to get freebies! If you're already on Facebook, you've probably "liked" various companies, organizations, bands, TV shows, and random funny pages (and Who Knew?, of course!). If you're not already on Facebook, it's time to give in to your friends and family members who have been urging you to join! It's a great way to stay in touch, but it's also a great way to stay apprised of free stuff that is being offered by the companies you love. Once you've signed up for Facebook, find the companies that make products you use regularly by typing each one's name into Facebook's search bar. Many companies—like Burger King, Babies "R" Us, Wheat Thins, Origins, Walgreens, and more—offer coupons and freebies just for "liking" their page. And don't worry, it's easy. All you have to do is go to the company's page and click the button that says "Like" (naturally).

Reader's Tip

If you like keeping abreast of all the latest sweepstakes, coupons, and giveaways on Facebook, you have to go to Apps.Facebook.com/promotionsHQ. They gather it all there for you so you don't have to hunt around.

—PATRICIA GREGORY

Free Patterns

Get free patterns from the leader in sewing—Butterick/McCall. Just go to Butterick.McCall.com/free-downloads-pages-1013.php. Sign up for their email program and get access to a wide variety of free patterns, most of which are for crafts. Another site for free patterns is FreePatterns.com. Just download and print out free patterns for sewing, quilting, knitting, crocheting, and even paper crafts. If you cross-stitch, get access to hundreds of free cross-stitching projects at Dawn's Cross Stitch. Just go to DawnsXstitch.PWP.Blueyonder.co.uk and click on "Alphabetical list of patterns" or "Patterns by category."

Free for Knitters and Crocheters

Grab your needles or hook and get ready for some new things to knit or crochet! For free knitting patterns of all sorts, check out KnittingPatternCentral.com, which offers patterns for afghans, rugs, garments, toys, and just about anything you can think of. (Try Crochet PatternCentral.com for crochet patterns.) The Lion brand yarn company also offers free patterns if you join their site—just visit LionBrand.com/patterns. Other sites for free knitting and crocheting patterns are FreeVintageKnitting.com and KnittingOnTheNet.com.

Make Easy Money from Home

There are many opportunities available for becoming a customer service representative right in your own home. Sign up with Alpine Access (AlpineAccess.com), Arise Virtual Solutions (Arise.com/work-at-home), or West Corporation (West.com) and you'll receive calls from customers needing help from major organizations like Sears, Office Depot, and the IRS. You usually need to provide your own computer with a high-speed internet connection, and sometimes an extra phone line, but you'll make up to $14 an hour and won't even have to change out of your pajamas.

New Favorite

Make money at home by helping web developers find out the ways in which their websites are confusing or not working well—become a website tester for UserTesting.com! They'll give you software to install on your computer that tracks your mouse's movements, and ask you to narrate a short video while you use the site. After answering a few questions, you'll be paid $10 per site you review. For more information, visit UserTesting.com/be-a-user-tester.

Online Teachers Wanted!

At Limu.com, people who know things are connected with those who want to know them! Set up an online class in your subject area using Limu's virtual classroom, and you even get to decide how much to charge per online student. You can also browse their listings of "wanted knowledge assets"—skills and knowledge people are looking to learn—and see if any of your skills match. Visit Limu.com/pages/teach.html for more information.

How About a House Party?

What's better than inviting your friends over and giving them a handful of freebies? HouseParty.com lets you do just that! Their company partners with products, TV shows, and more to bring you exclusive freebies, just for throwing a party in your home. Go to HouseParty.com, pick which products interest you, and sign up to host one of the many house parties that will all take place on the same day around the US. You'll be asked to post photos of the event, send out invitations from the site, and fill out extensive surveys about your experience. But in return, you can sample a wide array of free products. Recent giveaways have included Hasbro board games, Gerber baby food, Febreeze products, and Canon photo printers. The party host or hostess also receives special gifts like decorations, gift cards, or even camcorders! The only catch is that you don't always get chosen to host the parties you sign up for. Companies are looking for outgoing, social people who will promote their products, so make sure to answer their questionnaire with that in mind! Also, be sure to check the site in the late summer, when they often list TV premiere parties that will give you access to new shows before their debut on TV!

Free Everything, from People Like You

You can find hundreds of items—from furniture to books to clothes to exercise equipment—at Freecycle.org, a nonprofit website whose goal is to decrease landfill waste. Users join up and post about items they are giving away or need, and connect with other users who want the items or have what they're looking for. Just be careful—some free things are hard to resist, but do you really need that bedazzled couch cover?

Reader's Tip

If you're looking for a great all-around site to find lots of different kinds of freebies, try Freebies4Mom.com. Heather, the mom who runs the site, finds coupons and free samples from around the web and posts them daily. Recent finds include a free luxury bathrobe from Dove, free Pampers diapers, buy-one-get-one-free coupons for Snapple, and more. —SHERRILL PEARSON, BLOOMINGTON, IN

For Book Shopping

We love PaperbackSwap.com! Featured on the *Today Show* and in *Real Simple* and *Good Housekeeping*, the site allows you to list books (not just paperbacks) you don't want anymore. Once you send them to other users, you'll get credits you can use toward a new (to you) book of your own. What could be better than free books?

American Classics in Your Inbox
Sign up to receive a free story every week via email at Email.LOA.org/sotw_signup_index.jsp. These free stories aren't just any stories—they're revered classics from the Library of America, a nonprofit organization dedicated to publishing works by America's most treasured authors. As they say, each week's story "could be anything: a short work of fiction, a character sketch, an essay, a journalist's dispatch, a poem . . . . What is certain is that it will be memorable, because every story is from one of the hundreds of classic works of American literature published by The Library of America."

Looking for Love (Stories)?
Head over to RavenousRomance.com for a free, steamy short story each and every day! Then check out their great deals on full-length online novels. (Warning: Some of the stories are explicit!)

Free Sheet Music
The Mutopia Project might sound like a top-secret government plan, but it's actually an organization that compiles sheet music that has gone into the public domain. Go to MutopiaProject.org to download sheet

music for classical music by Bach, Beethoven, Chopin, Handel, Mozart, and many others.

Need Wood?

Looking for inexpensive, quality building supplies? Check out one of Habitat for Humanities' ReStores, which sell used and surplus wood and other building materials for low prices. To find a location nearest you, visit Habitat.org/env/restores.

Your Own Personal Shopper

At ShopItToMe.com, you enter your favorite brands of clothes and they do all the online searching for you. When items come up for sale on a department store's site, they'll send you an email, alerting you to the discount. The best part is, you can specify your size, so you won't have to waste your time wading through links only to find that the store is all out of extra-large!

Designer Duds at a Discount

If you're trying to save money, obviously it's probably a good idea to try to stay away from designer fashion labels. But if you just can't help yourself, Bluefly.com is the best place to go for a bargain. You'll find discounted prices on men's and women's designer clothing, including such labels as Kenneth Cole, Burberry, Armani, Marc Jacobs, Calvin Klein, and Prada. Just try to keep it to a couple of outfits and a handbag!

Kids' Clothes

Get gently worn clothes for your kids at ThredUp.com. Through this unique online community, browse boxes of clothes that parents have put together by gender, size, season, and more. Pay a low rate for shipping to get the entire box, then post a box of your own to share.

Online Shoe Shopping

At Zappos.com, you'll find more shoes than you ever imagined possible, including men's, women's, and kids' sneakers, dress shoes, boots, and sandals. Not only do they have free shipping, they also include a return shipping label with your order, so if you don't like the shoes once you try them on, you can easily return them for free. Another great site for shoes is 6pm.com, which carries lots of shoes that used to be on Zappos. You do have to pay shipping, but the savings can be worth it because the selection and prices are usually quite good.

ELF for Make-Up

Good make-up doesn't have to be expensive! For a great deal on cosmetics, head over to EyesLipsFace.com, where they have everything from lip gloss to nail polish for only a dollar apiece. They also have a great "Gifts" section, with cute box sets for unbelievable prices. For instance, eye shadow, mascara, eyeliner, a brush, and an eyelash curler for only $5!

Your Site for Salon Savings

Addicted to fancy shampoo? Find the brands you buy at your salon for much less at SalonSavings.com. Shampoos and hair-care products are 10–80 percent off, and skincare and fragrances are offered at much less as well. This site is also a great place to check if you have a favorite beauty product that has been discontinued.

Stop Squinting!

If you need new glasses and aren't sure how you're going to afford them, check out 39DollarGlasses.com. For around $45 (with shipping), you can get attractive (though bare-bones) glasses, including the lenses! Walmart also offers good deals on frames and lenses. If you're looking for something more stylish, try WarbyParker.com, which offers good prices on its own line of frames. Plus, you can try out their glasses online "virtually" by uploading a picture of yourself. Neat!

New Favorite

Here's an online shopping secret that can save you hundreds. When you're visiting a company's online store, make sure to hit up the "sale" section first. Many sites will also keep sale items in their original locations—without the prices marked down. Look in the sale section first to make sure you're getting the best price.

The 411 on Major Appliances

Washing machine just break down and you're not sure if it's under warranty? Need to replace a part in your dishwasher, but don't know what its specifications are? Want to buy a microwave and not sure what you should be looking for? Appliance411.com is here to help. They have purchasing information (including rebates), FAQs about appliances big and small, and best yet, online manuals and warranty information for just about any model of any appliance. If you're looking for help with any machine in your home, go here first.

Big-Ticket Coupons

Looking for coupons for big-ticket items in your home, like washing machines, TVs, and more? Stop by your local post office and grab a packet for people who are moving and would like their mail forwarded. Even if you don't fill out the forwarding card, these packets often contain coupons from stores targeting those who have recently moved.

Computer Help

For something called "Help," that particular menu item on any computer program is unbelievably unhelpful! The next time you find yourself throwing your hands up in frustration in front of the computer, head over to ProTonic.com. Type in a question, and get a free, prompt email response from a volunteer computer expert. Who needs an IT department?

A Great Site for Electronics

Looking for a good offer when purchasing a Macintosh computer, iPod, camcorder, TV, or other electronics? MacMall.com offers all kinds of special promotions, from free printers to iPod covers to hundreds of dollars off. Just make sure to send in the mail-in rebate before it's too late—many rebates expire in fewer than 30 days.

Reader's Tip

If you're looking for deals online, your first stop should be PriceGrabber.com. It lets you see what's on sale in various categories, then takes you right to the site to get the bargain. Best of all, you can see the prices at different sites side-by-side, and they include sales tax and shipping! I also love their "Rebates" section, which lists all currently available rebates on various products.   —BILLIE JO WOODS

Supermarket Savings

Want to save money every time you go grocery shopping? Check out MyGroceryDeals.com, where you'll see what's on sale at your local grocery stores before you go. Just enter your zip code and start saving!

Let the Coupons Come to You!

The best and easiest way to get coupons to most stores is to make sure you're on their mailing lists—both email and "real" mail. Though you may not like the idea of signing yourself up for junk mail, you'll also be surprised at the number of coupons you'll receive simply because the store knows you want them. Visit your favorite stores' websites to sign up for their email mailing lists; you may need to visit their customer service counter in the store to see if you can sign up for a mailing list to receive physical coupons in the mail. Many stores also have a loyalty program. Ask and see what's available!

Online Coupon Secret

When you're digging for online coupons, here's one tip you should definitely be aware of. You'll notice that when you log on to most coupon sites, they'll ask you to enter your zip code before showing you a selection of coupons. But here's a secret they don't want you to know: While the coupon company only wants certain zip codes to access certain coupons, your grocery store doesn't know the difference! When printing out coupons from sites like Coupons.com and RedPlum.com, try typing in a few different zip codes to see what coupons crop up.

Bring On the Coupons

If you love couponing but don't have a lot of people to trade coupons with, here's a great idea: How about making a "Take a Coupon, Leave a Coupon" box? Set it up at your office, or ask your library, church, or a local cafe if you can place one there. Everyone leaves coupons they can't use, and takes what they can. You'll love stopping by to see what you can get your hands on.

Know the Code

Ever go to buy something online and see that little box to enter a promotional or coupon code? Well now you never have to wish you had something to enter into that box again. At RetailMeNot.com, you can find hundreds of codes that will give you savings at a large variety of websites, including Kohls.com, Amazon.com, and JCPenney.com. If this site doesn't have a code for the store you're looking for, also try MomsView.com, DealTaker.com, or PocketDeal.com. Or simply type the name of the online store and the words "coupon code" into a search engine.

Navigate a "Customer Service" Nightmare

If you've ever gone mad trying to navigate the menu options when you call your cell phone provider, credit

card company, bank, or anywhere else, head over to
GetHuman.com first. GetHuman gives you the secret
phone numbers or combinations of keystrokes to press
to get an actual person on the line, listed by company.
So if you're calling USAA, for instance, you know that
your best bet for good customer service is hitting 00#,
then # again at the prompt.

Keep Unwanted Phone Calls Away

Never have to lie about who you are to a telemarketer
again ("Bruce and Jeanne Lubin are out of town!"). Put
your name on the official "Do not call list" by going to
DoNotCall.gov or calling 1-888-382-1222.

Last-Minute Deals in Travel

If you're looking for the best deals in travel, head over
to AirfareWatchdog.com, which catalogs the cheapest
fares as they are listed on travel and airline sites. The
nice thing about this site is that it polices all the different sites for you, rather than offering fares itself (like
Expedia, Orbitz, and other sites). If you normally spend
a lot of time trying different combinations of travel
dates and nearby airports, this site will take a lot of the
guesswork out of it for you.

Airline Points Gone Awry

Reward points getting out of hand? Check out
Points.com, which lets you keep track of your airline

miles at other rewards points, all in one place. Better yet, you can swap points from one reward program to another!

> ## New Favorite
> After you buy a plane ticket, visit Yapta.com. Enter your flight details and they'll email you if the price goes down. Even if you have to pay a fee to change your ticket, fares often fluctuate by hundreds of dollars. This is an easy way to make sure you're getting the cheapest price.

More Fun Than You Thought

All you need to know when you're searching for fun things to do at Goby.com is what you're interested in and where you are (and, if you want, when you're going). Whether it's getting coffee, going to a playground, hitting up a museum, or more adventurous activities like sailing and horseback riding, Goby will tell you what's out there, and even give you a map to see where it is. The best thing about Goby is its straightforward, user-friendly design: no huge ads, no "sponsored results," no long loading times or signing up. For those of us who have spent a lot of time searching for things online, it's a welcome respite.

Buy and Sell Tickets

StubHub.com is a must-visit site for event tickets of all kinds, like concerts, sporting events, theater, and more. They're put on sale by people who can't use them, so it's a great site for finding big discounts and tickets for events that are sold out. You can also sell tickets you can't use! Best of all, StubHub guarantees that they'll be legit, so you don't have to worry about a scam.

Online Dating Without the Fees

One in five people meet their mate online, but if you're interested in online dating don't pay for sites like eHarmony or Match.com. We've known just as many couples who have met on OKCupid.com—a great, free site that allows you to set up a profile and take compatibility quizzes to meet other singles in your area. Unlike other "free" dating sites, they don't try to get you to pay to have your profile listed first in search results, or for extra messaging privileges. The entire thing is free to everyone, which isn't a bad thing for your dating pool!

Visit on the Web, Then in Person

Love a particular chain restaurant? Make sure to visit their website and find out what deals they offer. Many sites offer a mailing list that will email you coupons, and other restaurants have a frequent diner program that will earn you free meals over time. Lots of chains have certain days each week in which they offer deals on particular entrees (especially for seniors). Ask your waiter or a hostess what the web address is (if it isn't written all over the menu!), or type the name of the restaurant into a search engine.

Reader's Tip

Before you head to the mall, head to their website. Many malls now post coupons to their stores right on their site!

—JODY GEHLER, PROVO, UT

Where the Kids Eat Free

No matter how hard we try, we always end up eating out way more than we'd like. It's easier to not feel bad about it when we go to a restaurant where the kids eat free. Visit KidsMealDeals.com to find a bunch in your area. Enter your zip code, and you'll find deals from chain restaurants and local joints alike, and they even have apps for iPhones and Blackberrys in case you need it on-the-go. Remember, a restaurant that offers deals for kids also usually offers frugal prices for adult entrees, so this site could potentially save you hundreds (or if you're as bad as us, thousands) per year. Bon appetit!

Free Stickers

If you have a kid who loves to collect stickers, you know that they'll save practically anything with a self-adhesive backing. For an extensive list of free stickers available online, Freaky Freddie is your go-to guy! Just visit FreakyFreddies.com/sticker.htm. They also list bumper stickers, in case it's time to plaster over that one from the 2000 election.

Our Favorite Kid Places Online

The next time your kids bug you to buy a computer game, go to KidsGameHouse.com instead. There, you'll find tons of free games (and not all just for kids), from logic puzzles to action and adventure games. You can play them all online, so there's no software to install. For educational or just-for-fun games suited to young kids, check out PBSKids.org, DiscoveryKids.com, NickJr.com, and Scholastic.com. If your child is a *Sesame Street* fan, head to PBS.org/sesame for a variety of free *Sesame Street*–themed games. You can also print out coloring pages, bookmarks, and other kids' activities. Best of all, you can search via character, so you can find activities based around your child's *Sesame Street* favorites.

Road Trip Entertainment

Never have to worry about what your kids are going to do in the car again with Rad Roadtrips. At their site, you can download free activity books for kids especially designed to keep them entertained in the car. The site also has individual coloring pages and a maze generator. Just go to RadRoadtrips.com and click on "Downloads."

New Favorite

Find out where the cheapest place to park is at your nearby airport by visiting BestParking.com. This site lets you know about public lots that are close to the airport, but aren't run by the airport itself—and are often half the price.

The Cheapest Gas

Before you go head to the pump, visit GasBuddy.com. Enter your zip code, and your new buddy will tell you the nearby gas stations with the lowest prices. You can also search to find the least expensive pump prices in your entire city or state. They even have cell phone apps! You'll never fill up, only to see a cheaper station on the way home, again.

Renting Household Items

If you have a household item you use rarely (or need extra cash fast), how about renting it? Zilok.com allows you to rent out your car, vacation home, tools, camera, lawn mower, TV, video game console, and more. (Unfortunately, you can't rent out your kids.) For more information, go to US.Zilok.com/support.

Are You the Mysterious Type?

Mystery shopping can get you free products and a bit of money on the side, but most of all it's downright fun. Visit a store, then fill out an online survey about your experience. The pay isn't much—usually not more than $15—but you'll be reimbursed for products as varied as designer sunglasses to lunch and a beer at a restaurant. If you're interested in mystery shopping, be careful of online scams. You should never have to pay to be a mystery shopper! Check out one of our favorite services, GAPbuster.com/mysteryshop, or search for mystery shopping and focus group opportunities near you at MysteryShop.org/shoppers, which is run by the Mystery Shopping Providers Association.

The Survey Says . . .

The folks at SurveySpot.com not only want your opinion, they'll pay for it. Join for free and you'll receive 5–7 surveys to complete each week. For each completed survey, they'll pay you $2–$10 or enter you in a sweepstakes (or both!). This and other survey sites like MySurvey.com, EPoll.com, and Toluna.com can be frustrating because you don't always qualify to take the survey and it can take a while to earn money, but if you enjoy answering questions and have a bit of free time, this is a great way to earn some extra cash while you're messing around on the web.

New Favorite
That half-off Groupon deal for your boyfriend's favorite restaurant seemed like a good idea—until the two of you broke up. Luckily, all is not lost (at least in terms of your finances). Visit Coup Recoup.com to off-load any unwanted deals you've purchased from sites like Groupon and Living Social. List your deal for someone else to buy and make your money back! And of course, if you're looking to get a great deal, this is the place to visit first!

What to Do with Unwanted Gift Cards
Has that gift card to Smitty's Birdbath Emporium been sitting on your desk for years? (Thanks, Aunt Doris!) Head over to PlasticJungle.com or GiftCardRescue.com to get cash from unused gift cards! They'll pay you a portion of the total cost of your card (around 80–90 percent) and resell it on their site.

Does a Company Owe You Money?

Hundreds of lawsuits are settled every day, entitling purchasers of products to money they don't even know about. At TopClassActions.com, find easy-to-navigate lists of recent settlements and how to get money from them. During one recent visit, we found out Costco owed us a free three-month membership and anyone with AT&T internet service could get $2.90 for every month they had subscribed!

Lost Money Could Be Yours!

There is over $24 billion worth of unclaimed property in the United States, and Unclaimed.org is the official government site that can tell you if any of it is yours. Search by name and state, and be connected to federal and state databases to see if there is any money, land, or property that has been left to you and is in government custody.

Find Free ATMs

Sick of paying up to $3 every time you have to visit an ATM? At AllPointNetwork.com, you can find all of the surcharge-free ATMs in your area by entering your city and state or your zip code. Many of the listings are for stores that offer cash back with purchase, but you never know when you'll find a free ATM you never knew about.

The Real Free Credit Score

Did you know that legally you are entitled to one free credit report per year? However, many credit report sites will make you pay to see your score, or charge you a membership or "credit monitoring" fee. We recommend AnnualCreditReport.com, the free site set up by government law. Take a look at your report and make sure there are no errors, or that there aren't any old credit cards listed that you no longer use (if so, cancel them as soon as possible). Even though they will show you your report, AnnualCreditReport.com won't give you your credit score for free. But to get a no-strings-attached estimation of your credit score, you can visit CreditKarma.com, which will also help you identify areas of improvement.

A Must for the Uninsured

If you don't have a prescription plan, or if your prescription plan has denied you coverage for an expensive medication, you may be able to get it for free or at a deep discount. NeedyMeds.com will tell you how to get the medicine you need from the government, private outreach programs, and even the pharmaceutical companies themselves. Simply find the name of your medication in the "Brand name" or "Generics" list and see if you qualify! You should never be without the prescriptions you need.

Free Contact Lenses

If you have a prescription for contacts, you can get a certificate for a free pair of Acuvue disposable lenses at Acuvue.com. Just click on the "Free lenses" link.

Begin the Journey to a Healthier Life

Trends in dieting seem to change with the season. One day you're being told to eat plain toast, the next, bacon—it all gets a little confusing! That's where FatSecret.com comes in. Create a personalized exercise and nutrition program, then share it with their online community for moral support and feedback. Plus, you can track your progress, keep an online fitness journal, and research different diets and fitness techniques. Another fitness site we love is MyHomePersonalTrainer.com, where you can calculate your ideal weight and heart rate, assess your cardiovascular fitness, and receive all sorts of free advice to help you start getting in shape.

CHAPTER 2

EASY WAYS TO SAVE MONEY

Shopping Smart

It may be a pain, but the best way to save on groceries is to shop at more than one market. You'll soon find that one store will have cheaper produce, one will have cheaper meat, and so forth. Explore grocery stores you've never shopped at—perhaps one that is closer to your workplace or gym rather than by your home—and you may find even lower prices. We've even found cheaper products at stores that are the same chain, just a different location. Write down the prices of your most frequently purchased items, or bring a receipt from an average grocery trip with you. That way you can be sure to remember where the prices are the most reasonable.

Weigh Your Options

When buying pre-packaged produce that has a unit price rather than a per-pound price, weigh it first to make sure you're getting the best deal. We've found that bags of things like carrots, apples, and potatoes are often heavier than their package specifies. Get the heaviest bag for more food at the same price!

Produce Purchasing Pointers

The best way to save on produce is to buy fruits and veggies when they are in season. Any crop will be much cheaper when a farm near you is harvesting it, because the price won't include the transportation from another country. When a harvest has been particularly good, expect deep discounts as distributors try to get rid of a product before it goes bad. Visit EatThe Seasons.com to find out what produce is in season in the US and Canada.

> ## New Favorite
> Companies release more coupons in November, December, and January than in any other months. More coupons are also available at the beginning of the month, so make sure to get a Sunday paper (or two) during these times for the most savings!

Grocery Bargains

Any time a new grocery store opens up in our area, we always stop by to take a look. It might be a little annoying to navigate differently laid-out aisles, but new supermarkets offer big sales and the lowest prices possible in their first few weeks and months of business, as an incentive to get shoppers to switch stores. Many stores also offer contests and giveaways to celebrate their grand openings, so visiting during the first week is a good idea.

Go Native

Especially in cities, stores by and for immigrants abound. Whether it's a Mexican, Indian, Ethiopian,

Chinese, or Korean grocery, you'll find cheap deals on foods that are native to that country. Bulk spices can be especially cheap, and you'll also find items such as inexpensive tortillas and avocados. We never buy rice unless it's from an ethnic market, as it's usually up to 80 percent cheaper than buying it at the grocery store.

Gift Card Assist

Need a little help budgeting your trips to the supermarket? Many chains now offer prepaid gift cards. Buy one for yourself and think of it as a portable checking account: Put money on the card, then "withdraw" from it every time you shop. With a dedicated grocery "account," you'll find it's easier to keep a tighter rein on your spending.

Reader's Tip

When you're at the supermarket, make sure to keep an eye on the prices at the salad bar. If you only need a few artichoke hearts, sun-dried tomatoes, or other specialty items that can also be found in salads, they may be cheaper to buy there by the pound than elsewhere in the store.

—LINETTE HASKELL DUNHAM

Steak Out a Great Deal

Did you know that the best time to shop for meat is in the morning? That is usually when the butcher marks down meat that is close to its sell-by date. If you won't make it tonight, freeze it for later!

Buying in Bulk

Ask at the deli counter of your supermarket for "bulk ends," and ask if there's a discount! These end bits of sliced meats are too small to slice in the machine, but can be sliced or cubed at home. They're often offered at half off!

Price Watch

When you're at the supermarket, make sure you keep a close watch while your items are being rung up. A recent study found that 10 percent of items are scanned in at the incorrect price.

Misleading Sales Circulars

Don't be fooled by sales circulars, especially the ones from supermarkets. They often advertise a product just to call attention to it, not because it's on sale. So before you snatch up what you think is a deal, make sure to consider the prices of similar items.

Beware of Sneaky Supermarkets

It's important to know that not *all* products are cheaper when you buy bigger sizes. Make sure to compare unit prices carefully at the store, because we have found that some items—like cereal and prepared frozen foods like French fries—are less expensive in smaller sizes. This is probably because the store knows these items are more likely to be purchased in bulk.

Break Free from Brands

When you've been buying the same brand-name product for as long as you can remember, it's hard to make the switch to generics. However, you'll be surprised when you find many generic and store-brand products taste exactly the same (or better!) for less than half the cost. Always buy generic baking ingredients such as flour, oil, and sugar. These generics are indistinguishable from their more-expensive counterparts. Frozen and canned vegetables are also usually exactly the same. As for products such as cereals, cookies, and crackers, basic is better—we've had good luck with plain granola, potato chips, and wheat crackers. No matter what the product, it never hurts to try. If you end up having to throw away one can of soup, you've wasted a few dollars, but if you like it, you can save a lot over the course of a year.

Look Down!

When shelving items, grocery stores customarily put the least expensive items on the bottom shelves. That's because most customers, when looking for a particular product, will just take the first item they see—at eye-level. When at the market, make sure to check the lower shelves for lower prices.

The Most Important Meal

For a quick and healthy breakfast, make waffles ahead of time, then freeze them. When you or your family is ready to eat, pop them in the toaster to reheat. Making waffles from scratch, rather than buying them in the frozen foods section, will save you money. You can also easily do this with French toast!

Low-Cost Take-Out

If you're considering take-out for dinner, think first of your grocery store. Supermarkets often offer pre-made foods at a low cost to attract shoppers, and you'll often find low prices on rotisserie chickens, French fries, cole-slaw, pasta salad, and more. Just make sure you don't make any impulse purchases once you're in the store!

Lunchtime Tip

If you often order take-out food, consider visiting your favorite restaurants at lunchtime. Most take-out joints offer lunch specials that are the same food as dinner for less. They'll often come in smaller sizes, but we've found that we usually don't need what the restaurant considers dinner-sized portions. Buy in the afternoon, stash in the fridge, and then reheat at dinner for savings!

Belly Up

As if you needed another excuse to sit at the bar, here's one more: Many restaurants offer the same food at the bar as in the main restaurant, but for cheaper prices. You may have to order a few dishes to share since the portions may be smaller, but your savings will still be substantial. And since most restaurants also have table service in the bar area, you can take the kids.

New Favorite
If you're a coffee fiend, you know how costly those delicious coffee-shop lattes can be. If there's a college or university near your home, check out the campus coffee shop for your caffeine fix—it's less expensive and just as good as the local Starbucks.

Not So Crummy

Don't spend money on store-bought breadcrumbs. Set aside a special jar and pour in the crumbs from the bottom of cracker or low-sugar cereal boxes. Also add crumbs from leftover garlic bread and a few dried herbs, and soon you'll have seasoned breadcrumbs! The great thing is that homemade breadcrumbs are even better than store-bought, since their uneven texture helps make them stick.

Intoxicating Tenderizer

Do you tend to buy those tougher, bargain-priced meats at your local supermarket? If so, you can tenderize them without spending extra money on powdered tenderizer. Just let your meat soak in a can's worth of beer for at least an hour, and that should do the job.

The Cheapest Days to Fly

If you're going on a trip and your flight days are flexible, try searching for trips that begin and end on a Tuesday or Wednesday. We've found that flights throughout the US and Canada are cheaper on these slow travel days.

Forgo the Foliage

The best summer vacation you'll ever take might not be in the summer. As soon as Labor Day goes by, the rates go down drastically on hotels and airfare to most vacation destinations. Some of the most-discounted areas are the Caribbean, Hawaii, California, and anywhere else there's a beach. In a warm climate, it will still be as hot as ever on the sand. But the price will be much less, and you'll get the added benefit of having fewer crowds. Check out a travel site like Travelocity.com for good deals to your dream destinations.

Where to Find Cheap Cruises

If you're dying to get away on a cruise, check out CruiseDeals.com, which has packages to Alaska, the Bahamas, Hawaii, Mexico, and just about anywhere else you'd want to go on a boat. The company negotiates with some of the world's biggest lines to bring their customers the best rates on cruises. If you want to hit the water, this is the best place to start.

Time to Go Camping!

Waking up to the sights, sounds, and smells of the forest can be one of the most peaceful things you'll ever experience—not to mention, the most inexpensive vacation you'll take in years. If you've never gone camping, it's time to start! If you don't have any equipment, ask friends if you can borrow theirs in exchange for lending them something of yours. You and your kids will enjoy working together while roughing it (and don't worry, "roughing it" can involve bathrooms and showers, electricity hook-ups, and even wireless internet). Best of all, with all that hard work each day, plus all the room in the world to run around in, your kids will get exhausted fast! To find campsites across the US and Canada, visit ReserveAmerica.com, and for a great article for first-time campers, go to RoadAndTravel.com/adventuretravel/campingfor firsttimers.htm.

Our #1 Piece of Camping Advice

Always, always pack duct tape when you're going camping. It's a must-have to repair rips or holes in tents and air mattresses, and it can be used to string up food out of bears' reach. You can even use it while you're hiking. Tape your pant legs to your boots with duct tape to avoid bites from ticks, flies, and mosquitoes.

Reader's Tip

Save money on car rentals by not renting at the airport, which charges rental car companies concession fees. Instead, take a cab to a nearby location—even with the fare factored in, you'll be surprised how much you save.

—DREY LUCA, CA

Cheaper Rental Alternatives

If you're renting a car for your vacation this year, try Rent-a-Wreck (RentAWreck.com), which offers older cars (that are far from being wrecks, by our standards!) at discounted prices. Do a YellowPages.com search for rental cars in your area and you may find more discounted rental car companies than you ever thought possible! Another plus about these discount companies is that some of them will allow you to rent a car if you only have a debit card (and not a credit card) to put down.

Let's Make a Deal

When digging for discounts on rental cars and hotels, always call the hotel or rental company directly for the best deals. If the only phone number you have is a national, toll-free one, look up the local number for that particular location and speak to them directly instead. The closer you get to your travel date, the better—in fact, don't be afraid to call the day before to confirm your reservation and ask for a better rate.

Keep Scrolling

When searching for travel deals online, make sure to scroll through a few pages of results before making your pick. Many sites have "sponsored results," which means that companies have paid to be featured at the top of search results.

Mail Your Luggage

Especially when you have to pack tons of presents, it's usually more frugal to ship the contents of your suitcase to your destination ahead of time. Most airlines charge between $15 and $30 for the first checked bag and much more for the second, while it only costs around $14 to mail up to 70 pounds via the post office.

Mailing Media

Mailing books, CDs, or DVDs as presents? The cheapest way to get them there is to take your package to the post office and ask for it to be sent "media mail." Though it will take a little longer to get there, this low rate—reserved for mailing "media"—will save you a lot of money, especially if your package is heavy.

Sending Flowers?

If you're sending flowers for a special occasion, skip the national delivery services and websites. Instead, find a flower shop that is local to the recipient and call them directly. Most national services simply charge you a fee, then contact these very same stores themselves.

Reader's Tip

Show your friends you care and save money by making your own cards to send for birthdays or other occasions. Look through old magazines for funny photos (or shots of your friend's celebrity crush) to use for the front. Or for something more complicated, visit Card-Making-World.com for ideas and free backgrounds and embellishments to download. —MICHELLE STEVENS, PORTLAND, OR

Inexpensive Gift Idea

Soaps never seem to lose their appeal as holiday gifts. They're useful and don't add clutter to people's houses (something we're always trying to avoid in ours). You can make your own by grating white, unscented soap into a bowl with warm water. For color, add a few drops of food coloring appropriate for the holiday. Next, add a drop or two of an essential oil (lavender or rose are lovely), then knead like pizza dough and make into little balls. As an alternative, use candy molds for fun shapes. Leave them to dry on wax paper for a day or so.

Suitable For Framing

Instead of spending tons of money on impressive, expensive frames, give your photos a personal touch. Buy the cheap frames at the store and repaint them yourself. Not only will they look almost as good as the expensive kind, you can customize them to perfectly match your home decor.

Housewarm with Houseplants

Clippings from a houseplant make great (and free!) housewarming presents. Cut your plant at the "knuckle" (or joint) section of the stem, then place in a cup of water until it grows roots. To present it, wrap the bottom in a wet paper towel and place in a plastic bag, tying it up with ribbon. Or plant in an old mug!

Free Air Filters

Purify the air in your home without an air filter by buying potted plants that naturally clean your air. Some good choices are rubber trees, corn plants, bamboo palm, ficus, mums, gerbera daisies, English ivy, peace lily, and philodendrons. Always buy houseplants in the spring, when you'll find a better selection and prices that are 20–60 percent cheaper.

When to Buy Home Appliances

If you're looking to buy large appliances or household furnishings like a washing machine, dryer, dishwasher, refrigerator, or sofa, the best time to buy is in October. At this time of year, businesses are busy making room for their holiday inventory, so you'll find tons of sales on last year's merchandise. Go ahead, celebrate a little early!

Furniture Buying

It's nice to be able to look at furniture in person before you buy it, but the internet usually has the cheapest prices. The solution? While you're at the store, write down the piece of furniture's brand and model number (which can usually be found on the price tag). Then type that information into Google and see what prices come up.

Shopping for Electronics?

If you're in the market for a new TV, DVD player, portable music player, or other electronic device, the best time to buy is in the late spring and early summer. Prices will drop because new products are usually introduced in the late summer and early fall. New computers are also often released in February, so shop in January for savings.

Use Your Phone to Check Prices

If you're lucky enough to own an iPhone, Android, or other smartphone, you're also lucky to have access to applications that make shopping easier. Once installed, you can use your phone's camera to take a snapshot of a product's barcode, or you can enter the UPC numbers underneath it. Your phone will then give you a list of how much the item costs at locations near you and online. Search your phone's app store for Barcode Scanner on iPhone and Android, ScanLife on Blackberry, and ShopSavvy for Windows phones. If you don't have a smartphone, you can still easily compare prices online. You don't get to use your phone as a scanner (which is half the fun), but you can enter the UPC code of any product to get prices from around the web by using Google's Product Search (Products.Google.com). Just type in the numbers found near the barcode and away you go!

Rah-Rah for Refurbs

If you're like most people, you probably shy away from buying refurbished electronics, but you shouldn't. We go out of our way to buy refurbs, which not only save cash, but also provide more or less the same level of reliability as brand-new items. Whether it's a cell phone, laptop, gaming console, or television, a refurbished item is arguably less likely to be defective than a new one, because these items are tested at the factory before they're resold. And in the rare instance where a refurb does fail, all of the other refurbs you've bought will have saved you enough money to replace it. Contrary to popular opinion, most refurbished units aren't simply broken items that have been repaired. They may have been returned to the maker for any number of other reasons. A customer may have returned a gift he didn't want, the packaging (but not the actual item) may have been damaged in shipping, the item might have a cosmetic blemish, or the item may have been missing a nonessential accessory. If you can live with those things, then refurbished items are definitely for you. Many of them even come with the original manufacturer's warranty intact.

Return to the Scene for Even More Deals

You're shopping in your favorite store and notice that there are tons of markdowns. After you fill your arms with bargains, go home and mark the day on your calendar! Most stores receive shipments of new goods every 9–12 weeks and discount current merchandise to make room for the new stuff. Return to the store during that time frame to find more deals.

How to Haggle

Before you go to the store, do a little research at competing stores or on the internet beforehand. If you ask a salesperson to match the price at a nearby store, there's a good chance she will. Make sure you're aware of "extras" that the competing stores may be offering. Even if you're not interested in an extended warranty or free engraving at the other place, you can use the incentive to your advantage when bargaining.

Twine Time

If you have a pair of espadrilles whose heels are looking ragged, patch them up with everyday brown twine you can find at the hardware store. Cut the twine into pieces that fit in the gaps and adhere with shoe glue.

Reader's Tip

If the heels on your nicest pair of shoes break or your shoes are starting to wear out, a shoe repair shop will be your best money-saving bet: They'll get your shoes in tip-top shape for much less than the cost of a new pair.

—BRIANNA BYERS QUIGLEY, CARTHAGE, MO

We Love Shoe Color Spray!

Not happy with the color of a handbag or pair of fancy shoes? Instead of buying new accessories, turn that unbecoming chartreuse into an elegant black with a can of shoe color spray. You can pick up an inexpensive can of shoe color from a repair shop, then revamp those heels yourself instead of paying someone else to do it for you.

Take It to the Tailor

Going to a tailor may seem like an expensive proposition, but it's often worth it if you unearth a good deal on a suit or other item of clothing that doesn't quite fit. Found some jeans for ten bucks that look great but are an inch too long? A jacket that's a steal, but a bit too baggy in the arms? For a small price, you can get these items custom-fitted at a tailor. And you'll still be saving a bundle from what the normal retail price would be.

Cut Your Clothing Clutter

Are you afraid you'll be buried in a fabric avalanche every time you open your closet? It's time to take control of your wardrobe. Going through your clothes and figuring out what you have and what you don't need has a lot of money-saving benefits. First of all, you can take unwanted clothes to a resale shop and either make some money or exchange them for new clothes. Secondly, you'll have a better handle on what clothes you need for the season, cutting down on duplicates and making impulse buying less likely. If you tend to buy a lot of items that are similar to each other, try organizing your closet by color, so when you pause by that black polo shirt at the store, you'll remember just how many black short-sleeved shirts you already own.

The Seasonal Shopping Secret

For the best deals on clothes, shop in the off-season. Buy spring and summer clothing in July and August, and fall and winter clothing in January and February. (You can often find the best sales right after the holiday season.) It's sometimes a bummer to buy something you're not going to be able to wear for six months, but when the time comes to switch seasons, you'll be happy you already have some new clothes to wear—all of which were purchased on sale!

> ## New Favorite
>
> In need of some new hangers? Try your local department store. When making a purchase, let the sales clerk know that you'd like to take the hangers too. If you notice any empty hangers lying around the register area, ask for those as well—it couldn't hurt!

Sneaky Cosmetics

When trying to compare a pricey cosmetic with a less-expensive one, you only have to look at one thing: the active ingredients list. Products that have the same active ingredients are going to do almost the exact same thing, even if the percentages are a bit off. (The only thing you might have to worry about is which smells better.) You'll be surprised how many expensive brands—especially hair products like shampoo—have the exact same ingredients in them for vastly higher prices.

Where to Buy Make-Up

No matter where you shop, department stores are usually one of the worst places to buy cosmetics. Because of sales commissions and the cost to rent the space at the store, they're never a bargain. Instead, check out your local grocery store or discount store such as Walmart or Target—they almost always have the exact same brands for much less. If you still can't find your brand, consider switching to another brand you can find. Choose one a good friend uses, and ask her if she'd be willing to buy it from you if you don't like it. It shouldn't be too hard to find one you like just as much that costs much less.

The Truth About Moisturizers

If you're looking for a way to cut back on your cosmetics budget, the first place to start is with your moisturizer. Whether it's night cream, day cream, anti-aging lotion, or anti-wrinkle solution, it's all pretty much the same. Pick a moisturizer with an SPF of at least 15—other than that, go with a less expensive brand whose smell you like. Your wallet will know the difference, but your face never will.

The Best Part of Waking Up

If you love the perfume section of the department
store, but sometimes get overwhelmed by all the scents,
try out this trick: Just bring a cup of coffee with you!
After you sniff one perfume, smell your coffee (or take
a sip). You'll be able to smell the next scent fully, as if
you just walked up to the perfume counter.

Stylists in Progress

Get your hair cut on the cheap by students who are
studying to be beauticians. You may risk a less-than-
professional 'do, but generally speaking, the students

are supervised by trained instructors, who can fix any mis-snipping that might occur. Student haircuts are also great for kids, whose simple cuts are usually hard to screw up. To find a beauty school near you, simply look up "beauty schools" in the Yellow Pages or online.

Trim on the Cheap

If you're used to getting an expensive haircut, it's hard to switch to a bargain salon such as Supercuts. But what you can do to save yourself hundreds of dollars a year is to get a hairstyle that doesn't need a lot of up-keep. When you need a trim in between cuts, go to an inexpensive salon. While hairstylists at the bargain salons sometimes can't give you the fancy cut you want, they can usually handle a simple trim, following the path of your normal stylist. If you just need your bangs cut, ask at your usual salon if they offer free bang trims in between cuts.

Skip the Dry

If you want to save at the hair salon, ask if you can get a discount if you skip the blow dry at the end. Many salons will knock at least $5 off the price. Even if you don't want to walk out of the salon with a wet head of hair, this is a great tip for kids' cuts, since kids often don't like getting their hair dried anyway.

Get Groomed for Less

The busiest days at the pet groomer's are Friday, Saturday, Sunday, and Monday. Find a groomer who offers discounts on Tuesdays through Thursdays, or ask your groomer if she will offer you a discount for coming midweek.

Pet Health Help

Pet medications are often insanely expensive. Luckily, we've discovered Omaha Vaccine, which offers great deals on meds that cost more elsewhere. Search for your pets' medications at OmahaVaccine.com, and get free shipping for orders over $35.

Save on Your Pet's Care

We all love our pets and will go to any lengths to make sure they are happy and healthy, but this shouldn't mean taking out a second mortgage to pay vet bills. Look at your local shelter to see what services they provide. Many will spay/neuter and administer vaccinations and annual shots for less than half the price of your friendly neighborhood vet.

Birthday Party Saver

Having a birthday party for your child? Consider serving cupcakes instead of one large cake, which will eliminate the need for forks and paper plates—and save you money.

Hire Some Birthday Fun

If you're hosting a party that requires you to hire someone like a clown, face painter, or bartender, head to your local college first. There, you'll find hundreds of young people who will do the job for a lot less than a pro. Put up an ad near the cafeteria, and stop by the careers office to see if they have an online "bulletin board."

Save on Your Tree Skirt

Don't waste your money on an expensive tree skirt this Christmas. Instead, look for a small, round tablecloth from a department store—they usually have a big selection and they're inexpensive, too. Cut a round opening in the center for the tree stand, and a straight line to one edge. Place the opening in the back of the tree and you're done.

Do It With Ribbon

Used wisely, a little holiday ribbon can go a long way. Wrap it around just about anything—a vase, throw pillow, lampshade, curtain, pillar candle, and the list goes on—to create a festive atmosphere at little or no cost.

Easy Easter Egg Dye

Never, ever pay for egg dye! Simply mix ½ cup boiling water with ½ teaspoon white vinegar, and add food coloring until you get a hue you like. For a striped egg even the Easter Bunny would be proud of, wrap tape around the egg before dipping. Once the egg dries, remove the tape, tape over the colored parts, and dip again in a different color. You can also use stickers in the shapes of hearts, stars, and letters.

Add Halloween Atmosphere

Adding stretchy cobwebs to the doorjambs and corners of your home is a great way to add Halloween flair to the entire house. Instead of buying the ones packaged as spider webs, though, simply go to a craft store and buy a bag of fiberfill. It's the exact same stuff, and a 16-ounce bag of fiberfill is less than half the cost. You can usually find bags of plastic spider rings for super-cheap at party supply or superstores—add them to the webs and on tables around your house for more atmosphere, and encourage your guests to take them home!

New Favorite

The cheapest time to refuel your car is on Tuesday and Wednesday. People fuel up on Thursdays and Fridays for weekend trips, and on Monday for their workweek. Therefore, most gas stations do their weekly price changes on Tuesdays or Wednesdays.

Stop Topping Off

Have you ever "topped off" your car's gas tank to round out the price at the pump? You should know that since the pump is only pumping out vapors at that point, they're automatically sucked back into the gas station's tank. In other words, even though you now have exact change, you didn't get any extra gas!

Gas-Buying Secret

Planning a road trip this summer? When it's time to fill up on gas, drive a little farther off the highway exit before choosing a station. The gas stations closest to the highway will often charge more per gallon than the ones located a bit off your course—you could save a few bucks by going the extra distance.

Key to Key Batteries

When your car's keyless remote needs a new battery, don't head to the dealership for a replacement—depending on the kind of car you have, it can cost any-where from $50 to $150. Instead, pry open your remote and check the size and type of battery you need. Then head to a hardware or electronics store for a much-cheaper alternative.

Free Floor Mats

If your car's floor mats need to be replaced, consider going to a carpet store and finding some samples to use instead. You'll always be able to find samples that are gray or another color to match your car's interior, and best of all, they're free!

New Favorite

Chips in your car's paint job can be expensive to fix, so before you head to the auto body shop, see if you can find a crayon that closely matches the color of your car. Fill in the nick with the crayon, and then buff gently. This works especially well with minor scratches!

Spend Less on Car Washes

Pricey specialty items used to clean cars are often found in big-box home improvement and hardware stores. However, you'll find the same items—squeegees, shams, and sponges—for much less in the cleaning aisle of your local grocery store.

Tuning Tip

The perfect time to take your car to the mechanic is while you're on vacation! The mechanic can take all the time he needs to fix any recurring problems and give it a tune-up, so you know it will get special care. Most mechanics don't mind keeping your car until you get back from your trip so that they can get more time to work on it!

Make Yours a Go-To Garage Sale

It's time for that yard sale you've been talking about all these years! Make it a success by advertising ahead of time—putting up flyers around your neighborhood and placing a free ad on Craigslist.org are two good ways to start. Ask your neighbors if they, too, have things to sell—people will be more likely to come out if you can state that it's a "whole-block sale" or a "multiple-family yard sale." Remember that people are bargain hunting, so don't set the prices of your items too high. Post a sign that states you're willing to bargain on the prices to make sure no one walks away because they don't want to pay the price you've set. And finally, remember to have fun! Look at it as an excuse to sit outside and meet people from your community, and you won't get too stressed.

New Favorite

The best time to have a garage sale is just after the 15th of the month. Many people will have just gotten paid, but paid their rent on the 1st. This means they'll have a little extra money to spend on your wares.

CHAPTER 3

USING FUEL FRUGALLY

It Pays to Restart Your Engine

Let us solve the "should I turn off the engine?" argument for you forever: If you are waiting longer than 30 seconds in your car, turn off the engine. You use more fuel idling after 30 seconds than you use to restart your car.

New Favorite

Backing into a parking spot so you're ready to just simply drive out when you restart your car isn't just a way to show off—it can save energy. Getting the car into a spot takes more energy than driving because you're moving the car into the different gears, as well as starting and stopping. Having the car do this work at the end of a drive rather than at the beginning of one saves energy because at the end of a drive your car's engine is already warm.

Keep It Shady

One of the easiest ways to save on fuel costs for your car is to park in the shade on summer days! The air conditioning is one of the most fuel-draining parts of your car. Having to cool your car back down to a non-sweltering temperature uses a lot more gas than you might think! Also make sure to invest in a sun-blocking windshield shade if you do have to park in a hot spot.

Chore Day

To save on gas, make one long trip for all your errands rather than making several short trips. Not only will you be driving a shorter total distance, but the Department of Energy also reports that several short trips beginning from a cold start use almost twice as much energy as a single trip of the same length. In other words, keeping your engine warm means your car doesn't have to work as hard.

Consider Your Route

When running errands, pick the best route for your fuel efficiency. Stopping and starting and going up hills will cause you to use more gas. Consider taking a route that will allow you to make fewer adjustments as you are driving, even if it takes a little longer.

Roll Them Up

Roll up your windows on the highway. Having the wind streaming through your hair might be fun, but it increases drag on the car and takes more energy to run. In this case, it's actually usually cheaper to run the AC.

It's In the Tires

One easy way to save on gas is simply to keep your tires inflated. It's much harder for your engine to get your car to move when your tires are even a little flat. Invest in a gauge, and make sure to keep them as inflated as possible without over-inflating.

Reader's Tip

Does your mechanic, tire store, or gas station offer nitrogen fills for your tires? Because nitrogen is lighter than regular air, it makes them move more easily, saving your car fuel. Look for places that offer them free with a tune-up or tire purchase. This is one add-on that's worth the money!

—DAN HUFFSTETLER, COLORADO SPRINGS, CO

All About Oil

Change your oil regularly and you'll have to fill up on gas less often. As oil ages, it gets thicker and harder to push through the engine, causing more energy to be used. By changing your oil regularly, you'll make sure you get the best fuel economy possible.

How's Your Filter?

A clean air filter can improve your car's mileage by up to 10 percent, so make sure yours is replaced regularly. It should be changed at least every 8,000 miles, but if you live in a sandy or highly polluted area, you should change it more often. A good rule of thumb is simply to have the filter changed when you get your oil changed.

Goodbye, Speedy Gonzales

One of the easiest ways to save on gas? Stay under the speed limit. Your car will begin to lose fuel efficiency once it gets over 60 m.p.h., so go a little slower and you'll not only save, you'll be safer.

Reader's Tip

We bought a mini-van that has a luggage rack, but we find that we almost never use it unless we're on a long vacation. If that applies to you, too, then you should remove the rack until you actually need it. Driving with the rack on top increases wind drag and helps kill your gas mileage. Removing it can be a real money-saver.

—FRANCESCA R., PORTLAND, OR

Lose Some Weight

To make your car more fuel efficient, remove any excess weight from inside. Take anything heavy out of your trunk or backseat that doesn't need to be there (kids don't count). An extra 100 pounds in your car can decrease your miles per gallon by 2 percent.

Roll Them Up

Roll up your windows on the highway. Having the wind streaming through your hair might be fun, but it increases drag on the car and takes more energy to run. In this case, it's actually usually cheaper to run the AC.

Spring for the Seat Warmers

Heated seats in your car may seem like a luxury, but they can actually be a huge money-saver. Heated seats don't have to use as much energy as your car's heating vents to keep you warm. If they aren't offered when you buy your car, consider getting a heated pad for your seat or even having heated seats installed after-market.

Keep It Humid

It's true that it's not the heat that makes you feel warm, it's the humidity. Humid air feels warmer than dry air, so in the winter, instead of cranking up the heat, run a humidifier. This allows you to turn down the heat, save energy, and still feel comfortable. Live, leafy plants also help raise humidity levels.

New Favorite

Do your kids have lots of stuffed animals? This winter, put those they play with less often to good use: Line them up in front of their bedroom windows to prevent drafts from coming in underneath.

Lock Your Windows

In the winter, don't just keep windows closed, make sure they're locked for the tightest possible seal. This could greatly reduce drafts.

More Radiator Power

Brrr, it's cold in here! Wrap a very large piece of corrugated cardboard in aluminum foil (shiny side out), and place it behind your free-standing radiator. The foil will reflect the heat, and you won't have to keep telling your landlord to turn up the boiler.

Dust Buster

Make sure to vacuum your heating and air conditioning vents regularly. When they get caked up with dust your furnace or air conditioner has to work much harder! For the best energy efficiency, make sure to keep them dust-free.

Reader's Tip

Close the heating and air-conditioning vents in rooms in your home you don't frequently use, like a guest room or laundry room. If your vents don't have closures, simply seal them off with duct tape. —BARBIE RODGERS, WILMINGTON, NC

Look for Leaks!

According to the Environmental Protection Agency, a well-sealed home can be up to 20 percent more energy efficient than its leakier counterpart. Most leaks occur in the basement or attic—look where you feel a draft or around wiring holes, plumbing vents, ducts, and basement rim joints. You'll be able to seal lots of leaks with a simple caulking gun, but for instructions on how to plug larger holes, go to EnergyStar.gov and search for "plug leaks."

A Ceiling Fan Can Keep You Warm Too

Don't let your fan go to waste just because it's no longer warm outside. To stay toasty during the frigid days of winter, hit the reverse switch to push hot air down into your room.

Ensure Accurate Temperature

For accurate temperature readings, make sure to place your thermostat away from sources of artificial heat, like ovens, appliances, computers, or direct sunlight. An inaccurately high temperature at the thermostat will cause the rest of the house to be colder than you want it to be. Similarly, make sure that cold air, such as that from windows or wiring holes, isn't making its way to the thermostat either. Also, ensure your thermostat is reading the inside room temperature and not the outside temperature.

Ease Your Energy Bill

Even when you're not using appliances, they still continue to use energy. So pull the plug when you're done with the blender, toaster, food processor, even your television—everything except appliances that need constant power to preserve a special setting.

Dishwasher Tip

Much of the energy your dishwasher uses is during the dry cycle, when it heats up water to the point of steam. To save energy, turn off the dry cycle (or simply open your dishwasher after the rinse cycle is done). Leave the door open a crack and let your dishes drip-dry. You'll save a lot by avoiding the heat-drying cycle on your machine, and your glasses will streak less.

Fabulously Full Freezer

Your freezer is more energy efficient when it's full of stuff, so don't be shy about stuffing it as much as possible. When you're running low on food items, just fill a few empty juice cartons or soda bottles with water and use them to fill up the space.

Leaky Fridge?

If your refrigerator is more than a few years old, the rubber lining that runs around the door (also known as the gasket) could be loose. To find out, close the door on a piece of paper. If you can pull it out without it ripping, your gasket is loose. To figure out where, turn on a battery-powered lamp or flashlight and place it in your fridge. Turn the lights off in your kitchen and close the door. Wherever you see light peeking through, cold air is leaking! Try regluing your gasket or buying a new one from wherever you purchased your fridge.

New Favorite

To save energy and keep your food cooler, first clean your refrigerator door's gasket (that rubber lining that goes around it), then rub it with petroleum jelly to ensure a tighter seal.

Your Dryer's Best Friend

Add a big, dry towel to the clothes dryer when drying jeans and other bulky items. It will cut the drying time significantly.

Make Sure That Lint Screen Is Clean!

Removing the lint from the screen in your dryer may not be enough to make sure it is running as efficiently as possible. The fabric softener used in dryer sheets can get caught in the mesh, even if you can't see it. To be sure you're completely cleaning the screen, remove it and clean it with warm, soapy water and a brush. Leave it out to dry completely before placing back in your dryer.

Heat Less Water

You never use your water on full-blast hot anyway, so it's worth it to lower how hot you keep your water heater. You can save up to $125 per year by simply lowering the thermostat on your hot water heater from 140° to 120°F.

Buy Your Water Heater a Jacket

A water heater insulation jacket (also called a blanket) costs $15–$35, but it can cut the cost to heat your water dramatically. By insulating your water heater, you'll cut down on the amount of energy it needs to use to heat standing water in half, also cutting down on the amount you need to pay. To find out if you need a water heater jacket, touch the side of it. If it's warm, it's leaking energy.

> ### New Favorite
> If your toilet runs for a long time after each flush, you're wasting water! If the problem is that the valve gets stuck open when the flapper chain gets tangled, here's an easy fix: Simply cut a straw so it's about 6 inches long, then thread the chain through it. It will keep the chain from tangling, ensuring that the valve closes properly.

Leaky Toilets Mean Higher Water Bills

Does your toilet have a leak? To find out, put a drop of food coloring in the tank and see if it shows up in the bowl. If it does, fix the leak to save up to 73,000 gallons of water per year!

Replace Those Showerheads!

If the showerheads in your home were installed before 1994, you should seriously consider replacing them with their modern, energy-saving equivalents. Check out your local hardware store for low-flow alternatives, and remember that just because it's low-flow doesn't mean it has to be weak!

CHAPTER 4

MAKING EVERYTHING LAST LONGER

Repair a Braided Rug

If your braided rug is coming undone, try repairing it with a hot glue gun. Just lay down some newspaper, then carefully apply a small amount of glue in between the braids. Press them back together again and hold for a few seconds for the glue to dry.

Make Colors Last

Brighten faded rugs by rubbing them down with a rag that has been soaked in salt water, then wrung out. You can also submerge throw rugs and drapes in a solution of salt water, then wash as usual.

Longer-Lasting Clothes

The easiest way to make your clothes last longer is to wash them less. Many of your clothes can be worn several times before you wash them, especially sweaters. Most items get more wear and tear from being in the washing machine than they do on your bodies! When you do throw in a load, make sure to turn knitted clothes and T-shirts with designs on them inside out when washing and drying.

New Favorite

Rotate through your bras rather than wear one for a few days in a row. You'll give the elastic time to contract and the bras will last longer. Who knew?

Restore Worn Velvet

If your velvet dress, shawl, shirt, or pants are getting a shiny mark from too much wear, you may be able to remove it. Try lightly spraying the area with water, then rubbing against the grain with an old toothbrush.

Sweater Saver

If your favorite cashmere or angora sweater is looking a little worn, put it in a plastic bag and place it in the freezer for half an hour. The cold causes the fibers to expand, making your sweater look new again! Who knew there was such a thing as sweater cryogenics?

Cuff 'Em

Are the cuffs of your favorite sweater starting to get stretched out? Make them like new again by blowing them with hot air from your hairdryer! Just wet the cuffs with water, set the hairdryer on its highest setting, and then blow-dry until no longer wet. The heat will shrink the cuffs slightly, bringing them back down to the right size.

Storing Sweaters

When putting away your sweaters for the spring and summer months, wrap them in newspaper and tape the sides. The newspaper will keep away both moths and moisture.

Never Lose a Button

Dab a small drop of clear nail polish on the front of a button to keep the threads in place and never lose a button again.

Shiny Pearls for Life

Pearl buttons, whether they're real or fake, can benefit from a coating of clear nail polish. They'll never lose their shine, and it will be harder to nick them.

Revive Water Resistant Items

Do you have a jacket, backpack, or tent that used to be water resistant, but has lost its effectiveness over time? Set your hair dryer to its highest setting and blow air evenly over it. The warmth will reactivate the coating on the cloth that makes it repel water.

Bag Your Purses

If you're putting away a purse you don't think you'll use for a few weeks or months, stuff some plastic grocery bags inside. This will ensure the purse keeps its shape—and give you something to do with those bags!

Medication Storage

Store all your medications in a cool, dry spot in your home, such as a linen closet or kitchen cabinet. Contrary to popular belief, medications do *not* belong in a bathroom medicine cabinet, where the heat and humidity will cause them to go bad more quickly.

Perfume Storage Secret

Perfume and cologne are very volatile—the fragrance breaks down rapidly when exposed to heat and air. If you're not going to use the entire bottle within 30 days, store it in the refrigerator to extend its life.

Make Perfume Last Longer

Before putting on a splash of your favorite scent, rub a bit of petroleum jelly on your skin. It will keep your fragrance from fading.

More Fridge Friends

The refrigerator is the perfect place to store hydrogen peroxide—the cold temperature will help it stay active for a longer period. Nail polish is another chemical that likes the cold. It will last longer if you keep it in the refrigerator, but bring it up to room temperature before your manicure.

Reader's Tip

Transfer your shampoo, conditioner, and body wash into pump bottles. Your products will not only be easier to dispense, but you'll make sure not to use too much. One pump is all you should need! —ALEXIS RAIZEN-RUBENSTEIN

A "Handy" Tip

If you've got kids who never seem to know when enough is enough, add water to your hand soap. Your hands will get just as clean, but the soap will last longer! You can also buy foaming soap dispensers, which are good for keeping the amount of soap you use to a minimum.

The Best Place to Store Soap

If you've just purchased a new bar of soap, take it out of its box or wrapper and place it in your linen closet. Being exposed to the air will make the soap harden slightly, which will help it last longer. Meanwhile, it will freshen your closet while it's waiting to be used in the shower.

Save Your Soap

Don't throw out those last few slivers of soap! Instead, cut a slice into the side of a body sponge and slip them inside. Now lather up and rinse. You'll get so many soapsuds, you probably won't need to repeat.

Strong Foundations

Some of the most expensive kinds of make-up are foundation and powder. Make it last longer by buying a shade darker than your natural shade, then mixing it with moisturizer (for foundation), or baby powder (for powder) until it matches your normal color. You'll have more than twice as much, and you'll never be able to tell the difference!

For the Fullest Lashes

To make your mascara last longer (and your lashes look fuller than ever), apply two coats every time you do your lashes. But here's the secret! In between the first and second coats, apply a thin layer of baby powder with a make-up brush. The mascara will adhere to the powder, making it stay on your lashes longer.

Out of Mascara?

Applying the finishing touches to your make-up and realize you're out of mascara? Here's a great tip to get that last bit out of the tube. Simply roll the tube quickly between your hands for 30 seconds. The heat generated by the friction is enough to soften the mascara stuck to the sides of the tube, so you'll have just enough to apply to your lashes before you run out the door.

Cosmetics Care

Many forms of make-up are sensitive to the sun due to their preservatives. Make sure to keep your make-up away from the window to ensure it lasts as long as possible.

For Fresher Flowers

Who doesn't love a bouquet of flowers displayed in a vase? Unfortunately, it's not always easy to keep your display looking fresh and beautiful. To prevent flowers from wilting, gently spray the undersides of petals and leaves with a little bit of hairspray. It really works!

Reader's Tip

Most powdered flower "food" works by lowering the pH level of the water, so that it's still good for fresh flowers, but bad for any bacteria that may want to grow. You won't be surprised to hear, however, that we've come up with a cheaper way to lower the pH of your flowers' water— aspirin! Just crush a tablet or two into the water each time you change it, and your flowers will last as long as if you were using the expensive stuff.

—ADRIAN AMOS, HASSON HEIGHTS, PA

Make Cut Flowers Last

Just bought a beautiful bouquet of flowers? Before you put them in the vase, make sure to trim off the ends of the stems under water. Cutting the stems gets rid of any dead part of the flowers, while doing it underwater ensures that air bubbles won't get caught in the stems while cutting. Without air bubbles, water travels up the stems more easily, keeping your blooms fresher for a longer amount of time.

Tip from a Pro

Florists do it, so why not you? If you have room in your refrigerator, place your entire vase of flowers inside when you go to bed each night. The cooler temperature will preserve your flowers when you're not awake to enjoy them.

Longer-Lasting Blooms

To prolong the life of your flower bouquet, simply replace the water each day, rinsing off the bottom of the stems as you do. This will discourage the growth of bacteria while making sure it gets the nutrients it needs.

Flower Food

To prolong the life of cut flowers without using commercial plant food, add 2 tablespoons vinegar and 1 teaspoon sugar to the water.

Refresh Potpourri

If your favorite potpourri loses its scent, it's easy to revive—with vodka. Yep, you read that right. Just pour a little vodka into a spray bottle and spritz the potpourri, mixing it up so each piece is saturated.

Endless Candles

Store your candles in the freezer. Once you light them, they'll go hours before they start dripping.

Eternal Flame

If you have a favorite candle, you might wince each time you go to light it, knowing it will eventually be gone. Yet letting it sit unused on the shelf seems like bad feng shui. As a compromise, try this: Let your favorite candle be a candleholder. When there's a big enough hole worn down the middle, put another, smaller candle inside and light that one. Votive candles work well and can be easily replaced when they burn down.

Rejuvenate a Cedar Chest

Cedar chests are wonderful because they not only look great, but their scent keeps moths away, too. But what to do when they begin to lose their scent? Get out some fine sandpaper and go to work! Gently sanding the inside of the chest will bring its scent back to life, making sure your clothes are safe and your room smells wonderful.

Reader's Tip

Don't keep your good wood furniture in direct sunlight, especially during the hot summer. It damages the finish and can bleach the wood. —ALPHONSO BANKS, DESOTO, TX

The Only Way to Dry Wood

If a piece of your wooden furniture or a wooden windowsill has gotten wet, resist the urge to dry it out with a space heater or hair dryer, as too much heat will make wood crack and warp. Instead, keep the area at room temperature and aim a fan at it.

Coffee Can-Do

If you need to repair a hole in a piece of wood, add a small amount of instant coffee to the Spackle, or to a thick paste made from laundry starch and warm water. The coffee tints the paste to camouflage the patched-up spot.

Staining Secret

If you allow wood to "weather" before you apply a stain, the stain will last years longer. It's a case where patience pays off. Let wood sit for several months before putting on the varnish.

Wham, Rattan, Thank You Ma'am

Make sure your wicker patio furniture lasts through the fall and winter, no matter where you store it. Lightly brush it with a small amount of vegetable oil and the wicker or rattan will stay supple. In the spring and summer months, keep it from yellowing in the sun by bathing it in saltwater with a wet rag at the beginning of the season.

Repel Rust on Furniture

Here's an easy tip for making sure your metal deck furniture doesn't rust: Just apply a small amount of petroleum jelly in any corners, where parts meet, and other places that tend to rust.

Feeling a Bit Rusty?

Don't just toss your garden tools in a bin or bucket when you're done with them; they'll eventually rust. To prevent this, submerge the metal parts in a bucket of sand whenever the tools are not in use. (Better yet, add some mineral oil to the sand.) Make sure the sand is stored in a dry place where rainwater can't get into it, though. If you decide you don't want to store your tools in sand, then a good thing to do is to toss a handful of tea leaves in whatever container you keep them in. For whatever reason, the leaves will help keep the metal nice, new, and rust-free.

Special Tip for Shears

Make sure your garden shears never rust with a little car wax. Just rub a little paste over the shears (including the hinge) to prevent them from ever getting stuck again.

Wooden Tools Need Love, Too

Care for wooden garden tools as you would your skin—moisturize! Over time, wood dries out and splinters. Apply a thin coat of linseed oil to wooden handles on rakes and shovels; it'll keep them safe and usable. A little goes a long way, so use the oil sparingly.

Store Your Hose Properly for Maximum Usage

Your garden hose will last twice as long if you store it coiled, rather than folded. Note that the hose will be easiest to work with when it's neither very cold nor very hot outside.

Coil Your Cord

Do you have a long extension cord you use with your electric mower, weed-whacker, or power washer? Keep it from getting tangled and running all over your garden's plants with a big bucket. Drill a hole in the bottom of the bucket and run the end of the cord through it. Then coil the rest of the cord inside. The cord will easily pull out and then coil back up when you're finished.

Beachy Keen

When you're headed to the beach, make sure to keep your electronics in plastic freezer bags. Sand can easily get inside cell phones, MP3 players, and other electronics, interfering with their inner circuits. To make sure your electronics last, keep them covered—plastic bags make the perfect see-through barrier.

For the Last Drop

If your electronic gadget starts to lose its juice, try this trick before you buy new batteries: Take the batteries out and rub their contacts with a pencil eraser. This will remove small particles of dust and dirt that keep the energy from flowing. Put the batteries back in and you'll be surprised at how much longer they last!

Free-Flowing Electronics

Use a pencil eraser to wipe off the metal contacts on rechargeable items such as your cordless phone and drill and they'll get a better charge. You can also use this trick for your cell phone and iPod.

New Favorite

An easy way to save money on batteries is to keep in mind what household appliances use more battery power than others. Some items, like remote controls, kitchen timers, wall clocks, and small toys need much less juice than digital cameras, large toys, wireless devices, and other power-intensive electronics. When the batteries in a high-powered electronic "die," use them in an electronic that uses less battery power, and you'll still get several weeks or more out of them.

Battery Booster

Batteries will last longer if they're stored in the refrigerator. To boost their energy, place them in the sun for a day before you use them.

Cool Charge

You've just realized your cell phone's battery is about to die, but you're at work and don't have your charger. Get a little more talk time by detaching the battery and placing it in your workplace's freezer, then allowing it to come back up to room temperature before you use it. The cold will keep your battery from losing a single drop of juice.

Safely Store Important Papers

The school year is over, and you need a place to store the kids' artwork and diplomas. Try rolling them tightly in paper towel tubes so they won't crease, then label the outside, so you know what's what. The tubes can also be used to store marriage certificates and other important documents.

Saving Newspaper Mementos

To preserve special newspaper clippings, dissolve a Milk of Magnesia tablet in a shallow pan with a quart of club soda. Soak the paper for an hour, then let it lay flat to dry. Afterward, it's best to keep the paper under plastic in a photo album.

Reinforce Folders

For a pocket folder you know is going to take a beating —like the one we keep near our tool kit that holds instructions—reinforce it on the sides and pockets with duct tape. It will last forever!

How to Store Stamp Pads

Always store stamp pads upside down. This will ensure that they don't dry out in between uses.

The Last Bit of Ink

Here's a trick used by office workers everywhere: When your printer's out of ink, remove the cartridge and shake it up for a bit. Stick it back into the printer, and you'll find it's got enough ink left for at least a few more print jobs.

New Favorite

You're trying to print out a document, but you just ran out of ink! Save yourself a trip to the store: Take out the ink cartridge, then blow hot air on it with a hair dryer. Once it's warm, put it back in the printer. The heat loosens the ink stuck to the side of the cartridge, giving you enough to finish the job.

Prolong the Lives of Your Cookbooks

A well-worn cookbook is a good sign, but company shouldn't be able to guess your favorite recipes just by inspecting the splatters. So here is yet another use for one of the million plastic bags taking over your pantry: Use one to cover the binding and pages surrounding the recipe you are using. Then to keep the book open and the pages clean, just place it under a glass pie plate—unless you're making pie, of course!

For a No-Scratch Stack

Stacking fine china? Insert paper plates between the real plates before stacking to prevent scratches.

Raise a Glass

To prevent glasses from becoming dusty, place them upside down on shelves. Arrange in order of size so they are easier to find and also to avoid breakages.

Saving Wine

Wondering what to do with leftover wine (besides drinking it, of course)? Keep it fresh by putting whatever is left in a small container such as a jam jar. This limits the amount of air the wine is put in contact with, keeping it fresh. Incidentally, that is the same thing those expensive "wine vacuum sealers" do!

Non-Sham Champagne

Champagne lost its fizz? Place a raisin in the glass and the last bits of carbon dioxide that remain will cling to the raisin, then be released again as bubbles. You can also try throwing a few raisins into the bottle before you make the final pour.

New Favorite

To make the bubbles in your soda last longer, decrease the amount of air that the carbon dioxide (which causes the fizz) has to escape into. This is easily accomplished by squeezing in the sides of the bottle after you pour a glass.

How to Save Your Cream

If your cream or half-and-half has begun to develop an "off" odor, but you desperately need it for your coffee, try mixing in 1/8 teaspoon baking soda, which will neutralize the lactic acid that is causing the cream to sour. Before you use the cream, however, taste it to be sure the flavor is still acceptable.

Tea Saver

Want to get more for your money when it comes to tea? Always buy the loose variety, and then use one-third of what's recommended. Just let the tea steep a little longer, and it will taste exactly the same as if you used the full amount.

Soften Brown Sugar

If you find that the contents of your brown sugar box have become one giant lump, wrap the box in a ball of foil and bake in a 350° oven for five minutes. It will be back to its old self in no time.

New Favorite
When it comes to preserving whole, unshelled nuts it's the freezer to the rescue again. Storing nuts in the freezer will keep their oils from going rancid, which means they'll keep for up to a year.

Better Buttering

When you finish a stick of butter, don't throw away the paper wrapper. Instead, fold it in half and store it in a plastic bag. Next time you need to butter a bowl or pan, use this paper—it's easy and neat!

Keep Leftover Cake Moist

If you have leftover cake, you have more self-control than we do! One of the best methods of keeping the insides of a cake from drying out is to place a piece of fresh white bread next to the exposed surface. The bread can be affixed with a toothpick or a short piece of spaghetti.

Celery Helper

Bread stays fresh for a longer time if you place it in an airtight bag with a stalk of celery. If you are going to freeze a loaf of bread, make sure you include a paper towel in the package to absorb moisture. This will keep the bread from becoming mushy when thawed.

Reader's Tip

If you find that your bread often goes stale before you use it, slice it and store it in the freezer. Separate out slices and let them sit for about five minutes at room temperature to defrost, or stick them directly in the toaster. Frozen bread is also great to use for grilled cheese sandwiches—it's much easier to butter, and it will defrost as it cooks in the pan.

—TORRANCE DUNLAP

Revive Stale Bread

Bread gone stale? Simply wet your fingers and flick some water on the top and sides of the loaf. Then wrap in foil and heat in a preheated 250° oven for 10 minutes. It will taste fresh again!

Fish Safety

Seafood is responsible for a lot of food poisoning, but it's perfectly safe and very healthy if handled correctly. If you can't use the fish immediately, remove it from its original wrapping and rinse in cold water. Wrap it loosely in plastic wrap, store in the coldest part of the refrigerator, and use within two days. Store ready-to-eat fish such as smoked mackerel separately from raw fish.

Perfect Leftovers

When storing a cooked roast in the fridge, place it back into its own juices whenever possible. When reheating sliced meat, place it in a casserole dish with lettuce leaves between each of the slices. The lettuce provides just the right amount of moisture to keep the slices from drying out.

Leftover Rice

Rice can be stored in the fridge for a longer amount of time if you store a slice of toast on top of it. The toast will absorb excess moisture and keep the rice fluffy and fresh.

Making Condiments Last

It's frustrating to have to throw out condiments like sour cream, mayo, yogurt, and mustard because you didn't use the entire container before it went bad. However, you can easily combat this by changing containers as you use up the item. Using a smaller container exposes the condiment to less air—and fewer bacteria. The trick, of course, is making sure you successfully transfer every bit of mayo possible from the jar to the tiny Tupperware. We usually do our container downsizing right before we're about to use the condiment on something. That way, we can scrape out what we don't transfer for our sandwiches.

Milk Saver

Adding a teaspoon of baking soda or a pinch of salt to a carton of milk will keep it fresh for a week or so past its expiration date.

Milk Matters

It's better to store milk on an inside shelf toward the back of the refrigerator, not on the door. Why? All dairy products are very perishable. The optimal refrigeration temperature is actually just over 32°F; however, few refrigerators are ever set at or hold that low a temperature. Most home refrigerators remain around 40°F, and the temperature rises every time the door is opened. Store cheese near the bottom of the refrigerator, where temperature fluctuations are minimal.

Freezing Milk

When you know your milk is going to go bad before you can use up the rest of it, separate it out into a few resealable containers and put them in your freezer. That's right, milk can be frozen! If you use skim milk, it can be thawed and drunk later, and you'll never be able to tell the difference in taste. For other varieties of milk, after thawing, use for sauces or baking. This is a great strategy for when you find milk at a deep discount. Buy as much as you can and freeze for later!

Reader's Tip

Inside the fridge, margarine and butter quickly absorb odors from other foods. Make sure you always keep them tightly sealed to keep them at their best quality.

—RACHEL CARR, BERLIN, NH

The Upside-Down Egg

To avoid the absorption of refrigerator odors, always store eggs in their original carton on an inside shelf of the refrigerator. Before you put away the carton, though, turn each egg upside down. Storing eggs with the tapered end down maximizes the distance between the yolk and the air pocket, which may contain bacteria. The yolk is more perishable than the white, and even though it is more or less centered in the egg, the yolk can shift slightly and will move away from possible contamination.

Save Your Yolks

Believe it or not, you can save egg yolks for later use. If you have used egg whites in a recipe and want to save the yolks, slide them into a bowl of water, cover with plastic wrap, and store in the refrigerator for a day or two. It beats throwing them out!

Forever Eggs

For eggs that last practically forever, separate them into whites and yolks, then freeze them separately in a lightly oiled ice-cube tray. When frozen, pop them out and store in separate plastic bags in the freezer. These frozen eggs are perfect for baking, and will last longer since they're separated. Egg-cellent!

Reader's Tip

To keep your ice cream from getting freezer burn, it's as easy as storing it in the freezer upside down, with a bit of plastic wrap under the cover. The inverted position will keep ice crystals from forming, and since it's frozen, you don't have to worry about the ice cream leaking all over your freezer.   —LIZ HOBKIRK, WADDINGTON, NY

Keep Cheese Fresher!

To keep cheese fresh and moist, wrap it in a cloth dampened in white vinegar and put it in an airtight container.

Sugar's Sweet Tooth

Cheese will stay mold-free longer if placed in a sealed plastic container with a tight-fitting lid. Add three or four sugar cubes, which will attract any mold if some does form.

Cheesy Freezer Tips

Believe it or not, you can successfully freeze many varieties of cheese without them losing their taste or texture. Cut into small blocks, place in sealed plastic bags, and then keep in the freezer for when you need them. Cheese varieties that can be frozen are Brick, Cheddar, Camembert, Edam, Gouda, Mozzarella, Muenster, Parmesan, Port du Salut, Swiss, Provolone, Mozzarella, and Romano. Small cheeses, such as Camembert, can even be frozen in their original packages. When removed from the freezer, cheese should be put in the refrigerator and used as soon as possible after thawing.

Reader's Tip

Before you store semi-hard cheeses like Cheddar, Swiss, or Gruyère, rub the cut edges with a little bit of butter. You'll never taste the difference, and the cheese will be less likely to dry out or become moldy.   —ELLEN FAUCI, NORMAN, OK

Cottage Cheese Flip

Because of its high water content, cottage cheese doesn't last as long as other food products in the refrigerator. To extend its life, store it in the container upside down.

Sour Cream Saver

To help sour cream last longer, add white vinegar right after you open it (1 teaspoon for a small container and 2 tablespoons for a large container). You won't notice the taste, and the sour cream won't go bad as quickly.

Should Produce Be Refrigerated?

If you've ever had a debate with a roommate or spouse about which produce should be refrigerated and which shouldn't, you're not alone. Refrigerating your produce can help it last longer, but not all produce does well in the cooler temperature. The majority of fruits and vegetables handle cold fairly well, but naturally enough, the exceptions are tropical fruits, whose cells are just not used to the cold. Bananas will suffer cell damage and release a skin-browning chemical, avocados don't ripen when stored below 45°F, and citrus fruit will develop brown-spotted skin. These fruits, as well as squash, tomatoes, cucumbers, melons, bell peppers, and pineapples, are best stored at 50°F—so keep them out of the fridge. Most other vegetables, including lettuce, carrots, and cabbage, will do better in your refrigerator. Potatoes, however, should be stored outside of the fridge and away from light.

Let Your Produce Breathe

Wrap all produce loosely; air circulation around fruits and vegetables reduces spoilage. A sealed, perforated plastic bag is ideal—but instead of buying them at the market, make your own by simply poking several holes in an ordinary sandwich or freezer bag.

Leave the Seeds

When using only part of a red, green, or yellow pepper, cut it from the bottom or the sides, leaving the seeds attached, and it will remain moist for longer. You can put the rest in a resealable plastic bag and use it up to 3–4 days later.

Celery That Keeps

Keep celery lasting even longer in your refrigerator by wrapping it in aluminum foil!

Mold-Free Melons

To keep melons from getting moldy as they ripen, rub the exterior peel with a teaspoonful of full-strength vinegar every few days.

Raisin Rejuvenation

Sad-looking raisins? To plump them up to perfection, place them a small baking dish with a little water, cover, and bake in a preheated 325°F oven for 6–8 minutes. Or, pour boiling water over the raisins and let them stand for 10–15 minutes.

❋ New Favorite

Fruit or veggies about to go bad? Give them a second life by cutting off any bruised or bad spots, then pureeing and freezing or refrigerating. (Process fruits and vegetables separately.) Pureed fruit works great in muffin recipes or mixed into ice cream, while pureed veggies add nutrients to pasta sauce, stews, and casseroles.

High and Dry

The moisture content of fresh berries is high, so make sure to dry them thoroughly before you stick them in the fridge, or wait until you're ready to eat them before you wash them. Otherwise, they can easily rot. Also make sure to store berries, especially strawberries, loosely covered in the refrigerator.

Grapes Are Easy

The best way to keep your grapes lasting longer? Keep them unwashed and attached to their stems until you're ready to eat them. This will ensure they don't become waterlogged and susceptible to bacteria.

Refresh Your Lettuce

You've left the lettuce in the crisper for a few days, and now it's too wilted to use for a salad. Perk up any green (including herbs like cilantro) by submerging it in a bowl of ice-cold water (and 1 tablespoon lemon juice if it's especially wilted). Let sit for 5–10 minutes and it will be as good as fresh.

Make Leftover Onion Last Longer

You've chopped up half an onion and you'd like to save the rest for later. Make sure the onion lasts longer in your fridge by rubbing the cut end with butter, then wrapping in plastic wrap.

Separate Your Onions and Potatoes

Potatoes hate onions . . . at least until they're cooked together. Onions should never be stored with potatoes because moisture from the onions can cause potatoes to sprout. Onions also release gases that will alter the flavor of a potato.

When shopping in the freezer aisle, avoid packages of frozen vegetables that have frost on them. It's a sign that the food has thawed and refrozen, and a percentage of moisture has already been lost. You should also give bags of frozen food a quick squeeze before putting them in your cart. If the food is solid, it has thawed and refrozen, and should be avoided.

Corn Purchasing Tip

When corn is piled high in supermarket bins, go for the ears that are on top. Why? Corn gets rapidly less sweet the warmer it gets, and even the heat generated by all the corn on the top of the pile can make the corn on the bottom start to lose its deliciously sweet taste.

Foil Foible

Never wrap foods that contain natural acids—like tomatoes, lemons, or onions—in aluminum foil. The combination of the foil and the acid in the foods produces a chemical reaction, which affects the taste of the food.

Popping Popcorn, Always

Are your popcorn kernels too pooped to pop? It's probably because they have lost too much moisture, but they can be revived. Soak the kernels in water for five minutes, then dry them off and try again. Or freeze them overnight and pop them when frozen.

Potato Chip Trick

It's 2 a.m.—do you know where your chips are? Yes, but unfortunately, they've been there way too long. Microwaving, which turns bread to mush, has the opposite effect on potato chips. Just give them a whirl for 30 seconds on a glass plate. Be careful when you bring them out: they may need to cool down a bit before you can eat them.

Reader's Tip

Don't throw away fresh herbs if you've got more on hand than you need. Just rinse the leaves, air dry, and place (on a single layer) on a plate with a paper towel. Then microwave them in 30-second intervals until they're crunchy (which can take up to four minutes). If you store them in an airtight container, they'll last for a year!   —ELLIE BIMESTEFER

Herbal Remedies

Fresh herbs are a wonderful addition to any dinner, but let's face it: They go bad quickly. To keep herbs fresh longer, loosely wrap them in a damp paper towel, store in a plastic bag, and keep in the vegetable crisper of the refrigerator. If you have more fresh herbs than you can use, hang them upside down to dry.

Give Them a Drink

Fresh herbs like parsley and cilantro will last for at least a couple of weeks if you store them in a jar or mug. Just clip the stems of the herbs, and place them in a jar with water in it, like you would with flowers. Cover loosely with a plastic bag and refrigerate.

Quick Ginger

Keep raw ginger in a sealed plastic bag in the freezer, and it will last pretty much forever. Best of all, you don't need to defrost it before you grate it!

New Favorite

Enjoy fresh herbs from your garden all year round (or preserve expensive herbs before they go bad) with this tip: Just chop clean leaves, pat dry, and freeze in ice cube trays with enough water to cover the leaves. Then pop into dishes for a fresh, summery taste.

Spice-Saving Secret

Do your dried herbs and spices lose some of their zest after sitting on your spice rack for years? Spices and dried herbs keep their flavor better if stored in a cupboard away from heat, light, and moisture, all of which impair flavor, change color, and shorten life. Make them last longer by putting half into a sealed, airtight container when you purchase them. Label the container and keep it in your dark cabinet, or better yet, your freezer. When the spice on-hand loses its aroma, replace it with some from your stash, and you'll never have to be irritated about throwing away an entire container of mustard seed or marjoram again.

Red Hot Idea

Both cayenne pepper and paprika are affected by light and heat, and have a shorter shelf life than just about anything else on your spice rack. In fact, take them off your spice rack and store them both in the refrigerator for a longer life.

Garlic Gift

If your head of garlic sprouts, it's still perfectly good to eat. Some of the flavor will go into the sprouts—chop them off and add to salads for a delicious treat!

Reheating Pizza

The best way to heat up leftover pizza is in the toaster oven, but if you don't have a toaster oven you don't need to endure the soggy crust that results from micro-waving yesterday's slice. Just place the piece in a covered skillet and heat over medium-low heat until warm.

Salt Shaker Shakeup

When your salt gets sticky in high humidity, keep it flowing freely by adding some raw rice to the shaker. Rice absorbs moisture and lasts for a long time.

INDEX

MY TIPS

Beauty

Cleaning

Clothes and Laundry

Cooking

Decorating and Entertaining

Health and Wellness

Home and Car Repair

Kids and Pets

Organizing

Outdoors/Pest Control

Saving Money

who knew?
online

Visit us on the web at WhoKnewTips.com!

* Money-saving tips
* Quick 'n' easy recipes
* Who Knew? products
* And much more!

Twitter.com/WhoKnewTips
Get a free daily tip and ask us your questions

YouTube.com/WhoKnewTips
Watch demos of your favorite tips

Facebook.com/WhoKnewTips
Daily tips, giveaways, and more fun!